Getting Started in

Real Estate Investing

The Getting Started in Series

Getting Started in
Real Estate Investing

SECOND EDITION

Michael C. Thomsett
Jean Freestone Thomsett

John Wiley & Sons, Inc.

New York • Chichester • Weinheim • Brisbane • Singapore • Toronto

This publication is designed to provide accurate and authoritative information in regard to the subject
matter covered. It is sold with the understanding that the publisher is not engaged in rendering professional
services. If professional advice or other expert assistance is required, the services of a competent
professional person should be sought.

Library of Congress Cataloging-in-Publication Data:
Thomsett, Michael C.
    Getting started in real estate investing / Michael C. Thomsett,
Jean Freestone Thomsett.—2nd ed.
        p.   cm.—(The getting started in series)
    Includes index.
    ISBN 0-471-24654-9 (pbk. : alk. paper)
    1. Real estate investment.   I. Thomsett, Jean F., 1947–   .
    II. Title.   III. Series: Getting started in.
    HD1382.5.T564   1998
    332.63'24—dc21   97-44934

Printed in the United States of America

10 9 8 7 6

Contents

Getting Started in

Real Estate Investing

The Allure of Property

W hy is real estate so universally popular as an investment? There are several reasons, and before considering real estate as a possibility for yourself, you may want to review the answers to this important question. You will see that, with its different investment advantages considered together, real estate is difficult to match by other investments.

First, it is one of the few finite investments. There is only so much real estate to go around, and when it is used up, prices have to rise. With a limited amount of space, the land available for development of housing, office, commercial, industrial, recreational, government, and lodging purposes is also limited. Not *all* land is appropriate for development. When the land is too steep, too wet, or in protected areas, it has to be eliminated as potential development land. When all of the topographically prohibitive land is removed from consideration, and when government-owned conservation lands are removed, there is only a relatively small amount of land remaining. Even beyond that, of the available land, not all of it can be developed due to zoning restrictions or due to the simple fact that the current owner does not want to sell. In comparison to the finite nature of real estate, corporations and most mutual funds can issue more shares if the demand from investors is strong enough. In theory, there is no limit to the number of investors in popular stock market issues.

Second, real estate has a track record that can only encourage investors. Real estate investments have gained in value in the past, partly because of the limited amount of real estate, and partly because of other factors, such as tax benefits. The historical record for real estate, like all markets, has had ups and downs. But over time, real estate has kept pace with inflation and has usually exceeded the Consumer Price Index (CPI) growth rate. The real estate cycle is highly predictable, following patterns based on normal supply and demand and varying regionally, but in the same manner for each cycle. This is not true of the other popular investment, the stock market, in which investing may often be compared to a blindfolded roller coaster ride—more exciting and potentially more profitable, but not always as stable.

Third, real estate investors enjoy exceptional federal income tax benefits. These benefits are unlike those available for any other investment. The 1997 "Taxpayer Relief Act" dramatically improved the tax benefits of owning your own home by eliminating the tax on profits for the first $500,000 when primary residences are sold. This may not directly benefit investors, but many possible strategies will evolve from this new law, and will be explained later in this book. For investors, too, tax benefits are significant. You are allowed to deduct all of the necessary expenses connected with owning rental property, such as for repairs, cleaning, accounting, interest, property taxes, and others. You can also write off the cost of buildings and other improvements over a period of years. The tax laws also provide exceptions for real estate investors to claim losses that would otherwise not be deductible.

Fourth, real estate is an investment you can see. There is something satisfying and reassuring about owning an intrinsic property. This gives you the opportunity to care for the investment and keep its value up, by direct actions you take right in your own community. Even by testifying before your elected officials in decisions affecting your property value, you are directly involved in protecting your investment and in influencing its future market value. In comparison, investing in stocks directly or through mutual funds yields you an account statement and perhaps a certificate; but you never get to see your money at work like you do with real estate. In the stock market, you own part of an intangible whole, and never directly own an actual piece of a company's real assets.

Fifth, real estate is considered one of the basic necessities. People need shelter, and housing provides them with that. Even commercial, industrial, and other types of property all relate to demand for those uses, based on local population. So investing in real estate means you are investing in the value of your own community. As a responsible investor, you are a participant in planning to maintain your town's way of life, while also putting your capital to work.

The primary emphasis of this book will be on investment in residential property. Most investors start out by buying houses and renting them out, so this is a sensible approach. As a general rule, investors in commercial and industrial property tend to specialize in those areas, because more money is at stake. Many real estate investors evolve into developers later on, but begin by buying one or two properties and becoming landlords.

As a real estate investor, your first challenge will be to figure out that conditions affect prices in your area, and to then estimate where you are in the real estate cycle. As a starting point, we recommend three steps:

1. Concentrate on studying local economic influences and cycles.

2. Gather the information you need to make an informed decision.

3. Set goals for yourself and make up a list of investing rules; then follow them consistently.

This book helps you to master the skills you need to succeed in real estate investment, and shows you how to apply the skills in your own situation. With that purpose in mind, this book is organized for ease of reference. Each chapter concentrates on a particular aspect of real estate investing, providing illustrations and examples for the major points. Important definitions of terms are supplied as you proceed through the book, so that those meanings are conveniently available in the context of the discussion and on the same page, highlighted in the margin. The same definitions are again summarized alphabetically in the Glossary.

Begin by defining your personal goals, as discussed in Chapter 1. Not everyone wants the same thing from an investment. For example, you might be interested in investing a large sum of money and becoming a developer of shopping centers. Or you might be more interested in buying one rental house a few blocks from your home, and finding a tenant to pay your mortgage for you; or perhaps you want to convert your present home into a rental when you move to a larger house. This book is aimed primarily at people who want to get started and are not sure where to begin, or who have an ultimate goal in mind and want to break in modestly and build equity for the next few years. You may want to gather information to better assess whether real estate holds the answers you seek as an investor, so that you will be able to make an informed decision about how to work with your capital.

Should You Be a Real Estate Investor?

Headline: "The big run-up in real estate values is now over."

Have you seen this pronouncement in your local paper, or in the financial press? Chances are you have gotten this news, and that you will hear it again—many times. At least once each decade, the experts advise us that we have missed the boat. These experts, though, fail to realize one important fact about real estate: that there are as many "boats" in the future as there were in the past, if not more. Real estate is not a onetime opportunity, and potential can and will arrive many times. Many factors— shifts in the job market, population growth rates, regional popularity, interest rates, and more—all mean that real estate opportunities occur not just once, but repeatedly and in very predictable cycles.

The many advantages of owning real estate are difficult to beat with other forms of investment. Real estate comes with the usual investment risks, but some very special risks related to real estate should also be kept in mind when you compare it to alternatives. With real estate, you gain tax advantages, direct control over the asset, and the ability to borrow money to purchase a property without being taxed on the money borrowed (in fact, by refinancing it is possible to keep your capital working while still owning the property). In exchange for these advantages, you need to buy an expensive property, place yourself in debt, and in most cases, be unable to get your cash out through a quick sale. You also cannot sell part of your investment as you can when you own stock or shares of a mutual fund.

Real estate provides you a combination of benefits and control. You can influence the value of a property with landscaping, roofing, a new coat of paint, and interior design, for example. When you buy stock in a corporation, that does not give you the right to go to corporate headquarters and sit in on management meetings, and you cannot own the specific assets represented by your shares. Stock ownership gives you a portion of ownership in an intangible unity called "equity," which collectively owns the company and appoints executives and managers. This is an important distinction.

One of the risks that many first-time real estate owners do not consider is that if you become a landlord, you will have to interact with tenants. That means they might call you in the middle of dinner or while you're trying to watch the game on Sunday. These problems keep many would-be investors out of the business entirely. But with careful screening of applicants and by the proper use of a telephone answering machine, you can achieve a relatively comfortable balance, while still acting as a responsible and fair landlord. All you really want as a landlord is a tenant who will pay the rent on time and do a reasonable job of caring for your property.

Looking beyond the potential problems of dealing with tenants, the potential gains from investing in real estate make it worth a serious look. Let's begin by establishing a few important distinctions. *Real estate* is land plus permanent improvements, which most often means buildings. You might also become involved in the *rights* attached to the ownership of real estate, broadly called *real property*. Also be aware of the important difference between the full value or price of real estate, as opposed to *equity*, which is the portion you own after deducting debt. Equity is the purchase price (or current value of the property), minus all outstanding debt balances.

 real estate
land and all permanent improvements on it, including buildings.

 rights
intangible assets added onto real estate, which have value not because of the land itself, but because of the advantages those rights provide.

 real property
real estate plus the rights attached to it, such as leases, easements, and estates.

REAL ESTATE AS A GROWTH FUND

Some investors buy real estate for the long-term appreciation and tax advantages it provides. In comparison, the *speculator* is an investor who attempts to make the greatest possible profit in the shortest possible time, and is willing to take higher risks than long-term investors, because short-term profits will be much greater. Speculators often are accused of being opportunists in the market, but that characterization is not always accurate. The speculator is simply taking a different approach to investing. The same distinctions can be seen in the stock market. Some investors buy long-term growth stocks, while others try to guess where short-term price run-ups will occur. In all such instances, speculators chase after higher profits, but they also assume considerably higher risks. With that in mind, some long-term investors believe that speculators often do not achieve as much in the long run, because real estate, by its nature, is a long-term investment. Both approaches have their good and bad features. Consider the following examples, comparing two investors who each have $50,000 to invest.

Example: Karen invested $50,000 as a down payment on a $160,000 triplex. Her rents more than covered her mortgage payment, and she held onto the property for eight years. At the end of eight years, she sold the property for $235,000, realizing a capital gain of $75,000. During the holding period, she enjoyed positive cash flow and tax benefits, and upon sale, she earned a profit on the investment. Mortgage payments and other expenses were covered by rent receipts.

Example: Adam paid cash for a run-down house in need of many repairs, mostly cosmetic. He landscaped the yard, painted inside and out, repaired the broken windows, and upgraded the plumbing and electrical systems. The total of his purchase price and repairs came to about $50,000. He sold the house about eight months after he bought it and, after closing costs, netted $60,000.

 equity
the portion of real estate you own. In the case of a property bought for $100,000 with a $58,000 mortgage owing, the equity is the difference, or $42,000.

 speculator
an investor who buys property with the goal of earning the greatest possible profit in the shortest possible time.

He made a net profit of $10,000 (before taxes) in less than one year.

A comparison between these two examples is more complicated than it seems at first glance, because the two people might be paying different tax rates and because there is no way to know what future appreciation might occur on the fixed-up house, nor what rental receipts could be earned by turning it into a rental unit. However, the illustrations demonstrate two different approaches. The first is the long-term strategy, aimed at achieving positive cash flow, tax benefits, and capital appreciation. This example is not unusual, but it is ideal. The second example demonstrates how short-term strategies might work. The risk here is that the cosmetic repairs might not add enough value to the property to make it worthwhile in such a short period of time but, again, the example is not untypical. These outcomes do occur if the speculator understands the market and knows good value when it presents itself.

The speculator made $10,000 on a fast turnaround of the property, which is a better annual rate than the long-term appreciation approach. However, the speculator gained no tax benefits or positive cash flow during the holding period. As you can see, the decision to be a long-term investor or a speculator depends on your tax circumstances, your ability to manage market risks, and even your personal temperament.

Another important question you should ask is: How does long-term strategy work in comparison to non–real estate investments? In the stock market, certain stocks are referred to as *growth stocks*. Generally, this means that the stock's value is expected to increase over time. If you buy shares today and the estimate of future price growth is right, your investment will grow in value steadily over many years. You would not be concerned with the day-to-day fluctuations in stock value.

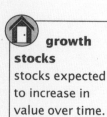

growth stocks
stocks expected to increase in value over time.

The same is true when you invest in growth-oriented mutual fund shares. The company's management buys shares in companies considered to be good growth stocks. If the mutual fund's management is right, your shares will grow over time.

With either direct purchase of stock shares, or mutual fund shares, you depend on the quality of management to achieve your goals. With many different choices on the market, you accept certain risks in the selection process, and that is always a part of the investment equation. These same risk elements apply to real estate as well. You always accept risk when investing, and real estate, like other alternatives, comes with specific risks. In real estate, these risks include these three possibilities:

1. The property investment may lose value or fail to appreciate according to your expectations. All investments contain this risk. Even insured savings accounts can deteriorate when interest rates are lower than inflation. The basic market risk is the best known and, for most people, the primary form of risk. It is fair to say that in most regions, real estate has to be held long enough for appreciation to occur and the real risk is that you don't know in advance how long that will be.

2. You may not be able to find tenants, or to charge rents adequate to cover your monthly expenses. When a large number of rentals are available and relatively few tenants, market rates level out or drop. In order to avoid vacancies, you might have to reduce rents. The opposite is true in periods of high demand. With too few units and many tenants, your market rates will rise.

3. Your tenants may not pay the rent that is due, or may not care well for the property. In real estate, tenant problems are frustrating because such problems force you to confront matters at once or lose money. Invariably, that means dealing with people who are having problems beyond the landlord-tenant relationship, or who are immature and irresponsible, or who simply want to avoid paying the agreed-on rent. Proper screening and review, and checking of references, reduce these problems dramatically and should be requirements of landlording.

These basic risks are not the whole story, but they are major considerations when you are evaluating the possibility of investing in real estate. These problems will not seem as formidable once you actually buy a property and begin managing it. With patience, caution, and maintenance, property will appreciate over time when it is carefully and intelligently selected. You will also learn by experience how to screen tenants, set fair rents, and confront problems before they turn into crises. Just as parents learn on the job, so landlords have to discover the problems that arise with tenants and learn how to avoid those problems in advance.

Risks are manageable, as long as you are aware of them. A common mistake is to look for ways to eliminate risk, when in fact smart investing calls for awareness and risk management. Some risks can be mitigated. For example, buying fire insurance protects you against a loss of a rental home; not to carry such insurance would be to assume more risk than you can afford. You need to evaluate the different types of risk involved with investing in real estate, and then determine how much risk—and what kinds of risk—you are willing to assume. The speculator is willing to take the risk that the real estate market might not support the strategy of buying and selling homes in a short period of time. If the speculator's timing is off, the strategy will result in a loss, or the property will have to be held for longer than intended.

Most people begin their real estate investments by studying and comparing prices. You should always keep in mind the risk rule in real estate: *The greater the risk, the lower the price.* For example, real estate in a poor location will naturally cost much less than real estate in a prime location. The risk in such a case has to do with potential for appreciation. The price in the poor location is less likely to rise at the same rate as prime property and, in fact, could even fall. As average market prices rise, the tendency is for better-than-average properties to rise faster than average, and for poorer-than-average homes to lag behind. Good investing requires foresight. In addition to estimating and calculating the risks and potential profits, you need to become adept at identifying the good and bad points about all of the factors affecting price and value: location, timing, and local economic conditions (now and in the future). This is exactly the same type of analysis all investors need to perform. However, instead of studying financial statements of companies and looking at market index trends, the real estate investor has to be able to read social, political, economic, and demographic trends within a city and region.

This book assumes that your goal is to invest for future appreciation. Certainly, speculation is one alternative, but that profile doesn't fit with most people in terms of available capital, financial goals, or market expertise. The main focus here is in showing you how to get started by buying one or two rental houses, then build up equity while managing property and coping with tenants, and ultimately create a profitable investment for your future financial security.

Long-term investing requires a commitment longer than two or three years. In fact, "long-term" generally means 10 years or more, because it takes that long to create *seasoned real estate*. As you make monthly mortgage payments and as property gradually increases in value over time, seasoning occurs.

 seasoned real estate real estate that has been owned long enough for market value and equity to accumulate.

THE REAL ESTATE CYCLE

Real estate investments react to economic cycles, as do all investments. The major points in the cycle—falling and rising prices, for example—are characteristics of *supply and demand*. The tendency dictated by this basic economic idea that prices rise and fall according to levels of supply and demand is the guiding force in selecting investments, timing purchases and sales, and selecting one investment over another.

In a pure *market economy*, prices rise and fall in accordance with the dictates of supply and demand. Higher demand places pressure on the supply, and prices rise; and lower demand softens the market, so that prices fall. The same features are found in the stock market, which often is called an "auction marketplace." That means that prices change specifically because the mix of sellers and buyers changes. When more buyers want a limited number of available shares of stock, that drives up the price; and when the number of sellers grows, it forces down the price of stock: An ongoing auction is underway when the market is open.

Real estate does not change hands on an auction marketplace. Stock exchanges are public and millions of individual trades result in tremendous share volume every day.

 supply and demand the economic conditions in the market that affect prices. When demand is greater than supply, prices tend to rise; when supply is greater than demand, prices tend to fall.

 market economy a market in which prices are not set, but vary with purely economic factors, specifically supply and demand.

In real estate, brokers are not bidding and negotiating from moment to moment; and real estate sells in large, single units rather than in millions of small shares. Offers are placed—in writing—through real estate agents and based on asked prices. Prevailing market conditions determine whether a potential buyer makes a full-price offer or tries to negotiate a lower price. The same conditions also affect the seller's response. A firm seller sticks to the asked price or stays close to it, but when the market is soft, sellers have to accept lower bids or their properties won't sell.

Although the rules of contracting for buy and sell prices and making and closing a deal are the same for stocks and real estate, methods are different. In the minds of most investors, the rules are different as well. For example:

✔ Many people who can afford to buy 100 shares of stock would be faced with much more demanding financial arrangements to bid on real estate. Accordingly, the stock market is available to many more investors, and trading can occur frequently and in relatively small increments.

✔ Stocks are often bought and paid for in cash, whereas real estate more likely involves financing.

✔ Real estate prices are naturally higher than shares of stock, so the entire process of buying and selling—comparing, negotiating, bidding, offering, and closing—tends to be more formal and take longer in real estate.

✔ Real estate does not trade hands as frequently as stocks, so the trading volume in real estate is much smaller, and indicators based on sales volume tend to cover periods of months and years rather than tracking methods used in the stock market, such as hour-to-hour or day-to-day volume.

Reasons for selling are different as well. Sellers of stocks often want to take short-term profits and move on to other issues, or simply want to move their money to another stock that they believe makes a better investment at that moment. The real estate seller may be anxious to sell for a number of different reasons. A *motivated seller* wants to find a fast deal in order to get the equity out and move on. Motivated sellers may have made an offer on another house, be moving to another area, or be making other major life changes. The degree of anxiety to sell will dictate how much negotiation the seller is willing to undertake. In a very soft market—in which many homes are for sale and few buyers are available—it might simply be impossible to sell a property, at least at the moment. In the auction marketplace of the stock market, there is always a ready buyer. The price may be low because demand is low, but shares of stock on a public exchange can be bought or sold at the current price, at any time.

The events and conditions influencing real estate values are referred to as the *real estate cycle*. While many factors affect the cycle, including population, the job market, interest rates, financing, construction levels, and many other economic changes, the real estate cycle moves in a fairly predictable sequence over time. The stages vary in length of time and rapidity of change based on the collective changes in market conditions; however, six distinct points can be identified in the course of the real estate cycle. These are summarized in Figure 1.1.

1. *Demand begins to rise.* Demand rises for many reasons, often for a combination of reasons. The fact that more buyers are looking for properties now than a year ago is a symptom of rising demand. It may be caused by growing population, job creation, and other factors. The forces that create demand cannot be isolated or easily identified; demand is usually a general trend involving many parts. One element of demand results from a decrease in construction activity, leading to housing shortages. In a truly efficient economy, developers would always build exactly the number of new homes required to meet the needs of the immediate future, while maintaining supply and demand in a healthy balance so that values gradually rise with moderate inflation. But that is the ideal world, and the real world rarely acts that way.

2. *Construction activity increases.* Why do developers increase their rates of construction? At the beginning of the cycle, the general perception is that demand is on

 motivated seller
a seller who is very anxious to sell, meaning that seller is more willing than a firm seller to negotiate on the price and other terms.

 real estate cycle
the trends in real estate values, affected by ever-changing levels of supply and demand. The cycle describes changes in construction activity, available supply of real estate for sale, credit available for financing, interest rates, population and job demographics, and attitudes among buyers and sellers at any given point.

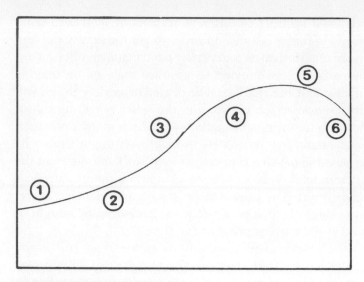

1. Demand begins to rise.
2. Construction activity increases.
3. Demand slows.
4. Supply exceeds demand.
5. Construction activity decreases.
6. Demand bottoms out.

FIGURE 1.1 The real estate cycle.

the rise. At that moment, the perception is correct. The trick, though, is to know when to stop building new homes. Construction activity is responsive. As demand increases, so do the construction rate and pace. That pace often exceeds actual demand, so that as the cycle tops out, the consequence is oversupply.

3. *Demand slows.* When we say that demand slows, we could mean that demand actually decreases or that the rate of new construction accelerates beyond a more moderate demand curve. As long as construction and demand are moving at the same pace, there is no relative change in the real estate cycle. When demand slows for either reason, this event signals that the top of the cycle is approaching. You will recognize this point by an increase in the time required for listed properties to sell. In some markets, homes under construction are being sold literally faster than they're being built. But if builders start accumulating an inventory of finished homes that are not selling right away, that is a sign that demand is slowing (or that construction has outpaced that demand).

4. *Supply exceeds demand.* The cycle tops out and begins to decline at the point when property available and on the market exceeds demand. This does not mean that no real estate is selling. It does mean the supply is larger than it needs to be, and demand is not great enough to move the inventory of available properties. As a consequence, prices tend to level off or fall. The cycle might stall—meaning that new construction is meeting demand, but prices do not rise because the inventory is perpetually higher than it should be.

5. *Construction activity decreases.* No market can sustain a holding pattern for long. When inventories of available property are too high, construction eventually falls off, at least temporarily. Builders and developers, like everyone else, do not always recognize the point in the cycle until it's too late. So at the point where prices have become soft and supply is too high, builders realize that they cannot continue to develop the market at the previous pace. Another problem in trying to watch and predict cycles, whether in real estate, the stock market, or other markets, is that you don't know whether specific signals indicate changes tomorrow, next week, or next year. Timing is the difficult part.

6. *Demand bottoms out.* At the end of the cycle, demand is at its lowest; construction activity has stopped for the most part; and no changes are in sight. A cycle might remain at its bottom for a few weeks, a few months, or many years. No two cycles follow identical wave patterns, and there may be numerous false starts along the way. The word "doldrums" appears in financial articles, and experts proclaim that the opportunities in real estate are over, once and for all. This statement is one of the predictable events at the bottom of the cycle. Remember, though, that such categorical predictions—like predictions that inflation is gone forever—are always wrong. The end of one cycle is also the beginning of another one.

A study of the real estate cycle can be simplified in theory, but in practice the actual cycles for your region will be affected by many complex social, political, and even historical factors. Forgetting for the moment about outside influences, you can reduce the real estate cycle to a fairly straightforward comparison between supply and demand. The waves of the cycle can reflect sales volume, prices, or units for sale. For the purpose of this simplified summary of the cycle, we will use market value—the best understood and most widely recognized result of changing cycles. The question often is expressed in terms of the prices of homes. They suddenly rise, or they remain the same for many months, or they fall. Why? Figure 1.2 summarizes this with two basic observations about the real estate cycle:

1. Supply rises and demand falls.
2. Demand rises and supply falls.

This cycle, like all cycles, involves the cause and effect of supply and demand. You are aware of the variables in the cycle and the complexity of influences that have to be added into this, but the basic equation remains the same. One way to better understand why cycles move the

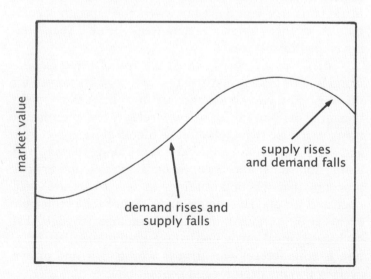

FIGURE 1.2 Supply and demand.

way they do is to understand that in the first half of the cycle—when prices are rising—the price curve tends to run ahead of the demand curve. On the other side, when prices are falling, the price curve lags behind the demand curve. The trends run out, and the cycle begins again—thus the wave effect.

Changes in relative levels of supply and demand are nothing less than the sum of all influences in the market at that moment. If developers ceased building altogether because of excess supply, demand would eventually use up that inventory, and the cycle would be forced to begin anew. If employers came to town, demand for new housing would accompany those new jobs. However, we can never have absolutes such as construction levels stopping altogether or a complete turnover in the job market. Such influences tend to occur incrementally rather than in single motions. So in reality, when we talk about supply and demand, we are really describing a trend that involves all of the complex economic, social, and intangible influences at work in the community.

REAL ESTATE RULES OF THUMB

You may have a thorough understanding of all the influences affecting real estate values in your community. Even so, the timing of any decision will have a lot to do with profit and loss. In all forms of investing, timing of buy and sell decisions is of critical importance. Depending on the stage of the cycle at the moment of that decision, the move could be judged on timing rather than on the analysis of cyclical information. Choosing the best moment is difficult, but not entirely impossible. The choice is probably easier in real estate than in the stock market, due to the differences between the two. Real estate cycles tend to be more easily identified in a longer-term perspective. Stock market trends, however, can change from moment to moment, and opportunities come and go quickly with those rapid changes.

You are wise to study real estate cycles and to be aware of the market in your community. However, the cycle itself is not the whole story. You need to be aware of six additional rules of thumb in real estate.

1. *Real estate is a long-term proposition.* It is not realistic to expect that you can make a killing in real estate in a very short period of time. While some people have profited from fast speculation, the opportunities are much clearer in hindsight. In fact, the most successful speculations are made at a moment when virtually everyone else is doing the opposite. You buy when everyone else is selling, for example. Going into real estate with the goal of getting rich quick is a risky idea, and the odds are working against you in that case.

2. *Real estate markets are strictly regional.* You have probably read in national magazines or wire service stories at various times about "the plight of real estate." You might also be aware that a lagging real estate market described in such stories does not necessarily describe what's going on in your town. That is because real estate is always subject to regional factors, and rarely is local real estate drastically affected by national trends. For example, Northwest prices move for Northwest regional causes, and not because of population and employment trends in the East.

Employment is a good example. Changes in the job market directly affect real estate supply and demand, and yet employment varies greatly from one place to another, often in places separated by only a few miles. Many people automatically assume that real estate conditions are the same everywhere, but this is a mistake. The assumption applies stock market thinking to real estate. However, while the stock market is national, real estate is strictly regional, so the rules are different. Never make up your mind about what's going on in your area based on a story written by someone living somewhere else. Depend on only regional news and statistics, and talk to real estate agents and bankers in *your* area before deciding the condition of the real estate market.

3. *The big run-up is never really over.* Whenever real estate prices soar in a relatively short period of time (five years or less), a period of pessimism follows. We are told that we have missed the chance if we did not buy real estate several years ago and, even worse, the opportunity will never come again.

None of that is true. If, in fact, a recent run-up has peaked, this is only the end of one cycle; and the end of a cycle is also the beginning of the next cycle. By waiting for the right signals, you will still be able to time your investment decisions to approximate the bottom and top points. Even if you did miss the "big" run-up of the recent past, you still have time to get in at the bottom of the next cycle.

Why do cycles repeat? In spite of the recurring predictions in the financial press that yesterday's opportunities are gone forever, there remains a constant and growing demand for real estate. The initial demand is for housing due to a growing population, and housing demands spur related demands in manufacturing, industrial, and other sectors. But can we depend on such demands increasing into the future? Yes. The population continues to grow. Even though the baby boomer generation may stop buying homes, their children (and grandchildren) will continue the demand. There is no reason to expect the demand for housing to decline in the future. The U. S. Bureau of the Census projects that the population of the United States will nearly double between 1996 (265.3 million people) and 2050 (estimated at 518.9 million).*

Much of the growth estimated for our future is credited to two factors. First is the trend in immigration. Second is what is called the "echo-boom" generation, people born from the late 1960s to the late 1970s and moving into house-buying age range by the year 2000. The home-buying block of the population will grow by 1.2 million over the next 15 years.[†]

Demand by way of population growth—whether caused by net increases in birthrates, immigration, decreased mortality, or a combination of these factors—is one important reason that real estate represents a sound in-

---

*U.S. Bureau of the Census, *Population Projections of the United States by Age, Sex, Race, and Hispanic Origin: 1995 to 2050*, 1996, midrange prediction.
†John F. Kennedy School of Government, Harvard University, The Joint Center for Housing Studies, *The State of the Nation's Housing*, 1996.

vestment. However, how can we know that trends in the past will repeat themselves? This is where some statistical studying is helpful and informative. For example, just because there was a baby boom in the late 1940s to mid-1950s does not necessarily mean the same trends will recur. In fact, the U.S. birthrate has declined steadily since 1960, and is expected to continue declining until the year 2000. However, between 1977 and 1994, 72 million children were born, and they are the real estate market of the future. This compares with the original baby boom dominating the housing market today, which produced 77 million births.*

Consider also the nature of real estate. The costs of construction and replacement grow with inflation, meaning that materials prices add to the cost and market value of property. Homeowners themselves work to maintain and increase values—not only because they want to profit from their investment, but because growing values are good for everyone: individuals, families with children, and the community as a whole. However, homeowners do not think like investors in many important respects. Long-term homeowners do not worry about relative price fluctuations, even when their property values fall, because they buy property and remain in one place for other reasons—quality of schools, safety, lifestyle, and proximity to work. To the homeowner, these are the important considerations. They are important to investors as well, but the investor's perspective is different. The investor is much more aware of the cyclical change in real estate, that 7- to 10-year fluctuation in supply and demand within the community.

4. *It is impossible to identify exactly where you are in the real estate cycle.* Investors invariably have trouble estimating where they are today. Their historical perspective is always clearer. Because "value" is a relative term, perceptions about today's real estate market have to be based on cyclical indicators other than price. This cannot be emphasized too much.

Price is only one way to measure cycles. When you're estimating future movements in the cycle, price is

*Edmondson, Brad, "Children in 2001," *American Demographics*, March 1997.

one of the least dependable methods to use. You can learn much more by running comparisons of other cyclical indicators, including:

✔ Number of housing starts in your area (compared to the past).

✔ Length of time housing is on the market between list date and sale date.

✔ Percentage differences between list price and sale price.

These are by no means the whole list, but you can see the value of these statistical indicators. All are designed for comparisons between periods. It is the same type of analysis performed in the stock market, where analysts are concerned with trading volume, high and low records for the 52-week period, changes in an issue's volatility, and other such indicators not directly related to prices. In real estate, price seems to be used all too often as the single indicator of the cycle, and that is not reliable as a means for developing the actual trend and identifying the place within a longer cycle.

Cycle identification is never an exact science, because duration and strength of movement in the cycle vary greatly. If cycles were predictable, it would be a simple matter to get rich in real estate, given a small amount of patience.

If you are troubled by the complexity of changing real estate cycles, you should take comfort in one broad fact: For the most part, *real estate prices rise over time.* This may not be true within one specific region over a lengthy period of time, but for most regions experiencing growth in population, expanding economic opportunities, or other changes, real estate generally keeps pace with inflation, and often exceeds it.

5. *Real estate is not a liquid asset.* Investors are always concerned—and rightly so—with the question of *liquidity.* This is the degree of speed with which an investment asset can be converted into cash. A savings account, shares of stock or mutual funds, or money market accounts, for example, are highly liquid. Real estate, by comparison, is considered an *illiquid asset.* Some portion

 liquidity
the condition of an investment asset in terms of how quickly it can be converted into cash.

 illiquid asset
any asset that cannot be converted to cash within a short period of time, such as real estate.

of every investor's total funds should be kept in liquid accounts, so that any emergency can be paid for without creating a problem. To get cash out of real estate, you have to sell or borrow against equity, and neither of those choices are desirable at any time. With liquid assets, you can always cash in or sell a portion of the total investment with little trouble and without harming the strategy and being forced to sell everything prematurely.

Because real estate is such a large-ticket item, you will probably have to finance the majority of the purchase price. Investors sometimes find that they need to scramble to find enough cash to cover their down payment and closing costs on investment property, for several reasons. Lenders generally want 30 percent down on investment property, whereas home buyers often can get by with only 10 percent down, and sometimes less. So real estate investors are sometimes forced to give up liquidity for a while, to make the deal work. Hopefully, they will be able to build up their "rainy day fund" within a few months so that emergencies that arise can be managed without taking drastic action.

6. *If you select real estate diligently, you will make money—eventually.* When you make an investment and it falls in value, you naturally think you have made a terrible mistake. But in real estate, as in other markets, a decline in price may be only temporary. It is rare that residential real estate loses value permanently. If you can afford to wait, chances are good that the investment will pay off. This claim, of course, comes with a series of "if" statements: if history is right, and if you buy residential property, and if you can afford to wait, and so forth. You also need to consider that a profit itself cannot be viewed simply—if you had placed your money elsewhere, you might have made *more* money. So real estate, even though profitable over the long term, might prove to be a relatively poorly performing investment compared to other choices.

It is also inaccurate to make absolute comparisons, because risks vary so much between investments. When you buy stock, you have no insurance whatsoever, although returns may be high in the short term. When you buy a certificate of deposit, you have insurance automatically, but returns are predictably disappointing, perhaps lower than inflation. So a true comparison has to be made with risk and return levels in mind, both actual and potential.

While it is always desirable to buy real estate following the basic maxim of "buy low and sell high," if you miss the absolute bottom of a cycle, that does not mean the opportunity has been lost. Real estate is one of the few investments that produces income at a considerable level, through rent. (Savings accounts come with interest and stocks pay dividends, but these are nothing compared to rents, which often are enough to pay your entire mortgage payment each month.) Rather than comparing real estate to other investments with dissimilar risk/return features, you may do better by setting goals and then determining whether you are reaching those goals. As long as your tenant is generating enough income to cover your monthly mortgage payment, taxes, insurance, and other expenses, you can afford to wait out the market. Even with marginal cash income versus outflow, you need to consider tax benefits as well. Ultimately, the only value that really counts is the value at the time you sell (or refinance), compared to the value at the time of purchase.

As an investor, you will consider these matters and, when the time comes to sell, you will calculate a profit or loss on some basis. Forgetting for the moment the pretax and after-tax calculations that are possible, the calculation of profit on real estate is somewhat complex—not because the numbers are difficult to find, but because it is not that clear which numbers should be used. To illustrate this problem, ask yourself: Should you base the calculation on the price of the home and the profit realized, or on the amount of money you actually invested?

Example: You bought a rental property two years ago and paid $100,000. However, your down payment was only $40,000 and you financed the balance of $60,000. You recently sold the house for $120,000 (not counting closing costs). What is your net profit?

If we base "profit" on the price of the home, then the net profit is $20,000. It was purchased for $100,000 and sold for $120,000, so the profit is 20 percent (on the investment):

$$\frac{\$20,000}{\$100,000} = 20\%$$

However, if we base the calculation on the amount of money put into the investment, the outcome is quite different. The down payment in this example was $40,000, and the profit was $20,000. That's a 50 percent return (on the equity):

$$\frac{\$20,000}{\$40,000} = 50\%$$

Another complication in the examples above is that the entire transaction took two years. So if you want to calculate the *annualized return*, you need to divide the results by two. This is necessary because returns will be different based on how long it takes to earn them.

Example: You bought two homes exactly six years ago. The first one was sold two years later for a return on the investment of 20 percent. The second home was sold after being held five years, and the return on investment was 35 percent.

On the surface of it, you might believe that the second home, which yielded a 35 percent return, was the more profitable investment. But that is not the case. Let's look at the average *annual* rate of return:

Home	Holding Period	Return on Investment	Annual Return
1	2 years	20%	10%
2	5 years	35%	7%

Even though the overall return on investment was greater for the second home, the real annual return was higher on the first. This becomes important if by selling after two years you freed up capital to reinvest. The calcu-

annualized return a rate of return expressed for the average 12-month period. When a return occurs over a period other than one full year, it does not reflect an accurate annual rate; the annualized return enables consistent comparisons between investments by expressing all returns as though earned in a single, average year.

lation for annual return is done by dividing the rate of return by the number of years in the holding period:

$$\frac{20\%}{2\ (years)} = 10\%$$

If the holding period involves partial years, the same calculation can be done using the number of months instead of years. The result of that calculation is then multiplied by 12, representing one full year.

Example: You held an investment for 76 months and sold it, realizing a return of 31 percent. To annualize:

$$\frac{31\%}{76\ (months)} = 0.4079\%\ (monthly\ interest\ rate)$$

$$0.4079\% \times 12\ (months) = 4.89\%\ (annualized\ rate)$$

These calculations become valuable for comparisons between different real estate investments. In order to evaluate your past performance or set investment goals for yourself relating to future performance, it is important to arrive at a consistent method for measuring return. Annualizing that return is especially important for real estate, which tends to be long-term. Accordingly, you will need to measure annualized returns on an averaged basis in order to have a meaningful comparison.

REAL ESTATE INVESTMENT PERFORMANCE

While it is possible that you just missed a great opportunity to invest in real estate at bargain prices, you have no way to know what phase the cycle is at right now. What really matters is how real estate prices will change in the future, not how they have changed in the past.

This claim can be made for any investment. For example, suppose the stock market has just completed a long-term run-up in prices and one stock you have been following has increased in value by 300 percent. Does that mean you should not buy it today? There is no way to know because you can't be sure what will happen in the future. The stock could continue to rise in value. For those going into the market today, the starting point is today's price. This does not mean you should ignore the past; it only means that historical information is of limited value when you are trying to estimate future performance.

Real estate is a long-term investment. On average, holding periods of a number of years produce not only profits, but real after-inflation profits as well. The longer the holding period—especially if you have financed the purchase—the greater the profits. That's because in the first years of a long-term mortgage period, very little of the monthly payment goes toward paying off the loan; most of it is paying interest.* And the average American home changes ownership every 12.6 years.† So for the average home buyer, 12 years or so does not allow much time for price appreciation, and very little equity will accumulate while mortgage payments consist mainly of interest. Real profits depend on the combination of accumulating equity and growth in market value.

How has real estate fared versus inflation in general? Between 1969 and 1996, real estate matched or beat inflation 20 out of 28 years, or 71 percent of the time. The only sustained period when real estate did not beat inflation was from 1980 to 1982, a time when inflation was exceptionally high. (This compares prices of existing homes to the Consumer Price Index.)

The point to be made is that investing in single-family housing has been profitable over time. Prices continue to rise every year *and* beat the rate of inflation most of the time. Markets for condominiums and cooperative housing units and for apartment buildings are not included in these statistics, but since most first-time investors purchase existing homes (rather than newly built homes) to use as rentals, this comparison is valid for the first-time investor.

Table 1.1 summarizes these results. The first column

---

*For example, for an 8 percent interest rate loan repaid over 30 years, only 16 percent of the borrowed amount is paid off after 12 years. The rest of those payments have gone entirely to interest.
†Chicago Title and Trust, annual study, cited in *Builder Magazine Online*, January 1997.

TABLE 1.1 Housing Values and CPI			
Year	Housing Increase	CPI Increase	Difference
1969	8.5%	5.4%	3.1%
1970	5.5	4.9	0.6
1971	7.8	4.3	3.5
1972	7.7	3.3	4.4
1973	8.2	6.2	2.0
1974	10.7	11.0	−0.3
1975	10.3	9.1	1.2
1976	7.9	5.8	2.1
1977	12.6	6.5	6.1
1978	13.5	7.7	5.8
1979	14.4	11.3	3.1
1980	11.7	13.5	−1.8
1981	6.8	10.4	−3.6
1982	2.1	6.1	−4.0
1983	3.7	3.2	0.5
1984	3.0	4.3	−1.3
1985	4.3	3.6	0.7
1986	6.4	1.9	4.5
1987	6.6	3.7	2.9
1988	4.3	4.1	0.2
1989	4.3	4.8	−0.5
1990	2.6	5.4	−2.8
1991	5.0	4.2	0.8
1992	3.4	3.0	0.4
1993	3.0	3.0	0
1994	2.8	2.6	0.2
1995	2.8	2.8	0
1996	4.5	2.9	1.6

Sources: Bureau of Labor Statistics; National Association of Realtors.

shows the year; the second column, called Housing Increase, is the percentage of increase in value of the median price of existing homes on a nationwide basis.* The third column is the percentage of increase in the Consumer Price Index (CPI).† (And the last column shows the difference between housing and CPI increases, or the degree to which housing increases exceeded the CPI (or, when housing prices fell below inflation, the degree to which housing prices lagged behind the CPI).‡ The same results are summarized in Figure 1.3.

While past performance can never completely show the way to future performance of real estate or any other investment, historical information is valuable. From the comparison of increased value in existing home prices and the Consumer Price Index—or inflation—you can see that real estate has generally proven to be a successful investment. When values have met or exceeded inflation 71 percent of the time over 28 years, it is safe to say that performance of real estate has been not only successful but consistent.

Part of the reason for this consistent record is that housing prices are actually a part of the CPI, so they cannot be compared as mutually exclusive. However, when housing increases are compared to the CPI calculation as a whole, it is clear that the growth in value has exceeded overall inflation. The conclusion: As an investment, real estate operates as an asset whose value grows over time *and* beats inflation.

When you add the other beneficial features of real estate to this, it is apparent why real estate remains popular with investors. Real estate is a stable and sensible

*The annual percentage of increase in the median prices of existing homes is based on information provided by the National Association of Realtors. An *existing home* is a home constructed during a previous year but sold during the reported year.
†The increase in the Consumer Price Index for each year is developed from data compiled by the Bureau of Labor Statistics CPI for All Urban Consumers with a base period of the year 1967.
‡The rate of difference represents the degree to which increased existing home prices exceeded (+) or did not exceed (–) the same year's reported change in the CPI.

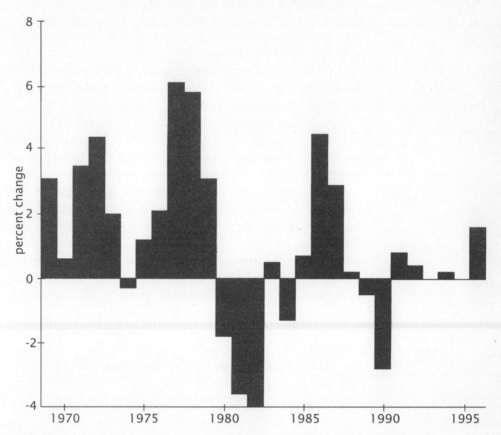

FIGURE 1.3 Existing Home Prices and CPI—1969 to 1996. *Sources:* Bureau of Labor Statistics; National Association of Realtors.

investment, the value of which is related directly to supply and demand. People need housing. Thus, the factors that affect value grow from necessity and not from strategy or timing exclusively. One observer has described the stock market as being naive,* which is a way of observing that momentary changes in market values tend to be erratic and not based on logical indicators. In comparison, real estate is anything but naive (if such human traits are to be attributed to investment markets), but

*Jonathan Pond, quoted in "Basic Steps to Prepare for Inflation," *Builder Online*, 1996.

rather is prone to react to real and meaningful indicators—supply and demand that grow from changes in actual economic conditions.

Other important benefits include the generated cash flow from rents, which cover mortgage payments, property taxes, insurance, and other expenses, either entirely or significantly. You also enjoy the tax benefits of owning real estate, being allowed to deduct not only interest, taxes, and other expenses, but also to claim depreciation on the buildings and other improvements. Finally, if your property follows past trends in the real estate market and increases in value, you may be able to refinance your mortgage in the future and take out cash to use for other investments.

The major drawback with real estate is that in order for the appreciated value to be realized, you need to allow time—usually a period of several years. If you are willing to accept the risks that come with investing in real estate, the benefits will likely be worth your patience and commitment. The next question is, Where do you get the money? If you are like many other first-time investors, you will probably consider using your own home equity as seed money to start up your real estate investment plan.

YOUR HOME AS AN INVESTMENT

People generally select real estate as an investment because of its historical record. Real estate is also tangible. For many investors, owning a visible asset is comforting in comparison to getting only a certificate and a monthly statement, or merely having an account number at a brokerage firm. Stock is part ownership in the intangible entity of the corporation, which in turn owns and manages all of the tangible assets. You cannot see and touch your ownership shares.

Real estate, in comparison, is tangible. As the owner, whether of your own home or of a rental, you can see it, fix it up, and create increased value through improvements and simple maintenance. One way that many people first invest in rental property is by using the equity in their own homes. You can refinance and get cash out, or acquire a second mortgage or a line of credit. But in a very real sense, this is placing your home at risk to create an investment portfolio. That might be a good idea, but you should go through a checklist and answer six questions first to ensure that the decision makes sense.

1. *Is there a demand for rentals in your area?* You certainly don't want to threaten your family's security, so before you buy rental real estate, you should be reasonably confident that you will be able to find tenants. This is an important first step.

You need to make certain that if you do buy a rental house, the demand for rentals is at a reasonable level. Without regular income from rents, you will have to make your mortgage payment on your own. So, if there is a high number of vacancies in your community, the timing is not good for buying residential real estate.

To get information about vacancies, inquire at property management companies, local lenders, and real estate agents. If your community has a landlords' association, that would also be a good source of information about local conditions. Don't depend on national averages or even your state's averages, since only local regional conditions matter.

2. *Can you afford the mortgage payments, even if you don't have tenants for two or three months?* Even in a good rental market, there might be periods of vacancy. You should not place yourself in a position of being unable to afford one to three months' mortgage payments without corresponding rental income. Here, more than with any other form of investing, having an emergency reserve is critical.

Even if rental demand is high today, there is no guarantee that will still be true tomorrow. In addition, demand may be seasonal. For example, if a large portion of your local population consists of attendees at a local university, you may expect higher than average vacancies from June to September, when many students go home for the summer. Plan for the worst-case scenario and develop a contingency plan.

The pressure of affordability will be greater if you finance your investment by refinancing your home or taking out a second mortgage or line of credit. That means higher payments than you're making today, thus more financial pressure if you do have a vacancy.

To be realistic, you should plan on having to carry potential negatives in rent for up to five years (or more). Annual rents (net of vacancies) may not cover your mortgage payment, taxes, insurance, and other expenses, requiring that you put additional money into the investment. As rents gradually increase over time, the cash flow relationship tends to improve.

3. *Does investing in real estate fit with your long-term financial goals?* Ownership of rental property should fit with your personal goals, which are not the same for everyone. For example, if your child will be going to college in three or four years, this is not a good time to begin a real estate investment program. However, if your children have 10 years or more before college age, real estate could be an excellent way to save for the future *and* enjoy some tax benefits along the way.

If you are considering using home equity to start your investment program, it is very important to ensure that this idea fits your long-term plan. If you cannot afford to tie up all of your equity for 5 to 10 years or more, it's probably premature to get into real estate right now.

4. *Are you willing to deal with tenants?* Many would-be investors stay out of the business or get out early solely because of the problems associated with tenants. In the chapter concerning landlording (Chapter 10), you will see that there are many steps you can take to minimize the potential difficulties landlords face. For example, by taking a written application and checking references, you will eliminate many potential problems before they even come up.

In some communities, the law favors tenants to a degree that landlording risks are high, perhaps even unreasonable. In other communities, the laws are more balanced. It pays to check with others who know— specifically other people who have rental properties or an attorney—to discover exactly how the law works in your area. Take this step before deciding to invest in rental property. The risk of regulatory difficulties is considerable. Some tenants, wise to the unfair advantage provided by overly punitive laws, know how to take advantage of landlords to live cheaply and hide behind the complexities of the legal system. You may want to completely avoid becoming a landlord if you live in an area where bureaucratic regulations have destroyed landlording as a business.

As a general rule of thumb, you stand an excellent chance of having a reasonable relationship with tenants, as long as you screen carefully and, after the tenant is in your house, keep an eye on conditions. As long as you maintain the property and act in a reasonable manner, most people will respond in the same way.

Landlording is both an investment and a business. Substitute the word "customer" for the word "tenant" and you will see why this applies. As with any other business, you need to be selective. At the same time, you expect to be paid, without exception. If the arrangement is not working out, get different tenants. It's that simple.

5. *Are you confident that real estate values will increase in your community during the coming decade?* You do not have to be an expert to have an opinion about the future, and experts are not necessarily more right or wrong that the average person, for two reasons. First, they may have more clouded judgment because they are too close to their market. Second, they may have a very strong bias. Real estate agents, escrow officers, lenders, appraisers, inspectors, real estate attorneys, and other professionals all depend on a strong real estate market to make a living. So, naturally, they tend to overestimate the future strength of the market.

Experts have the advantage of being exposed to more information than the average citizen as well as having direct experience. But, because cycles don't work in the same way twice, you should take expert advice carefully. Always ask for documentation supporting estimates, rather than just taking someone's word for it. Remember, *your* money will be put at risk, and not the expert's money. You have everything to gain by thoroughly researching the question of the current real estate cycle.

6. *Can you afford to go into debt?* This is a critical question. Most real estate investors depend on lenders, and when you acquire a mortgage you are going into debt. That carries an obligation to make payments every month, regardless of whether a tenant pays you on time.

The affordability of debt can be reflected in many ways. First, are you comfortable with the idea of being in debt? You should be able to sleep well at night even knowing that you owe the bank a lot of money and that you are depending on tenants to pay their rent in order to make your mortgage payment. Some people cannot get comfortable with that idea. Second, is your income high enough and is your credit strong enough to pass the lender's tests? If you do not have an excellent credit rating, you probably cannot get into real estate investment. However, if your credit is good, then you will probably have little trouble financing investment property. Third, are you sure that you can afford to cover the additional mortgage payment if and when you have vacancies?

EXPANDING YOUR PORTFOLIO

Many first-time investors get excited about the potential for expansion of their real estate base—often before finding out through direct experience exactly what is involved in owning real estate. Unfortunately, some so-called experts are ready to claim that you can get rich quickly, with little or no money down, little effort, and no experience.

The reality is far different. Making money in real estate is easier if you know what you are doing and understand your limitations. As you gain experience, you also discover some of the realities of the business. One of the first lessons is that lenders will only lend you what you can afford to carry in terms of debt. This is restricted by your income. This alone naturally limits everyone's ability to expand a real estate portfolio.

Another reality is that you probably are not going to be willing or able to put in the time and energy required to manage more than one or two properties. Managing your real estate can be very demanding. If you are working full-time and taking care of your investments on the weekend, how much leisure time are you left? With four or more properties, chances are high that you will always be dealing with at least one crisis. If you go far beyond five or six properties, you will have little or no time left for your family. With more than six properties, managing your investment will sometimes take all of your time, unless you want to give up some of your income and delegate these problems to a management company.

No doubt, you have heard the promises of how to become a real estate tycoon. First, you buy one house for nothing down, then borrow against the equity to buy another house. You continue this plan until you have 35 properties. You are also promised that you can sell within a few months, gaining $50,000 in profit each time. And, of course, all of this requires no real effort or time on your part. The illustrations and examples work on paper and sound good, but the reality is far from these promises. Nothing is said about the leaking roof, major plumbing problems, or the septic system you have to replace. Appliances in rentals break down, tenants forget to take care of the yard, and some tenants may trash your property.

The point here is not that landlording is a bad business; the point is that you need to understand the contingencies before expanding beyond your means to manage the investment—financially and personally. Landlording is actually a great business as long as you can remain in control. If any investment is taking away from your quality of life, you might as well put your money into a mutual fund and forget about property. As to the get-rich-quick scheme? The truth is, you will not become a millionaire buying foreclosure properties with nothing down. The only people who make money in that area are the high-pressure companies selling kits for $500 each, telling you how it is done.

As a general rule, you should be as involved in rental management as you want to be, and no more. If you have the time and resources to manage effectively up to three homes, don't buy a fourth. If you can handle 10 properties, keep your investment at or below that level. Only through experience will you discover the best investment level for you, based on your credit, available cash, temperament, and available time.

Suppose you decide to buy a few rental properties over the coming two or three years, but the banks won't

seller financing

a financing arrangement in which the property owner agrees for the buyer to purchase the property partly with cash and partly by the seller providing a mortgage. The seller assumes the role of lender, and the buyer agrees to make monthly payments to the seller, with interest.

carry

a term describing a seller's holding a note for part of the debt owed by the buyer. The seller helps a buyer close the deal by providing part of the purchase price as a loan.

work with you. Perhaps your income is too low or you have had credit problems in the past. In this instance, you might need to take a creative approach to getting into real estate.

If you consider yourself a good risk taker, one approach is to finance your down payment using existing credit cards or lines of credit. This is an extraordinary risk, and most people should reject this immediately. Repayment at high interest rates makes a poor investment, if only because interest is likely to take up all of your profit and perhaps more. Meanwhile, the demand for making high payments will inhibit your ability to continue paying other recurring expenses.

A more realistic approach is to look for *seller financing*. Some sellers will agree to *carry* a loan. For some people, this idea makes a lot of sense—especially if there is no other way to get a loan. The seller, by carrying a note, gets profits from the sale over a period of time *and* earns interest on the unpaid balance.

A word of caution: If you find a deal in which the seller is willing to carry a note, that might indicate that the seller wants to earn interest. But it could also indicate that there are problems with the house, severe enough that the seller knows a conventional lender will not grant a loan. For example, if the foundation is substandard, it might be impossible to get a bank loan. As an investor, you should always remember this point: If the seller has a problem with the house, that problem becomes *your* problem as soon as the deal closes.

As a general rule, the more financing the seller is willing to carry, the more such problems you might expect to find with the house. This could mean that the value is simply not there, because the problems are so severe. If the house has a lot of *deferred maintenance*, that condition takes away from current value. You will have to perform repairs one day and the longer you wait, the more damage will accumulate.

Example: A buyer was looking for seller financing because he knew he would not qualify for a bank loan. One seller was willing to carry up to 80 percent of the purchase price. But on close examination of the property, the buyer decided not to go for the deal. The house had thousands of dollars of deferred maintenance: a leaking roof, an inadequate foundation causing slanting floors, leaking plumbing, unsafe electrical systems, and many other problems. These costs were far too high. The "bargain" wasn't really a bargain at all.

The fact that a seller is willing to carry part of the financing does not always mean that there are big problems. However, it often happens that seller financing indicates problem houses and attracts buyers with poor credit. This is just one potential trap to look out for and avoid. Be aware that deals requiring the degree of deferred maintenance that goes far beyond cosmetic repairs are the most likely ones to involve seller financing. You might end up acquiring a big headache with no real market value, rather than finding a good deal. In setting a price, take into account the amount of work required to fix those problems and, if you do make an offer, discount the price with those repairs in mind.

Remember, every investment buyer eventually becomes a seller. Evaluate every potential investment property in terms of the problems you will encounter when you want to sell. The methods you can use to find the best values in real estate are the subject of the next chapter.

 deferred maintenance work required to properly maintain or upgrade a property, which has accumulated over time and has not been done. Examples include old, chipped paint; broken windows; leaking gutters; unrepaired pest damage; sagging foundations; outdated plumbing, electrical or heating systems; and leaking roofs.

Chapter 2

How to Choose Property

Everyone prefers hot markets to cold markets. In a hot market, everyone believes they can make a profit. Buyers and sellers alike prefer to believe that they foresaw the hot market coming. In short, when the market is hot, everyone can be right.

In some very heated markets of the past, people could make money with virtually any property. The danger (in all markets) is that eventually you reach the top. There is always one "latest buyer" who turns out to have timed the market badly. When markets are so hot that any property will work, that does not mean you should buy carelessly. It always makes sense to choose property using intelligent guidelines. Shopping carefully and taking the time you need, in spite of pressure from others, is always smart investing.

The advice to "buy low and sell high" is usually used in reference to the stock market. The same rule applies to real estate, although "low" and "high" mean different things at different times. Because real estate values tend to plateau at the end of the cycle, there may be no actual low points in real estate that compare to price movements in the stock market. One cycle's high may become the next cycle's low, and the term "low" may, in fact, come to mean flattening out. So, choosing property is largely a matter of timing.

CONDITIONS OF THE MARKET

An old real estate maxim is that there are three things that determine real estate value: location, location, and location. However, it is not really that simple. Property should be evaluated not only on the basis of location, but also on current market conditions. All investments can be classified broadly as "good" or "bad" depending on timing. You will recall the previous chapter's discussion of timing as the essential ingredient in the real estate cycle. This applies to all investments. For example, you would not want to buy shares of stock at the all-time high price level—on the risk of a market correction—and the same rule applies to real estate.

Value in real estate changes due to changes in current market conditions. A bargain is a relative judgment. For example, one long-term resident of a community might be shocked that a newcomer would be willing to pay $115,000 for a house, because the long-term resident can still remember when that house was worth only $40,000. This ignores the reality of the current market. It may be that $115,000 is a bargain given the relative values in today's market.

The market can be generally described in terms of who has the greater advantage, buyers or sellers. This is an excellent distinction. When demand is low, a potential buyer has the advantage and when demand is high (and supply is limited) the seller is in command.

A *buyer's market* is typified by many bargains, given the current oversupply of properties. Because there is too much supply, the buyer has the leisure to compare many properties; can take time to make a decision; can offer a price well below the seller's asking price (with every prospect of having an offer accepted); and has tremendous advantages in negotiating other terms and conditions in the offer. In a *seller's market* a bargain is more difficult to find. A limited supply of properties is available, but many buyers compete with one another or, at the very least, buyers move in quickly enough so that the inventory of available properties is low.

 buyer's market
a condition in which there is a plentiful supply of properties on the market, and not enough available buyers to purchase the entire inventory; from the seller's perspective, a slow market.

 seller's market
a condition in which many buyers are competing for a relatively small inventory of available properties; a fast market, in which prices tend to be driven upward by high demand.

Bargains can be found in several forms. For example, when interest rates are high and money is scarce, an acceptable property with attractive financing is considered a bargain, even if the price is on the high side. In markets with extremely high interest rates, being able to get a deal with low interest becomes the deciding factor. Price is not as important. It may even be possible for a seller to get a highly inflated price if that seller is also willing to carry a mortgage at a relatively low rate.

A bargain may have vastly different definitions at different times and in different markets. It might also mean different things to you as a homeowner, and to you as an investor. Value and the potential for future value are important in either event; but perception of those factors affects your buying decision directly.

Demand for investment property is somewhat different in several respects. Investors don't look at properties in the same way as homeowners, for obvious reasons. For example, as a homeowner, you might want to buy a particular house because the kitchen is large, modern, and well-designed. An investor might look at the same kitchen and consider it an extravagance that is reflected in the price, but not necessary for a rental.

The difference in attitude is reflected in the market value of properties. Homeowners are constantly evaluating property on the basis of personal comfort, space, quality of life, traffic levels, safety, and the age of the property, as well as convenience to schools, shopping, transportation, and recreation. Investors think about resale value, utility of the property as a rental (meaning providing basic necessities tenants expect, but little in the way of custom design), and the tenant market rather than the neighborhood.

That comparison of priorities is critical in the decision about which investment real estate to buy. It is entirely possible that a market will reflect high demand for primary residential housing and at the same time low demand for rental units (or vice versa). For example, one employer might decide to relocate headquarters and move an entire corporate structure to one community, creating demand for five thousand houses. It may also be that most of those new residents will want to buy their own home.

This creates an obvious aberration in the local real estate market. At the same time, that community might be suffering from overbuilt conditions in the apartment market.

Another example makes the same point. If a community of 50,000 includes 12,000 local university students, there will tend to be high demand for rental apartments and houses; this does not necessarily mean that home ownership will be in great demand at the same time. Rental demand may be high while the market for primary residential real estate is very slow. The markets are entirely different, and they are driven by different economic groups. It would be a mistake to evolve a series of assumptions about one market based solely on information about the other. The overall demographic mix can mislead investors, and one common trap is to classify "the market" as one unit, reacting to the same supply and demand factors when, in practice, markets tend to work separately from one another. These divisions can be quite detailed. In residential markets alone, your community might have different factors at work for:

✔ College students (apartments, rooms, and share properties).

✔ Middle-class working families.

✔ Migrant populations.

✔ Retirees (condos and small housing).

✔ Tourists (time-share, seasonal condo living).

Further subgroupings are possible. The point is that each of these groups places different kinds of demands on the real estate market. We are not even considering the effect of nonresidential development, including commercial (downtown buildings as well as mall developments); light and heavy industrial; government (prisons, public works, and administration); recreational parks and facilities; and other land use that affects different residential markets.

As a real estate investor, you will probably start out buying residential housing. If that is true, then you need to be able to judge the relative conditions of that market. For this, the most reliable indicator is the current *vacancy rate*. A high vacancy rate indicates that too many units are

vacancy rate
the percentage of rental units in apartments and other multiunit buildings that are not occupied by tenants. Average vacancy rates are used as an indicator by lenders and appraisers to estimate average annual rental income.

available; and when vacancy is low, it indicates that demand is high for rental units. Demand drives up rental market rates, an important fact to remember as an investor. That, in turn, favorably affects the value of rental properties.

Although the traditional vacancy rate is a study of multiple-unit housing, the rate directly affects rental houses as well. If you buy a house to rent out, the local vacancy rate will determine whether you should be able to find and keep tenants. Within every market, there is always a segment of renters who want houses and will pay more to get them. They may prefer living with other people and sharing rent or living alone in a desire for maximum privacy and space. No matter what the motive, high demand for apartment units also creates a high demand for rental houses.

High vacancy rates have the opposite effect, and market rental rates are consequently held down. Remember, high vacancy rates directly reflect low demand. This is unavoidable. So investors in such markets cannot expect as much cash return on their investments. Not only are rents held down by low demand, but the vacancy rate may also translate to losses of two, three, or more months per year.

The discussion of demand for apartment units is a form of market demand. In comparison, high demand among investors for income property is caused by completely different influences. The causes may have little to do with the current conditions of demand for rental units. Even when vacancy rates are very low and tenant demand is high, this does not necessarily mean that the market for investment properties is hot among would-be investors. If a high number of rental properties are for sale at the same time, the supply and demand is not set by tenants, but by the number of potential investors (buyers) compared to the number of sellers. So the "market" has to be defined carefully. As a holder of rental property, your market is the number of tenants versus the number of rentals available. As a seller, your market is the number of potential buyers versus the number of rental properties for sale. There is significant difference between market demand among tenants for available rental units and among investors for available investment properties.

This is a dilemma. Logically, you might reason that a high demand among tenants would drive up the value of rental real estate. In fact, over the long term, it does. But we have to also remember that markets are not entirely orderly, and the timing and sequence of developments tend to be random and chaotic in the short term. In other words, it may take time for the effect to catch up to the cause. It is true that demand among renters will ultimately lead to the development of more rental units, but short-term responses may not reflect that at all. Remember, *economic logic is not the same thing as market logic*. A reasoned, analytical, and unemotional study of the market may dictate one obvious course of events. However, the market is unreasoning, nonanalytical, and emotional. That's what makes a study of supply and demand so interesting. Real opportunities arise when observant investors recognize momentary opportunities and take advantage of them. Such moments arise from the disparity between the obvious (economic) and the current reality (illogical) factors within the market.

Another example of the disparity between economic forces and market forces can be seen when governments attempt to interfere in the real estate cycle. Some communities have seen the consequences of rent control, for example. In its attempt to hold down rents, governments fail to trust market forces; they believe that the cost of living can be artificially kept down by making it illegal to raise rents beyond a predetermined level. The real consequence of rent control, however, is that developers have no incentive to build more rental housing; therefore, demand continues to grow while supplies remain dormant. The effect of rent controls is much higher rents for newcomers (or the creation of an underground market in rentals), and greatly inflated pricing of new rental property because the supply is discouraged. In this instance, market forces are not allowed to work, so the real supply and demand factors are subverted, making things worse rather than better. The real market is destroyed by the regulatory restriction.

FACTORS ADDING TO VALUE

Earlier, the real estate maxim concerning location was introduced. Another maxim that says a lot about value is expressed in the form of advice: "Buy the worst house on a good block." This statement sums up the importance of location and its effect on future value. With location in mind as the important selection standard, you first need to locate that "good" block. This means an area not next to a freeway, a cement plant, or a state prison. Price will reflect the relative desirability or undesirability of location. So a house on a busy street will have lower market value than an identical house one block away on a quiet, relatively traffic-free street. Such factors as proximity to high traffic, industrial uses, freeways, and other unattractive features also hold down future value. A "good" block should be:

✔ Quiet in terms of traffic flow.

✔ Well-maintained by current owners.

✔ In an area of low crime.

✔ In a built-up area (no vacant lots, for example).

✔ Close to conveniences such as shopping and transportation.

✔ Zoned for residential or residential-commercial mix (as opposed to unregulated zones, characterized by intensive uses combined with residential).

Let's say you locate the ideal block containing all of the attributes and, equally as important, lacking any undesirable features. All the lawns are well-manicured, the houses are newly roofed and painted, the cars parked on the street and in the driveways are obviously in good condition, all of the houses are occupied (none are boarded up); and these conditions apply to every house, with one exception. That one house has overgrown weeds in front, it is unpainted, and the roof is in obvious need of repair. In short, it is not being cared for and the obvious problems are cosmetic. (Other problems may be found as well, but the visible problems are what make it the worst house on a good block.)

In these circumstances, that one house—the one with all the deferred maintenance—will appreciate in value well beyond the average house on that block, for one very good reason: In its current condition, its value is far lower than the houses that are being well cared for, so that improving the obvious problems will have an immediate and dramatic effect on value. Its condition reflects market value far below the average house on that block. It is a bargain. With a little cleanup, the cosmetic fixes can be done quickly and with little additional investment capital (not to mention without requiring much in the way of specialized skill, either). The easy fixes will increase equity almost as soon as the work is done.

"Good" may describe the attributes of the neighborhood—crime levels, zoning, noise, traffic, population density, quality of schools, convenience. "Good" may also refer to the price levels of property. Some neighborhoods demand much higher prices than others for identically sized homes. So you can get more home for the same money in a neighborhood with less status. At times, the status is derived from local opinion and reputation rather than from any tangible reasons.

Other factors have to be remembered when studying real estate value. If you will be investing strictly in *residential property*, you should be aware of the effect of *mixed use* on current and future value. The advantage of zoning is that it provides for reliability among property owners. If you buy a home in a residential neighborhood, you have a right to expect that the character of that neighborhood won't be changed by a future decision to allow commercial or industrial development across the street. For investors, the same need for reliability is important because such unexpected changes could adversely affect future property values.

Many of the same considerations arise for investors in *commercial property*. This type of property has specific requirements relating to visibility to high-volume traffic (which is opposite of the requirements for "good" residential property); space for parking, delivery, and storage; and other considerations special only to commercial use.

residential property
property designed for living, including single-family homes, duplexes and flats, triplexes, apartments, and other multifamily buildings.

mixed use
zoning that allows residential as well as other uses (commercial, industrial, recreational) in the same area; or an area that lacks zoning altogether.

commercial property
nonresidential property, operated for business use. It requires adequate traffic and parking, delivery areas, and room for storage of inventory.

industrial property
property used for manufacturing, trucking, storage, warehousing, transportation, and other specialized uses. Industrially zoned areas tend to have noise and traffic levels and other hazards not compatible with residential land use nor with most types of commercial land use.

highest and best use
the use of property for the most profitable, efficient, and appropriate purpose, given the zoning and other restrictions placed on the land. Property not being utilized at its highest and best use will have less value than other, comparable properties, based on this standard.

So a long-term commercial property owner will be inconvenienced if residential development is allowed to encroach on commercial zones.

The final major classification is *industrial property*. Such property tends to have high noise levels, and may involve dangers such as environmental or topographical hazards and flammable or toxic material storage, to name a few. For obvious reasons, locating such intense uses in a residential neighborhood would not only affect local property values, but would also pose great dangers. For these reasons, industrial zoning tends to be designated in carefully chosen areas with minimal impact on residential zones.

Another point affecting the value of real estate is the use of land and improvements. Value is affected directly by the degree of utilization of land. Value is maximized when property is being used at what is called its *highest and best use*. This means that land used at maximum potential allowed under zoning laws and reasonably practical given other features (topography, location, etc.) will also achieve its highest potential value. For example, if a building lot in a residentially zoned area is left vacant, it is not being put to its highest and best use. The market for such land will be determined by its potential use rather than by the more desirable standard of highest and best use.

The current use also affects *market value* of property. Zoning is one important aspect of market value. The failure to properly zone land will, naturally, restrict the potential for that property to achieve the market value it would otherwise be expected to command. The example of an empty building lot makes this point, because the land is being left idle rather than being used for the properly zoned purpose. Other examples include the failure of a local government to change zoning of property due to local antigrowth pressure, even when the need is obvious.

Example: In one area, a parcel of 200 acres of rurally zoned land was being considered for a rezone to industrial. A local antigrowth group organized to lobby the local council in opposition to the plan. Their efforts delayed the rezone for five years even though the land contained all the right attributes. It was flat, isolated, and underutilized, and the soil was too poor for farming. It was also crossed by rail lines and siding, so that industrial use would have been the most appropriate, or highest and best use. Once it was rezoned and development began to occur, land values increased to reflect highest and best use.

Market value is also affected when property is located in inconsistent zones. For example, a residence situated in the middle of a commercial zone will not command as high a price as a similar house in a strictly residential area. The commercial use, traffic, and overall theme of the area will hold down the value of that property as a residence; however, if the house were converted to commercial use, it would probably appreciate. Given the nature of zoning in that area, commercial zoning would represent the highest and best use. Few people want their homes located in the middle of highly traveled commercial areas, not to mention near train tracks, cement plants, quarries, service stations, and similar facilities.

As you evaluate property with the idea of investing, you should also be aware of the importance of *conformity*. This is a tendency for construction in one area to be similar in nature to other nearby sites. For example, if a neighborhood typically contains three-bedroom homes, then a home with five bedrooms will be nonconforming. For purposes of appraising homes or estimating market value, conformity is considered as a positive feature. Conforming homes are generally more marketable. Nonconformity becomes especially troubling when it results from *overimprovement*.

As a general rule, overimprovement places limits on how much value a property will realize upon sale. While typical homes in one area that conform may rise in price along a similar schedule and timeline, a nonconforming home may not be able to recapture the value of investment in overimprovements.

Example: In one neighborhood, most homes are on single building lots, have three bedrooms and two baths, and average 1600 feet in living space. One home, however, was built in the middle of a double lot, has five bedrooms and three baths plus an office and a den, and has about 2700 square feet of living space. It is a nonconforming home.

market value
the current value of property according to the price it would command on the market, which reflects current supply and demand levels and whether the property is being utilized at its highest and best use.

conformity
the tendency for property in one area and with common zoning to be similar to other properties in the area and with the same zoning. Conforming homes, for example, tend to be similar in lot size, number of rooms, and other features. Nonconforming properties tend to be limited in their potential market value.

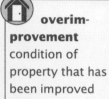

overim-provement condition of property that has been improved beyond the scope of other properties in the same area, so that the property is nonconforming.

The typical house in this neighborhood has a market value of $175,000. When the nonconforming home goes on the market, the typical price of other homes in the neighborhood will tend to hold down the market price of the nonconforming home. It is not likely that the seller will be able to realize the full value of the improvements.

In this example, several features make the property nonconforming. For example, building on a double lot will not mean that the land is worth twice as much, because the highest and best use of that land would be to build two homes. Nonconforming homes tend to be appraised at a level below their replacement value. In the example above, the house might sell for more than the average home; but it will not be marketable at the price level it would achieve if it conformed to the size, style, and features of other homes in the area.

Be aware of the problems created by nonconforming property. At some point, you might actually want to buy a nonconforming property; but before you do, you need to know about restrictions on equity growth that come with such an investment. When you become a seller at some time in the future, the nonconformity of the property will limit the market value.

RENTAL TRENDS

No region is immune from changing trends in real estate. The demographic forces at work in an area—population, employment, income levels, and so forth—should be evaluated long-term. In other words, how are today's conditions likely to change in the future, and how will that affect real estate values?

The mix of local population is one such factor. If there is a large number of renters in your area (such as a college population, for example), prospects are high that this trend will continue well into the future. That is a positive indicator for investors, because high demand for rental apartments and homes ensures that you will be able to afford your mortgage payments. With the exception of slow periods (such as summer in a college town), you can expect low vacancies well into the future.

If your area does not have an easily identifiable renter population, how can you judge the trends? One way is to check the market directly. How many rental ads appear each day or week in the newspaper? Talk to rental agencies and management companies in your area. How many For Rent signs do you see around, and how long do they stay up? Also check with your chamber of commerce and with landlords directly. You can get in touch with other investors by joining a local landlording association. Ask the right questions:

- ✔ What is the average vacancy rate?
- ✔ How long does it take to find tenants?
- ✔ What are the market rental rates?
- ✔ What do you see taking place in the future?
- ✔ Most important of all: What are the trends?

Once you have calculated current rental conditions in your community, think about how the future might change. This is where you really gain insight as an investor—in how well you can calculate future changes, based on today's conditions and trends. Are employers relocating here and hiring people? Are they providing family-wage jobs and attracting workers and managers to the area? Does the local government encourage economic development? Are new retail outlets opening? (*Note*: If many retail establishments are coming into town and hiring many minimum-wage workers, that makes for a higher-than-average renter population. In comparison, the real estate market as a whole is better served when the employment base is stronger, because that translates to more future home buyers.)

Also check population estimates for your region, which may be published by a state agency or studied by a local economic development association. Is the population growing? Is that growth below or above state and national averages? How does that growth rate translate to housing prices and rent levels?

MAKING YOUR MONEY GO FURTHER

Evaluating real estate as a possible investment is easier in many respects than evaluating the other popular alternative—stocks. The stock market changes rapidly, on a daily and sometimes hourly basis, often for reasons no one anticipates. In comparison, real estate tends to react to more rational indicators. It is true that the effects of cycles may not keep up with the causes, but over the long term, real estate can be accurately judged.

If you determine that real estate is a worthwhile investment, and that the timing is right, you will need to decide how to invest your capital. Of course, if you have enough money available, you could purchase property for cash. However, few people have the luxury of a large sum of cash. Most investors have to finance their real estate purchases. With the right opportunity, you can turn this into an advantage.

The greater the level of borrowed money (financing) on your investment, the higher the risk. This is true because you need to generate rental income in order to make your mortgage payment. So if you do not have a tenant, or if your tenant does not pay the rent, you still have to come up with that mortgage payment in some other way. This is a drain on your other capital. Many people who have never invested in real estate see the rental income covering the mortgage payments, and immediately envision the possibilities. You could—in theory—have an indefinite number of rental properties without any real net cost. In truth, that may not work out. The less money you put down on a property, the higher your payments; so the cash income will not always cover all of the mortgage payment *and* other expenses. The truth is that you will be limited in the number of properties you can afford to acquire—both by money and by risk.

The greatest risk of all comes from *leverage* of capital. This means using a limited sum of capital to finance more than one investment. This is the greatest risk, but it also offers the greatest potential for future equity growth. The challenge is to find an appropriate and reasonable balance between potential gain and acceptable risk. When you place yourself in a situation that maximizes profit,

leverage
the use of a limited amount of capital to purchase more than a single property, increasing potential gain as well as risk level.

that also means that you have to live with correspondingly higher risks.

All forms of financing are variations of leverage. If you want to escape leverage risk completely, you need to pay all cash for real estate, which is impractical for most people and not necessarily the best way to invest, either. The risk is there because borrowing money obligates you to make repayments. A mortgage is a loan, and it must be repaid. So by any measure, you will probably not be able to escape some degree of leverage risk. As the term is usually applied, though, it refers to the purchase of multiple properties at the same time.

Example: An investor had $50,000 in capital. He purchased three properties. The first one cost $45,000 and the investor made a down payment of one-third, or $15,000. The second property cost $50,000 and was acquired with a 20 percent down payment, or $10,000. The third property cost $125,000 and was bought with $25,000 down.

In this example of leverage, the investor was able to purchase $220,000 in property value with only $50,000. That means that the financed balance, $170,000, is the leveraged portion of this investment. Figure 2.1 summarizes this example of leverage.

Example: Another investor also had $50,000 to invest, but wanted to avoid leverage altogether. She bought only one property, a small two-bedroom house that needed some work. With only $50,000 in capital, the market was limited to only the low end. The investor has to wait to fix up the property because all of her capital was used up in buying the house.

This example shows how the desire to avoid leverage can impede your investment program. Not only was the investor restricted to only the low end of the market spectrum, but also since all of the capital was used to buy the property, nothing was left over to make needed repairs.

When you use leverage, there is the possibility that the market value will not grow quickly enough to make

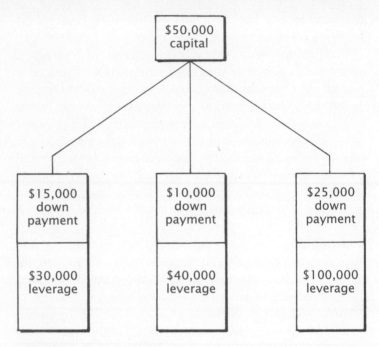

FIGURE 2.1 Leverage.

the investment profitable. Your potential profits may be converted to interest, so that lenders actually profit rather than you. In that instance, leverage defeats your purpose. However, if tenants are making your mortgage payments for you, the investment is paying for itself.

You should seek a happy medium between what are actually two extremes. Excessive leverage threatens the entire investment plan as well as your personal financial security. On the other end, avoiding the risk altogether is too limiting and prevents you from being able to take advantage of a healthy market when the opportunity presents itself. You have probably heard the claim that you can make a lot of money in real estate with high leverage. But it's also important to recognize that leverage is both opportunity *and* risk. If you take on too much risk, it does not take much to upset the whole plan.

Without any doubt, leverage is the way to make money in real estate. But the risk that is associated with leverage needs to be managed carefully, planned and controlled. Buying real estate as a long-term investment works well when you are aware of your financial limitations. For example, you know that you depend on rental income to make regular mortgage payments. In comparison, when you own property *free and clear*, it is much easier to survive a period of vacancy, because you do not have to make payments to a lender.

Leverage gives you the opportunity to put your capital to work at maximum level. So the more properties you own (or, more accurately, the more properties you control through leverage), the greater the potential for future appreciation. This assumes that you select properties carefully on their own merits and maintain them well over time so that they hold their market value. When you consider the advantages of controlling several properties, you can see why avoiding leverage altogether is a poor idea.

 free and clear
a term describing real estate owned without any outstanding debts. The owner is free of mortgages and other liens, and has clear title.

Example: An investor with $50,000 of capital purchased three properties with total value of $220,000, including leverage (mortgages) of $170,000. Five years later, all of the properties had doubled in value. Tenants paid rents adequate to cover mortgage payments, but there was no cash left over after paying for related expenses (maintenance, taxes, etc.). The investor sold all three properties, and realized $440,000. Profits are computed as follows (*note:* all of these illustrations are calculated before allowing for tax benefits or calculating tax consequences):

Sale price	$440,000
Less: original cost	−220,000
Profit before taxes	$220,000

Example: Another investor purchased one property and paid all cash of $50,000. After five years in which rent payments covered the mortgage obligation, the investor sold the property, which had doubled in value. The pretax outcome:

Sale price	$100,000
Less: original cost	− 50,000
Profit before taxes	$ 50,000

Neither of these illustrations considers the benefit both alternatives enjoy—that rent payments cover the mortgage. But the difference is clear. Leverage enables the first investor to earn a $220,000 profit, whereas the second investor earns $50,000. That is the benefit that accompanies the higher risk. If you argue that the illustration is not realistic because it assumes that values will double, remember that the same assumptions are used for both cases. You may apply any form of assumption and the answer will be the same. The investor who uses leverage assumes greater risks but makes more money. And in either alternative, it is also fair to assume that rents cover mortgage payments.

How should you deal with the question of potential reward versus risk? Consider using leverage to the degree necessary, but within limits that you can manage. Owning more than one kind of property allows you to spread the risk around within your *portfolio*. For example, you might own one single-family house for future appreciation as well as a six-unit apartment building for current income. In the future, you may also trade up to larger apartments or expand to own several houses. This may improve tax advantages and bring you more cash at the same time. Putting parts of your money into different types of properties spreads the risk.

Even in the residential housing market, you can achieve this risk-spreading. For example, suppose you own three houses. One is on a full acre, which may give you future potential gain through splitting the land into two building lots. Another is in a very desirable neighborhood and near a school, which means maximum potential for future appreciation. And the third has been split into a duplex and produces far more rental income than required to make the mortgage payment. Each of these properties has distinct and different potential, so that your market risks have been spread among dissimilar properties.

This strategy is called *diversification*. It is the same process stock market investors use by buying stocks in different industries.

portfolio
an investment term describing all of the holdings owned by one investor. In real estate, the portfolio refers to all of the properties owned or controlled, plus other investments. It may include equity assets (ownership of property) as well as debt investments (loans made to others, which earn interest).

QUESTIONS TO ASK

When you go to an open house; be aware that the agent probably has several other listings. The open house is, first of all, an opportunity to see the one house, but even more, is an opportunity to get a range of market information.

The real estate agent is usually an expert. Experts have their bias, of course, because their livelihood depends on earning commissions, and that happens only when they make a sale. The agent is highly motivated to show you a house that he or she has as a listing, and that is going to be a strong bias, because every agent's listings are naturally limited in range and number. And because commission-earning people tend to be optimistic, you cannot consider their market predictions as reliable or necessarily fact-based on all occasions. With these points in mind, ask an agent the following questions:

diversification a strategy of spreading risk among different markets, regions, or types of property, with a potential for future price increase. This lowers the risk that a single change in the market will adversely affect all properties in the same manner.

1. *Do you think we are in a buyer's market or a seller's market?* A real estate agent's opinion is valuable. The agent lives in the cycle and is aware of it constantly. Agents know from day to day how much inventory is available, how long it takes for properties to sell, and what kinds of offers are made against asked prices. In other words, they know the market.

Don't ever depend on one person's opinion about the market as your only source for your own opinion. Gather a lot of information from as many sources as possible, but develop your opinion primarily from observation. What the real estate agent tells you might be valuable information, but ultimately, you are responsible for gauging the market for yourself.

2. *How do you see the market changing over the coming year?* Just as agents tend to understand the market as it is today, they also tend to know the direction in which it is headed. But be very careful in listening to the answer, remembering that the agent's income depends on inducing people to take action now, not a year from now. You will probably not find a real estate agent who will advise you to hold off buying property until next year. Their information is not objective, since they are paid to get people to buy and sell property.

This is a valuable question, since agents may provide you with insights about trends and, equally valuable, the reasons for anticipating changes in near-term trends. That is the key to good timing: knowing what is about to happen. For example, the agent might be aware that a new employer has recently signed an agreement to build a major new plant in town, and that will mean hundreds of new jobs within a few months. Such a change will directly affect the real estate cycle.

3. *In what part of town would you suggest buying a rental property, and why?* Agents are great sources of information about where markets are hot, and where they are not. You should specifically mention your interest in rental properties, because a reference to the "best" part of town may mean different things to you as a landlord than it means to most people as homeowners.

From the agent's response, you will quickly discover whether they have any sophistication in the rental real estate market. Most do not. The majority of contacts real estate agents have are with homeowners, whether as buyers or sellers. A small number of real estate agents understand the investment side of the market, and you will need to find those few people to work with as you develop your own investing skills.

You might have your own bias about a particular part of town, only to discover that the real estate agent sees neighborhoods differently—often for very good reasons. It helps to modify or reinforce your opinion with someone else's point of view or to completely shatter your preconceived ideas with new, contradictory information. For example, a part of town might be good in terms of renter demand due to convenience to transportation routes and shopping or proximity to a university; but potential growth in market value could exist in other parts of town. That is the typical subtlety that you can gain from listening to a real estate agent's point of view.

4. *Is today's market better than last year's?* This is somewhat loaded as questions go, because agents depend on commissions. Most do not want you to think you have missed a market opportunity, so the future will always appear more promising than the past. You might expect to hear from many agents that the market right now is the best it has ever been, but a delay will mean missing the opportunity forever. This kind of information is difficult to digest and impossible to translate. It is tainted because, even though the agent is a professional and a good source of information, that sales agent is also a salesperson. Whether the product is real estate, cars, or financial products, salespeople have to convey a sense of urgency, coupled with the message that you must act now.

When it comes to buying real estate, that is the worst approach. Do not let anyone pressure you into premature action. There are always opportunities and, due to the cyclical nature of real estate, you do not need to rush into anything. In order to sift through the information you are given, ask the agent about relative value. By doing so, you might learn about factors affecting market value and demand that you did not realize before; or you might conclude that, in fact, this is *not* necessarily the best time to buy. That means you should back off for a few months and then check out the market again.

If, though, you decide that this is a good time to buy, your next stop should be the local lender. Always look into the financing before you look for property. The lender is a first stop before talking seriously to a real estate agent, because financing terms will determine whether you can get the deal. The first question should be: Can I qualify for financing? The next question should be: Where is the best financing deal?

The next chapter explains the range of alternatives you have for locating financing for your real estate investments.

Chapter

Financing Your Investment

O ne sure way to become a familiar face at the local bank is to begin buying rental property. This is a difficult business to run without borrowing; your lender will be an indispensable resource.

THE SUPPLY OF AND DEMAND FOR MONEY

money supply
the amount of currency in circulation at any given time, plus demand deposits (savings accounts immediately available to depositors) in banks and other financial institutions.

Banks and other lenders cannot just create money to lend on real estate. They are limited by their own resources, which is the combination of their own assets plus the amount that they can borrow. Since banks are required to set up reserves when they lend money, they cannot grant an unlimited number of loans, either. As the *money supply* changes, so do interest rates; and so does the bank's capacity to make loans.

As a borrower who is subject to changing policies among banks and other lenders, you should keep this important point in mind: *Whenever a lender makes a loan, the lender is required to set up a reserve.* This means the bank has to keep cash on hand to provide coverage for those loans that become bad debts. The bad debts can be closely estimated, so the reserve requirement is a reliable safety measure. Without these *reserve requirements*, banks would conceivably be able to lend as much money as they wanted, assuming they could find the money somewhere (from borrowing elsewhere, for example). But the safeguard protects everyone's economic health. Once a lender reaches the limits of its reserves, it cannot make additional loans.

Since the bank cannot merely create more money when it needs to make more loans, it is restricted by its own set financial capability. The bank's own borrowing power is limited. When the Federal Reserve Board wants to create more money (ease the money supply) or restrict the amount (tighten the money supply), it can achieve its desired result by making it easier or harder for lending institutions to borrow. Typically, a lending institution borrows money from the Federal Reserve banks and lends it out at higher rates. But just as real estate is subject to the forces of supply and demand, lenders do not always have absolute discretion over whether they can grant you a loan. They too have a supply and demand market in money.

Your local bank has to set up and enforce lending standards. These standards change as the national money supply changes and as interest rates move up or down. Banks that belong to the Federal Reserve System base their policies on the dollar amount they are allowed to borrow from other banks. They have to pay interest just like other borrowers, at a rate called the *discount rate*.

With the reserve requirements restricting the lending activity of a bank, it would seem that a smaller bank would not be able to generate new loans once its more limited reserve levels were met. There is a way around this problem. With *conventional financing*, loans granted by the original institution are rarely left on the books of the original lender. Loans are usually resold on the *secondary market*. So a bank or savings and loan association makes a loan to a homeowner or investor, and then sells the loan to one of the secondary market agencies. These agencies include the Federal National Mortgage Association (FNMA), also known as "Fannie Mae," and the Government National Mortgage Association (GNMA), also known as "Ginnie Mae." These agencies form mortgage pools and sell shares to investors. Just as investors in mu-

 reserve requirements the rule stating that lenders have to establish reserves for loans granted and keep a minimum required amount of cash on hand to cover future losses.

 discount rate the interest rate charged to banks when they borrow from other Federal Reserve banks.

 conventional financing lending obtained from traditional sources, such as banks, savings and loan associations, and mutual savings banks.

secondary market
the market for the purchase of loans written by conventional institutions. Agencies in this market buy loans to form pools; shares in pools are sold to investors who want to earn interest. The pool works like a mutual fund for mortgages rather than stocks.

first mortgage
a mortgage that has first priority for payment in the event of default and foreclosure. When a borrower fails to make required payments on a mortgage, the lender forecloses. The first mortgage holder is paid first; other mortgage holders are paid from the remaining equity, if any.

tual funds own small units of a large stock market pool, investors in these pools own units of larger blocks of mortgages.

Agencies in the secondary market will generally buy only a *first mortgage*. These are mortgages that have first right, or priority, to be repaid in the event the borrower defaults. That is the best form of mortgage security. A *second mortgage* would be in second place in the event a borrower defaults on the mortgage obligation.

So even when a relatively small lender has reached its maximum reserve level, it can start all over again simply by selling its loans on the secondary market. This may occur four times per year, so lenders are able to turn over their portfolios quite frequently.

The secondary market imposes several restrictions on lenders, which are passed on to borrowers. These restrictions are important to the lender, because they qualify the loan for sale in the secondary market. For example, as an investor, you will be required to make larger down payments than homeowners are required to make. This tends to limit the potential for financing an indefinite number of rentals with conventional lenders who also work with the secondary market.

Your local bank probably sells most (if not all) of its loans on the secondary market each quarter. You may not even be aware that this occurs. In some cases, the local bank continues to service the loan, meaning it will collect mortgage payments and perhaps escrow deposits from you, make insurance and tax payments, and forward the money to the secondary market (minus a fee).

In some cases a bank will be willing to grant a loan that does not meet the secondary market conditions. Because that loan cannot be sold, chances are the bank will charge higher fees and a higher interest rate. When a bank keeps a loan rather than selling it on the secondary market, it is called a *portfolio loan*. Many banks are unwilling to deal with portfolio loans. Even though interest rates may be higher, most lenders can make more profit on turnover with the secondary market.

If you do not qualify under prevailing secondary market rules, you may also try to arrange seller financing—asking the seller of the property to carry a loan. This occurs when there are problems with the house that prevent conventional loans from being approved or, on the other side, when a buyer does not qualify with the lender for some reason.

In shopping for ways to find the most affordable form of financing, you will quickly discover that the secondary market rules are difficult to follow. They are complex and tend to change over time, so even full-time bank loan officers have to struggle to keep up. It pays to research and compare, and to shop around among different institutions, credit unions, and private sources.

TYPES OF LOANS

Anyone who has shopped for a mortgage knows that a complex and bewildering array of choices awaits you. There is no standard loan to apply for, and no universal rules about how lenders operate. If you shop around enough—and if you are willing to pay enough—you can probably find a loan for just about anything.

Cost is the big factor in loan shopping. The most apparent form of cost is the interest rate itself. As an investor trying to figure out how to finance real estate, you need to be prepared to pay a higher interest rate than would be paid by a homeowner for the same property. You will not get the most attractive rate possible, because you will not be occupying the property.

There are five features to be aware of on all loans:

1. *Interest rate.* Most people begin comparing loans by emphasizing the interest rate, often forgetting to look at the other terms. While the total package should be reviewed, be aware that the interest rate on a long-term loan is extremely significant. The payment difference between 8 percent and 9 percent interest on a 30-year loan for $100,000 is $71 per month. This adds up to a difference of more than $25,000 over the full term of the loan.

Another important factor to consider is whether that interest rate will remain the same throughout the loan term, or is subject to change. (For more details, see the discussion later in this chapter.) You should be aware that

second mortgage also called a "junior lien," a mortgage not in first position in the event of default. The second mortgage holder is paid only after the first mortgage holder is paid, and only if enough equity remains in the property.

portfolio loan a loan kept on the lender's books and not sold on the secondary market, or kept for a specified period of time before being sold; lenders tend to charge higher fees and interest rates for portfolio loans.

assumption
a feature in a loan providing that the borrower can allow a future buyer to take over payments on the loan, as well as responsibility for repayment, without permission from the lender.

due on sale clause
a clause in a mortgage agreement stating that the entire outstanding balance of the mortgage loan is due and payable immediately upon sale of the property.

point
one percent of the loan amount; an additional charge in the form of advance interest payment, added on as a fee assessed for getting the loan. Points are also called "loan fees."

you will be charged a higher rate today for the privilege of locking in a rate for the entire life of the loan.

2. *Assumable, or due on sale.* Can the loan be transferred to someone else? Some loans have rules relating to *assumption*. This means that if you sell the property in the future, you can transfer the loan to the buyer without permission from the lender. In practice, most lenders will state that they allow assumption, but only on approval and only if they have the right to modify the loan terms. (Translation: Sure, you can have a new person "assume" the loan, but all terms and conditions can be changed.) When a loan is described as fully assumable, that means there are no limitations on your right to transfer the loan to someone else. When a loan is not assumable, you will recognize that by the inclusion in the loan contract of a *due on sale clause.* This clause states that if you sell, the loan must be paid at once.

3. *Points.* Comparisons between dissimilar loans are made more complex by the *point* system. Lenders charge varying numbers of points, also called "loan fees," as a cost of acquiring the loan. This charge amounts to extra interest. One point equals 1 percent of the amount you are borrowing. For example, each point for a $100,000 loan is worth $1000. So if you are told the loan fee will be two points, that means the lender will charge you $2000 up front just to get the loan—above and beyond your monthly interest payments.

The more points you are charged, the higher your actual costs. Depending on the length of the loan, the amount borrowed, and the interest rate, an otherwise competitive loan with high points could be a worse bargain than one with a higher interest rate and fewer points.

4. *Impounds.* In many cases, lenders will insist that you include *impounds* in your monthly loan payments. Usually, impounds include property taxes and homeowner's insurance. While some lenders offer this service as a convenience or on a voluntary basis, investors often are required to include these extras as part of the deal. In that way, the lender knows that property tax and insurance payments are made, because it has control over the impound account. The impound account is held in escrow and therefore is sometimes called an escrow account. The total payment that includes mortgage payments as well as impounds is called PITI (principal, interest, taxes, and insurance).

5. *Call feature.* Does the lender have the right to make you pay off the loan early? Be sure you know what you're getting when you sign a loan document. You should thoroughly understand all of the clauses in the contract. One clause that may be a problem for you is the *call feature.* If your contract includes a call feature, the lender has the right to demand full payment after a specified number of years. That right will not necessarily be exercised by the lender. But if that lender can get a much higher interest rate, or if the borrower is late on payments every month, there is a good chance the loan will be called.

FIXED-RATE AND ADJUSTABLE-RATE LOANS

Loans for real estate can be divided into two major classifications, fixed-rate and adjustable-rate, based on how interest will be treated in the future.

Fixed-Rate Loans

With a *fixed-rate mortgage* (FRM), the interest rate is permanently fixed as a part of the contract. This means that for the entire loan period—usually 15, 20, or 30 years—the interest rate will not vary.

A word of caution: As explained above, some loans include a call feature. Some lenders offer fixed-rate mortgages based on the 15-, 20-, or 30-year term, but include a call feature after five years, for example. This means that although the rate is fixed, the lender has the option of canceling the deal and demanding full payment. This version of a fixed-rate mortgage is not the same as the traditional long-term, fixed-rate contract. *Read your mortgage contract thoroughly and carefully.*

The advantage of the fixed-rate contract (assuming it contains no call feature) is the certainty it provides you. You can plan for practically the indefinite future, knowing the level of mortgage payment each and every month. If

impounds charges added to interest and principal to cover property taxes and insurance, and possibly other costs. The lender collects an estimated amount necessary to make periodic payments, and then submits those payments on the borrower's behalf.

call feature a clause in the mortgage contract giving the lender the right to demand full payment of the unpaid loan balance at some point in the future. Lenders may "call" a loan if market interest rates have risen far above a loan's fixed rate, or if the borrower is chronically late with monthly payments.

fixed-rate mortgage (FRM) a loan in which the interest rate will not change during the contract period, as a matter of contract.

adjustable-rate mortgage (ARM) a loan in which the future interest rate may change, with that change determined by an index of rates. The frequency and amount of change are limited by the mortgage contract.

future interest rates rise, you will not be affected, because your rate is locked in. Conversely, if rates fall, you also have the right to shop for a new mortgage at any time. The fixed-cost feature of the fixed-rate mortgage is significant for long-term planning, not only for homeowners but for investors as well.

Adjustable-Rate Loans

Lenders often induce borrowers with a lower initial interest rate on an *adjustable-rate mortgage* (ARM). The adjustable rate protects the lender against future inflation. If market rates rise, the increased cost of money is passed on to borrowers with adjustable-rate mortgages.

Several important features come with an adjustable-rate loan. The degree to which interest will change in the future is determined by changes in an index of interest rates. Several index measurements are published, and the one the lender will use is specified in the contract. For example, some lenders adjust their rates based on auction interest rates for U.S. government securities; others use prime rate, the bank's district rate, or a regional rate. The important point to remember is that the index is included in the original contract; the lender cannot change the index later on.

As the borrower, you take the lower initial rate as a trade-off for protection against the possibility of higher rates in the future. In other words, the risk is that your interest rate will rise; the benefit is a lower initial cost. For some borrowers, this is an acceptable risk; for others, there is no choice. Some people have to go for the adjustable-rate loan because of the initially lower monthly payment involved. To qualify for a loan, your income is compared to the monthly payment level. If the payment exceeds a predetermined standard, the bank turns you down. So to qualify when it's a close call, an adjustable-rate loan frequently makes the difference.

An adjustable-rate mortgage does not contain unlimited risk. The contract includes a *cap* on the percentage increase the lender is allowed to impose—both yearly and for the entire term of the contract. For example, a loan might specify that the annual cap is a 2 percent increase, and the lifetime cap is 6 percent. That means that the most your interest can go up is 2 percent each year; and the most it can go up over the entire repayment period is 6 percent.

To attract new business, some lenders offer an exceptionally low initial interest rate on their adjustable-rate loans; however, in the fine print, it's disclosed that after 6 or 12 months, that rate is replaced with a much higher rate. This low initial rate is called a *teaser*. While the cap is an important feature in an adjustable-rate loan, the teaser can work as a deceptive way to get people to sign up for new loans. In considering an adjustable-rate loan, evaluate the cap and teaser provisions and estimate the effect they will have on your monthly payment.

Example: One lender offered an adjustable-rate 30-year mortgage specifying the following terms: The initial rate was 7 percent, with an annual cap of 2 percent and a lifetime cap of 6 percent. These terms meant the borrower could expect to pay 7 percent for at least the first year; then the rate could increase by as much as 2 percent each year thereafter (if the index being used allowed that much of an increase); but the maximum overall increase for the loan's 30-year duration was limited to 6 percent above the initial rate, or a rate of 13 percent. Both annual and lifetime caps are maximums, so that in practice more gradual increases could occur over the entire period of time.

It is wise to consider the worst-case scenario. However, your own rate may not increase to the maximum, and it may even decline occasionally. The outcome of an actual adjustable-rate mortgage is likely to look more like the example in Figure 3.1.

In this figure, the actual interest rate varies from year to year. Compare the actual rate with the annual and lifetime cap rates. The borrower's interest level may rise, but only within the confines of those cap rates.

cap
a limit on the amount of increase a lender may impose under the terms of an adjustable-rate mortgage. The annual cap specifies the maximum annual increase, and the lifetime cap specifies the overall increase the lender is allowed to pass along to the borrower.

teaser
an initial interest rate charged on an adjustable-rate mortgage, well below the current market rate, offered by a lender in order to attract new business. After a few months, the teaser is replaced with a higher interest rate.

CREATIVE FINANCING

Some terms attached to loans force real estate investors to become creative in the ways they finance their purchases. Depending on your credit rating, the amount available for

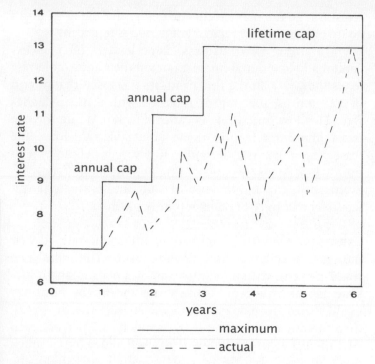

FIGURE 3.1 Adjustable-rate mortgage.

 creative financing
any variation on the standard fixed-rate or adjustable-rate loan, or alteration in the terms of the mortgage contract, designed to make a financing deal work.

 balloon mortgage
a mortgage containing a series of payments over a period of time (often three to five years), followed by a single "balloon" payment representing the entire outstanding balance of the loan.

a down payment, and current supply and demand features, you might need to accept some terms for your loan that do not usually come up when you're buying your own home. Five forms of *creative financing* are described here.

1. *Balloon mortgage*. The *balloon mortgage* is designed for those who cannot qualify for full payments on a loan or who want to minimize monthly payments for a few years. For those interested in a balloon mortgage, the plan should be to refinance or renegotiate the loan by the end of the term—or alternatively, to be confident that the property will be sold before the due date of the balloon mortgage.

The typical balloon mortgage includes payments of little or no principal, often none at all. The interest-only payments, as shown in Figure 3.2, extend for the entire term, ending with a single payment of the entire loan amount.

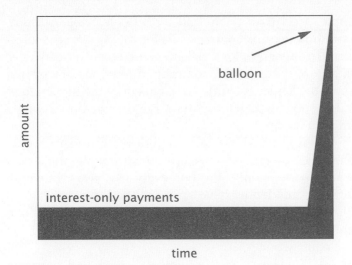

amount

balloon

interest-only payments

time

FIGURE 3.2 Balloon mortgage.

2. Rollover mortgage. The *rollover mortgage* is similar in many respects to the balloon mortgage. However, when the rollover comes due, the interest rate is renegotiated and a new set of terms goes forward. With a balloon mortgage, there is no requirement that the lender continue the loan in force. The renegotiated loan implies that the borrower has a right to go forward (although many lenders contract other terms, such as a requirement that the past year's payments were all made on time).

The rollover mortgage may be negotiated for an entire term, such as 15 years or 30 years; however, the interest rate is reconsidered at different intervals, often every five years. This makes the rollover a longer-term variation of the adjustable-rate mortgage. The contract, though, does not limit the methods to be used by the lender in establishing the new rate. It is truly a matter of negotiation, to be based on current rates as well as whether the lender wants to continue the loan. Setting the rate too high is likely to force the borrower to look elsewhere, having the effect of opting to not continue with the contract.

The important distinction between the two forms of loan is in the lender's agreement to continue the loan (rollover) or to demand full payment (balloon). For ex-

rollover mortgage a mortgage containing fixed-rate terms for a specified period of time, after which the contract continues but the interest rate is renegotiated, or "rolled over" for a new term.

amortization
the repayment terms of a loan, including the required principal and interest, based on the interest rate and the period of time allowed to pay down, or amortize, the loan to zero.

 **buy-down mortgage**
a mortgage in which an initial interest rate is reduced by pre-payment. The rate is reduced according to the prepayment, which is also called "discount points."

ample, a contract might call for a 30-year *amortization*. Assuming that the contract calls for rolling over the terms every five years, as long as lender and borrower can agree on a rate, the loan will continue in force. If they cannot agree, the lender is entitled to payment of the full amount, and the borrower will negotiate a replacement loan with a different lender.

Figure 3.3 shows how a rollover mortgage works when the rate is renegotiated. In this example, the lender is allowed to modify the rate every five years, but both borrower and lender have agreed to the same payoff date, 30 years from the original contract date. In a balloon mortgage, the amortization rate is agreed on, but the due date comes sooner.

3. *Buy-down mortgage.* When lender and borrower cannot agree on the rate of interest on a loan, one possible compromise is the *buy-down mortgage.* This is also a possible negotiating tool investors can use to induce a lender to

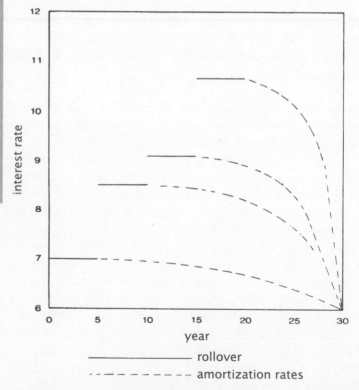

FIGURE 3.3 Rollover mortgage.

lower its rate. The lender agrees to reduce the loan rate in exchange for a prepayment of part of the interest. The payment and rate of reduction are both negotiable. The amount paid for buy-down is also called "discount points."

4. *Bridge loan.* Some people want to buy an investment property right away and don't want to risk losing the deal by having to wait to sell a different property; however, they do not have cash for a down payment. This is an awkward situation. In this case, you might be able to get a *bridge loan*, which is designed as a temporary measure to help you close your deal without having to wait. A lender agrees to finance your transaction, and you agree to pay interest until the other property sells. The lender also places a lien on the property you are selling as collateral for the loan.

Bridge loans often are used by real estate companies to help complete sales. When real estate companies make it easy for investors to buy property, they are able to close more deals. Naturally, when real estate companies lend money, they do not want the obligation to be outstanding indefinitely. Like all lenders, they place a deadline on repayment. So even if your older property does not sell by that deadline, you will be obligated to repay the loan. (In practice, if you are working with one real estate company that also is marketing your property, *and* if you are doing a brisk business with that company, you will probably be able to get an extension on the bridge loan.)

5. *Lease option.* Some people cannot come up with a full down payment right now, but they have identified a property they want to buy. For them, one of the more interesting forms of creative financing is the *lease option.* This is also used when someone wants to keep open the possibility of buying a property in the future, but is not yet certain—and is willing to pay a price to keep that alternative open. Also called "lease with an option to buy," the lease option contains two parts. The "lease" is like any other rental lease. The owner is entitled to regular rent payments, and the tenant agrees to maintain the property and to make payments on time. The second part, the "option," is separate. You, as potential future buyer, give the owner a sum of money—either all at once or as part of the periodic monthly lease payments—to obtain an option to buy the property. The option specifies the sale price of the

bridge loan
a loan granted temporarily, pending the borrower's finding permanent financing. Bridge loans are used by investors who have a property for sale but want to close a new deal immediately, without having to wait for one transaction before closing the other. Also called "gap financing," the bridge loan may require a higher interest rate than the market rate, but provides flexibility to the borrower.

lease option
an arrangement in which someone leases a property and buys an option to purchase that property for a specified price on or before a specified date in the future.

 loan-to-value ratio
a ratio used by lenders to limit the amount they will loan on a property. The appraised value is multiplied by the maximum percentage the lender will allow, resulting in the maximum possible loan amount the lender will approve. The ratio is expressed by dividing the proposed loan amount by the appraised value, with the answer representing a percentage.

property and the deadline. If the option is exercised before the deadline, the seller is obligated to sell according to the terms of the option. If the owner of the option does not exercise the option, it expires and becomes worthless. (An option can also be extended or renegotiated, which would involve changing the terms of the option.)

PACKAGING YOURSELF TO THE BANK

Whether you can boast of high income and excellent credit, or have marginal income and less than perfect credit, you will improve your chances of getting a loan when you make a strong, positive impression on the bank. It helps tremendously when you present yourself so that the lender will want to approve your loan.

Financing is truly the lifeblood of real estate investing. You need the lender in order to pursue your dream of investing in real estate; this means you need good credit and a good track record. You also need to understand that the lenders are governed by rules of their own. Because most lenders turn over their loan portfolio to the secondary market, they need to ensure that you and your loan will qualify.

Approach lenders realistically. Be aware of the limitations under which they operate, and proceed based on factual information rather than with a wish list. All lenders are going to require you to have some equity in a property. Otherwise, why should the lender take a risk?

To purchase rental property, the bank is probably going to require that the *loan-to-value ratio* be no more than 70 percent (this may vary between lenders or based in changes in the prevailing secondary market rules for non–owner-occupied properties). This means the total of *all* loans on the property cannot be more than 70 percent of the appraised value; or, putting it another way, you will be required to have equity equal to at least 30 percent of the property's appraised value.

Example: An investor made an offer on a property with an appraised value of $170,000. The bank imposed a requirement that the loan-to-value ratio not exceed 70 percent. In this case, the maximum debt allowed on this property was $119,000.

$$\frac{\$119,000 \text{ (loan balance)}}{\$170,000 \text{ (appraised value)}} = 70\% \text{ (loan-to-value ratio)}$$

By determining—in advance—the bank's policy regarding required equity, you will be able to select properties more realistically. You will know ahead of time how much you can afford. Two tests lenders apply use this ratio. You can ask yourself these two questions to determine whether you will be able to get a loan:

1. Do I have enough cash for a down payment?
2. Can I qualify for the loan with my monthly income?

Calculating the Down Payment

Once you know the numbers involved, you can quickly decide whether you have enough cash to make the deal work. In the example above, a $170,000 property is being considered, and you know the lender has a policy that the loan-to-value ratio is limited to 70 percent. So you can calculate that:

$$\$170,000 \times 70\% = \$119,000$$

and that means you need:

$$\$170,000 - \$119,000 = \$51,000$$

for a down payment. This money has to come from the sale of other property or from savings. If you simply cannot get that much for a down payment, there is no point in asking the lender to consider a loan.

Qualifying for the Loan

The idea of "qualification" goes beyond having good credit. The lender compares your monthly income to the monthly payment you will be required to make on the loan. If the monthly payment is too high when compared to your income, you simply won't qualify. To determine the monthly payment, you first need to find out the rates the lender charges for investment properties. Knowing the amount you intend to borrow, you can next calculate the monthly payment using amortization tables. (See Chapter 4.) Next, ask for the bank's policies about loan payments versus income. Based on its calculation, you can determine before applying whether you'll be able to qualify. If you don't qualify, the solution is to put a higher down payment on the property to get the monthly payments down to a level for which you are qualified.

You can simplify your search for potential investment properties by knowing in advance how much of a loan a lender will approve in your case. You can go through the *prequalification* process with a lender. This process involves checking your credit and taking a full application from you. The lender will be able to tell you whether you are qualified for a loan and, equally important, the maximum amount the lender will approve for an acceptable investment property. Prequalification will involve a review fee of some level, which pays for a credit report as well as the bank's time; it is worth the effort, however, to determine in advance that you can get a loan.

BORROWING TO INVEST

Many people would agree that borrowing money to invest is a controversial suggestion; many would reject the idea out of hand. For example, going into debt to speculate on the stock market is a high-risk, dangerous idea and for most people an unacceptable one. But depending on the investment, borrowing might be prudent and even necessary.

The vast majority of real estate investors have gone into debt to buy property. Tenants pay rent adequate to meet the required mortgage payment, or most of it. This makes the debt manageable—as long as the rent comes in. The difference between borrowing on the stock market and borrowing to buy real estate involves four important distinctions:

prequalification
the process of review by a lender of the income, assets, and credit of a prospective borrower. The purpose is to determine, first, whether the borrower is qualified to borrow and, second, the maximum amount the lender will be able to approve.

1. *Income is earned and mortgage payments are due monthly.* Rental income is a regular, recurring event. It makes managing debt possible because income and expense are matched up. So income and mortgage payments are the two sides of real estate investment. In comparison, if you borrow money to invest in stocks, you may not receive monthly dividend payments.

In addition, the level of dividend payments is beyond your control. A corporate board of directors has the power to vote to not pay a dividend, to lower it, or to cancel the dividend program altogether. Many companies do not pay dividends on their stock. As a landlord, you control rental income. You typically have the right to raise the rent, restricted only by market forces. If your rent is too high, you will lose tenants.

2. *You have direct control.* When you own rental property, you are in direct control. You decide if and when to make major improvements, change the landscaping, select one tenant over another, or raise the rent. When you own stock, you do not have the same kind of control; in fact, you have no direct policy-making powers whatsoever. You are not given a voice in management, and are allowed only to vote for members of the board of directors (who, in turn, appoint a management team). Most people who own publicly listed stock have such a small share of ownership that they have no effective voice. With real estate, your voice is virtually the only one, because you are in direct control of policies and decisions. Even though the lender's debt might be far greater than your equity, the lender has no influence over how you manage the property. (The lender can require that you carry insurance and may demand impounds from you to ensure that taxes and insurance are paid, but lenders do not have the right to tell you how to manage the property.)

3. *Real estate has less risk of sudden and severe loss.* The stock market is volatile and at times reacts to economic news in extremes. While overreacting price movements are corrected given enough time, the stock market is "on-the-edge" investing; there is a constant sense of uncertainty about what will happen in the market.

While many investors are drawn to the uncertainty of the stock market, long-term investment may require a more dependable and sensible form of market. Real estate values do not fluctuate on a daily basis, but tend to change according to economic indicators rather than in reaction to rumors or perceptions of the moment. Prices thus tend to be more predictable; this limits the short-term price potential as well as the short-term risk.

4. *Real estate provides significant tax benefits.* When you buy shares of stock, your dividends are usually taxable income each year. And if you sell and earn a profit, you are taxed on the capital gain. You do not have the opportunity to shelter income unless you invest strictly through a qualified retirement plan, in which case you cannot take out equity or borrow against it.

With real estate, you enjoy several powerful tax advantages. They are available today rather than years later, after you retire. For most people, tax breaks are worth more during their peak earning years, so real estate is attractive from the tax perspective. Among these tax breaks are deductibility of interest paid on mortgage loans, as well as property taxes and other expenses. You can also depreciate buildings and other improvements, providing even more deductions. Finally, there are ways to defer your capital gains on investment properties by purchasing other properties within six months or less. (Tax advantages and strategies are covered in greater detail in Chapters 5, 8, and 12.)

REFINANCING

You can refinance your home and use the money to buy investment property. This is one way to go into debt to become a real estate investor. If you have enough equity in your home, you can get a new loan and take out cash to use as a down payment. But don't overlook the risks this creates. Refinancing is just another form of increasing your debts—including higher monthly payments and removal of equity from your property. Many lenders' ads admonish homeowners for letting their equity sit "idle" when that lender can show you how to "free up" the equity and "put it to work." When you do that, it is a form of borrowing secured by your home's equity. As long as you view refinancing realistically, you will be able to evaluate the risks involved. Borrowing always increases risk. There is no way to escape that fact. It also increases the potential for using money to invest so that future profits will be realized. When you borrow to invest in ways that do not produce monthly cash flow, it is less advisable.

Another alternative is to seek an *equity line of credit*. With this type of loan, you pay interest only on the amount you actually draw from the line of credit. You do not have to draw the cash until you need it, and you can repay at any level above the minimum payment (established by the amount borrowed), without penalty. The lender approves the maximum line of credit based on equity in the property. Like any other mortgage loan, it is based on the equity in your home.

equity line of credit
a form of loan in which the lender provides the borrower a maximum line of credit secured by equity in real estate. The borrower can draw as much as necessary up to the maximum.

While equity lines of credit generally are granted on primary residences, it might be possible to get such a line of credit on investment properties as well. You will need to shop for these lines of credit, as most lenders limit equity lines of credit to your home only. However, as a tool for managing investment equity, it is worth investigating. If a lender in your area is willing to grant you a line of credit on an investment property, it could be worth considering.

When lenders grant you an equity line of credit, they place a lien on the property equal to the maximum line of credit. The minimum monthly payment you are required to make is based on the interest rate and the outstanding balance that has been drawn on the line of credit.

An equity line of credit is an excellent tool if managed responsibly. If you can discipline yourself to use it only for investment purposes, and not to buy a new car or boat, or to consolidate other debts—actions that do not produce investment income or improve your net worth—then it is worth looking into. The primary advantage is that you can draw on it as needed without having to apply for a new loan.

Example: An investor was granted an equity line of credit based on his home equity. The maximum was set at $75,000. He used the line of credit for down payments on two investment properties. The plan was to sell one within a year, and that goal was reached. When the sale closed, the investor used the net proceeds to pay down the equity line of credit. Because he made a profit on the sale, he was able to pay down more than he borrowed for that down payment. The equity line of credit was available for future use, and the current balance outstanding was less than the amount taken out for the second down payment.

If this investor had not used the proceeds from the sale to pay down the equity line of credit, then the outstanding balance would remain, demanding recurring monthly payments and interest expense. It is critical that the debt be managed. If you do not repay from profits, then continuing interest eventually offsets those profits.

Having credit or cash available is very tempting, and successful real estate investors need to be highly disciplined. As necessary as cash and credit might be, you need to exercise control so that they are not misused. You need to be a future-thinking person. If you would find it too tempting to have access to a line of credit, then applying for that type of financing would be a mistake. However, if you are confident that you could properly manage instant credit, then the equity line could prove a good way to go.

The way you manage your debt is at least as important as the way you select and manage the property itself. As a real estate investor, you also need to become an expert debt manager. The next chapter explains how to read and use interest tables.

The Cost of Borrowing

Assuming you can qualify for a loan, and that you can afford the payments, your choice of financing is the greatest challenge to successful real estate investing. The use and management of leverage enables you to be a player in this market because, for most real estate investors, the whole plan depends on one thing: getting the money.

If financing were easy, everyone could succeed in real estate. With an unlimited line of credit, you would be able to borrow not only to buy more property, but also to make up any shortfalls along the way. That would be nice; but, realistically, we are all limited in the degree of borrowing we are allowed to accumulate.

Remember this important point: The real cost of buying property is not just the price of the property. It is the overall level of payments you make over the many years that you finance most of that purchase price. The interest rate you pay and the time required to repay the mortgage ultimately determine the real cost of buying real estate. This is often overlooked by investors, who may be overly concerned with getting the "right price," to the extent that financing is a casual afterthought. But, a few thousand dollars' difference in the price is insignificant if you are penalized many more thousands of dollars as a consequence of failing to properly shop around for financing.

Consider the impact of getting a loan that is not the best available. If you shop diligently, you can reduce your interest rate as well as the initial costs of borrowing. However, if you look only for a bargain price, you will not be thinking long-term, merely emphasizing the immediate concern. Certainly, you should try to get the best possible purchase price, but that is only part of the picture. You need to understand how interest calculations are performed, because even a slight variation in the interest rate could mean the difference between only marginal profits (or even losses) and a satisfactory return on your capital.

Example: You bought a house for $125,000 with a down payment of $25,000. The balance, $100,000, was financed with a 30-year, fixed-rate mortgage loan at 9 percent interest. Your monthly payments are $804.63, adding up to $289,666.80 over 30 years; $100,000 of this amount is principal, and the remainder—$189,666.80—is interest. Together with the down payment, the total cost of this house will be $314,666.80.

Down payment	$ 25,000.00
Principal payments	100,000.00
Interest payments	189,666.80
Total	$314,666.80

A good break in the interest rate in this example would have been worth a lot more than saving a couple of thousand dollars in the price. For example, if you could have negotiated this deal at a rate of 8 percent instead of 9 percent, it would have saved more than $25,000.

Now imagine accepting a price $5000 higher on this property, but with a lower interest rate. You would obviously be better off paying a higher purchase price with lower interest on the financing. This is not to argue that you should pay more than the best price you can negotiate. After all, a $5000 savings is worth $5000. The point to remember, though, is that the price is only part of the whole deal; you also need to shop around for the best mortgage deal you can find.

At this point, many people say, "But it doesn't matter if I pay more interest. I can write it off on my taxes." If you want to become serious about investing, you need to challenge this way of thinking, and to recognize the fallacy of the idea that spending more than you need to is, in some manner, actually an advantage. It is never to your advantage to pay more than you need to pay. If you could get 8 percent, but you settle for 9 percent, it means only one thing: You are throwing away money. If your overall federal and state income tax rates add up to 40 percent, your after-tax expense is still 60 percent of every dollar you paid in interest. So, in the previous example, a pretax difference of $25,000 would represent an after-tax difference of $15,000 (60 percent of $25,000). If you can eliminate a degree of interest expense, it saves you money—both before and after calculating the taxes.

Some investors are satisfied with affordable payments on the loan, as a sole criterion for selection. With rental properties, this means that a loan is affordable as long as rent income is high enough to make payments of principal, interest, taxes, and insurance (without allowing for unexpected repairs or for vacancies). Covering costs is important, to be sure. If you are spending more money than you're bringing in, you should question whether it makes any sense to make the investment at all. However, for some investors, losing money each month makes sense—on the theory that future value justifies today's investment. It is even possible to have negative income before taxes, but positive income after taxes.

The truth remains, though, that even with satisfactory matching up of income and expenses, a higher interest rate adds to the cost of the property, reducing your eventual profit, and in the case of vacancies, adding to your cash burden. Why pay more if you do not need to? There is truth in the idea that when rental income is adequate, the tenants make the payments for you. However, a lower rate is better than a higher rate, if you can get the better deal. Paying a higher rate makes sense only when you have no choice. For example, if you do not qualify for bank financing but the seller is willing to carry your note, that offer might involve a higher rate than the bank is offering. In this situation, you need to pay the higher rate because of the circumstances. That is not the same as merely failing to shop around for better deals when you do qualify for them.

Three general guidelines worth following are:

1. *Figure out your interest cost—be aware of what you pay to borrow money.* Computing your interest cost is not difficult. The next section of this chapter explains the importance of interest in determining the real cost of property, and how easily you can calculate your long-term interest cost.

Think about the long-term consequences of high interest. If you keep a property for a 30-year term over which a loan is repaid, what happens to your profit? The truth is that you may pay two to three times the purchase price when interest is considered. In many situations, you end up converting increases in market value not into your profits but rather into profits for the bank. The cost of borrowing is not limited to the monthly affordability of the payment level. It could also mean you will pay all of your profits to the bank in the form of interest. This is, perhaps, the greatest long-term problem associated with real estate investing. Long-term deterioration of profits due to conversion to the lender could make real estate investments poor in comparison to other investments, so you need to control that cost.

2. *Keep an open mind to the possibility of refinancing in the future.* Just because you have a long-term loan does not mean you have to keep it. Even when today's economic picture seems fairly stable, remember that everything can change in the future. With hindsight we are amazed at how dramatically changes have occurred. Expect more of the same in the future. For example, in the 1970s, when interest rates rose to 8 percent, that level was considered disastrously high. By the early 1980s, 8 percent was considered rock bottom, with market rates exceeding 15 percent. But by the 1990s, 8 percent was again the midrange rate.

Just as you shop for property bargains, constantly be looking out for financing bargains, too. The cost today for financing might seem good, but by tomorrow's standards, it might then be wise to refinance and get an even lower rate.

3. *Don't settle for just covering your costs—look for ways to increase profits.* Very few business owners would tell you that a marginal rate of profit is acceptable. They constantly try to maximize their profits, to squeeze a little bit more net return from their sales dollar. The same rule applies to you as a real estate investor, because you have your capital at risk; and because you are interested in earning a profit from your efforts and from exposing yourself to risk. A key point to always remember: *The less you pay in interest over the term of the loan, the greater your profit will be in the future.*

Never think fatalistically about the cost of borrowing. In other words, don't just assume that all loans are the same. Look for the best deal you can find and keep your eye on the lending market in the future. Be sure that today's best deal continues into the future, and, if rates fall, consider refinancing.

THE SIGNIFICANCE OF INTEREST

Anyone who has made payments on a mortgage loan already knows the frustration of seeing how slowly the loan balance inches downward. The gradual change in the relationship between principal and interest is painful to observe. The major portion of each early-year mortgage payment goes to interest.

Once you figure out how interest is computed, you will begin to appreciate the importance of shopping for financing. A .5 percent or 1 percent difference in your loan rate translates to thousands of dollars in interest. A rate increase for an adjustable-rate mortgage loan means not only that your monthly payment goes up, but also that the long-term interest cost rises. People are aware of the month-to-month consequence of change in the adjustable-rate loan rate, but may not stop to realize the larger significance. When the lender increases the adjustable rate, it means you pay more interest. And *the more interest you pay, the more you are paying for the property*.

Interest represents such a huge cost in the acquisition of property because it is computed based on the outstanding balance of the loan at the beginning of each month. It takes a number of years for the principal to begin declining noticeably, because in the earlier years, the majority of the payment goes to interest.

If you ever decide to become a lender—perhaps selling a property and carrying a loan yourself—you will come to appreciate this as a benefit. For the lender, interest income is significant not only because it lasts for many years, but also because it is computed based on a slowly declining balance. Investors are cautioned by experts to be aware of how well they are keeping their capital at work, because of this very fact. Whether you are borrowing money as a buyer of real estate, or lending money to someone else, you need to understand the *time value of money*. When you accumulate interest in a savings account, for example, your interest income accelerates at a growing pace. That's because the more interest your account earns, the higher your base for the next interest period. Interest grows as the base grows. The opposite is true when you are the borrower. When you have to *pay* interest, the amount of interest tends to gradually decrease over time as the principal balance slowly falls.

Banks and other lenders recognize that you could not afford extraordinarily high payments on a mortgage loan in the earlier years, so monthly payments are calculated at a specified level designed to pay off the entire loan by a target date (30 years, for example). This is called *level debt service*. Whether you are paying off a home mortgage, an investment property mortgage, a car loan, or any other type of loan, you are probably making payments in the same amount each month. Even in adjustable-rate mortgages, the payment is the same as long as the interest rate doesn't change. Once the rate changes, a new level of monthly payment is calculated. Figure 4.1 shows how the monthly payment is divided. In the earlier years, most of the payment consists of interest. The curve accelerates toward the end of the term, until the loan is repaid in full.

As a depositor in a bank or shareholder in a mutual fund, you will benefit from the time value of money as capital increases at an ever-accelerating rate. The advice most commonly given is to "reinvest your dividends." This means leave your earnings in the account so that you earn

time value of money
the basic series of rules concerning accumulation of interest over a period of time; compounding and its effect; and return to lenders (or, on the other side, the cost to borrowers). The longer the period of time that money accumulates with interest, the higher the time value of the money. The time involved determines the real benefit or consequence of interest.

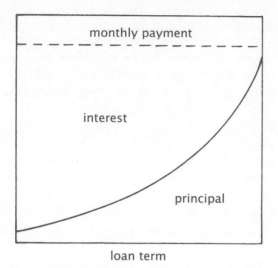

FIGURE 4.1   Level debt service.

level debt service
periodic payments that remain the same every month. While the payment is level, it consists of principal and interest, divided according to the current outstanding loan balance. As the loan balance becomes lower, the portion of the level payment going to the principal gradually increases.

increasing amounts in the future. If you withdraw your earnings each month or quarter, you never benefit from the time value of money. The same basic premise works with real estate (to the benefit of the lender). The longer you take to pay off your mortgage, the higher the interest cost.

HOW INTEREST IS COMPUTED

As a borrower, you have to live with the realities of *compound interest*, which is calculated at the beginning of each period. A "period" can be a month, as in the case of a mortgage payment; interest can also be computed:

✔ Every day (daily compounding).
✔ Four times per year (quarterly compounding).
✔ Twice per year (semiannual compounding).
✔ Once per year (annual compounding).

compound interest
interest calculated on the remaining balance of debt; or the accumulation of interest based on both the principal and accrued interest.

Most people understand compound interest when it refers to their income from savings accounts, but have more difficulty understanding how it works against them as borrowers. If you have cash deposited in a savings account at your local bank, interest is earned each month. You will observe that, as long as you leave all of the money in the account, the interest earned increases each month. Figure 4.2 summarizes this with the example of $100, earning interest at 7 percent compounded monthly.

The same rules concerning the time value of money work against you when you are borrowing money instead of saving it. Unfortunately, your loan amount might be substantially higher than the balance in your savings account. As a consequence, your interest *expense* will be much higher as well. You should know exactly how to compute interest on your mortgage, for three reasons:

1. *You need to know.* You might borrow money from a private party at some point in the course of investing in real estate. You will need to know how to figure out the interest in order to claim the deduction when reporting to the Internal Revenue Service each year, and in order to

Month	7% Interest	Balance
		$100.00
1	.58	100.58
2	.59	101.17
3	.59	101.76
4	.59	102.35
5	.60	102.95
6	.60	103.55
7	.60	104.15
8	.61	104.76
9	.61	105.37
10	.61	105.98
11	.62	106.60
12	.62	107.22

FIGURE 4.2 Monthly compounding.

keep your books accurate as to the balance due on the loan. Additionally, if you ever lend money to someone (for example, if you sell a property and carry a mortgage), you should know how to compute the interest, if only to check to make sure your borrower is computing it properly.

2. *You need to compare costs.* When shopping for mortgages, you will need to know how to determine your monthly payment—not to mention the importance of knowing how a rate of interest translates into the true overall cost of buying property.

3. *It is always wise to monitor the lender.* If you intend to keep your own books, you should break down your monthly payments on your mortgage between principal and interest. The principal portion reduces your liability, while the interest portion is a deductible expense. Some lenders show the breakdown each month for you, but many lenders today use payment coupon books, so you don't receive a monthly statement. You need to know how to make the calculation yourself. If you think you're doing the calculation correctly, but the lender's year-end numbers are different, you should find out why. If you're off by only a few dollars, it could be due to rounding, and you can accept the bank's calculation. Otherwise, ask the bank to recheck its numbers or to explain to you how it calculates interest. Lenders—even those with computers—can and do make mistakes, so it's up to you to ensure that your loan is being calculated properly.

Some lenders use variations on the standard formula. For example, they may calculate interest on a daily basis. However, most use a strict monthly calculation, meaning that the annual interest rate is divided by one-twelfth—representing the monthly rate—and that is applied against the outstanding balance.

There is a four-step procedure for calculating the interest and principal portions of your monthly payment:

1. Multiply the balance of the loan at the beginning of the month by the annual interest rate.

2. Divide the answer by 12 (months) to determine this month's interest expense.

3. Subtract this month's interest expense from the total monthly payment to determine the month's principal payment.

4. Subtract the principal payment from this month's beginning loan balance. This gives you the new balance on the loan.

Example: An investor obtains a mortgage at 7 percent, with a beginning balance of $85,000, and a repayment term of 20 years. In such a case, the monthly payment is $659.01 per month.

1. Multiply the balance of the loan by the interest rate.

$$\begin{array}{r} \$85,000.00 \\ \times\ .07 \\ \hline \$\ 5,950.00 \end{array}$$

2. Divide the answer by 12 to compute this month's interest.

$$\frac{\$5,950.00}{12} = \$495.83$$

3. Subtract this month's interest from the monthly payment. This is the principal payment.

$$\begin{array}{r} \$\ 659.01 \\ -495.83 \\ \hline \$\ 163.18 \end{array}$$

4. Subtract the principal payment from the loan balance at the beginning of themonth. This is the new loan balance.

$$\begin{array}{r} \$85,000.00 \\ -163.18 \\ \hline \$84,836.82 \end{array}$$

The procedure is repeated each month. In this example, next month's beginning balance will be $84,836.82. If this procedure is carried forward for the entire term of the loan, it will be repaid in full (the balance will be zero) at the end of the period—in this example, in 20 years.

Table 4.1 shows how this loan is amortized for the first year. Notice that the part of the payment going to principal increases by only about one dollar per month. As time goes by, the payments to principal will increase. But it won't be until the 13th year that this particular loan will be half repaid. The second half is repaid during the

	TABLE 4.1	Loan Amortization		
Month	Total Payment	Interest (7 percent)	Principal	Principal Balance
				$85,000.00
1	$ 659.01	$ 495.83	$ 163.18	84,836.82
2	659.01	494.88	164.13	84,672.69
3	659.01	493.92	165.09	84,507.60
4	659.01	492.96	166.05	84,341.55
5	659.01	491.99	167.02	84,174.53
6	659.01	491.02	167.99	84,006.54
7	659.01	490.04	168.97	83,837.57
8	659.01	489.05	169.96	83,667.61
9	659.01	488.06	170.95	83,496.66
10	659.01	487.06	171.95	83,324.71
11	659.01	486.06	172.95	83,151.76
12	659.01	485.05	173.96	82,977.80
Total	$7,908.12	$5,885.92	$2,022.20	

remaining seven years. This $85,000 loan will cost $73,162.40 in interest.

USING AMORTIZATION TABLES

It's important to know the monthly payments for a specific rate and mortgage amount, if only to determine whether you can afford that level of payments. Time also affects not only the monthly payment, but the total cost. The longer the mortgage term, the lower the payments, but the higher the overall interest cost. Most people have to compromise between the dollar amount they can afford each month and the interest cost they are willing to pay—assuming the analysis is performed at all. The best way to gather this information is by mastering the art of reading an amortization table. A typical page from a book of mortgage payments is provided in Figure 4.3.

interest
rate

term

| 7% | | | | | |
Amount	10 Years	15 Years	20 Years	25 Years	30 Years
$20,000	$232.22	$179.77	$155.06	$141.36	$133.07
25,000	290.28	224.71	193.83	176.70	166.33
30,000	348.33	269.65	232.59	212.04	199.60
35,000	406.38	314.59	271.36	247.38	232.86
40,000	464.44	359.54	310.12	282.72	266.13
45,000	522.49	404.48	348.89	318.06	299.39
50,000	580.55	449.42	387.65	353.39	332.66
55,000	638.60	494.36	426.42	388.73	365.92
60,000	696.66	539.30	465.18	424.07	399.19
65,000	754.71	584.24	503.95	459.41	432.45
70,000	812.76	629.18	542.71	494.75	465.72
75,000	870.82	674.13	581.48	530.09	498.98
80,000	928.87	719.07	620.24	565.43	532.25
85,000	986.93	764.01	659.01	600.77	565.51

mortgage
amount

monthly
payment

FIGURE 4.3 Amortization table.

Books of amortization tables reveal the payment amount, such as the one in the Figure. It is useful when the amount to be borrowed is a round number. It's a bit more difficult when you are borrowing an uneven amount, and a few more steps are involved.

Example: You will be borrowing $83,550 on an investment property. You have found a loan for 7 percent and a 30-year term. But you have not been told what your monthly payments will be. Using a book of amortization tables showing only rounded amounts, you need to add up several balances to find the monthly payment:

	Amount	Payment
	$80,000	$532.25
	3,000	19.96
	500	3.33
	50	.36
Total	$83,550	$555.90

For most situations, it is reasonable to round the borrowed amount up or down and then compare different repayment terms. You can also calculate periods between table levels. For example, referring back to Figure 4.3, what if you want to know your monthly payment if you contract for a 27-year term? Although that calculation is not listed, you can get a rough idea by looking at the payment levels for 25-year and 30-year terms. For an $85,000 loan, you know the 27-year payment will be somewhere between $565 and $600 per month. That's a fairly narrow range.

The same type of calculation can be performed vertically. For example, payment amounts are given for $80,000 and $85,000, but not for $83,550. For a 30-year term, you know the payment will be somewhere between $532 and $565—again a narrow range. Once you are familiar with amortization tables, you will see how they can be useful for gaining ballpark estimates of the cost of borrowing at different levels and for different numbers of years.

The figures showing payments for various terms and amounts, based on 7 percent interest, provide you with all the information you need to figure out which is the best route to go. These amortization tables contain four essential ingredients:

1. *Interest rate.* Payments vary according to the interest rate. If you observe the differences in payment amounts for various interest rates, you will see that the rate is extremely important in terms of your overall interest costs. The monthly payment might not seem very significant—until you multiply it by 360 months. You need to consider the differences over a 30-year term to appreciate how much a slight difference in the interest rate will affect your total cost.

2. *Term.* The term is the number of years or duration of the loan. The shorter the term, the higher the monthly payment. And the shorter the term, the lower the overall interest cost. If you recall that compound interest is figured on the outstanding balance each month, a shorter repayment period translates to less interest expense. It also means you will accumulate equity more rapidly. If you decide to sell before you have paid off your loan, a shorter term translates to more equity at closing, and more money returned to you.

3. *Mortgage amount.* The mortgage amount is the amount borrowed, or principal. Since interest is compounded strictly as a percentage of the principal balance, the higher your amount, the higher the interest. The higher the amount borrowed, the higher the required payment has to be to repay that loan by the end of the term. Notice that the payment for a $20,000 mortgage is always one-half of the required payment on a $40,000 mortgage at the same rate and term, and one-third of the $60,000 mortgage. So if your proposed mortgage amount is not on the table, it is fairly simple to figure it out.

Example: Your payment tables go only to $100,000, which is typical. But you want to borrow $120,000. What is your monthly payment? You can calculate the payment on a $60,000 mortgage and double it; or add together payments for $100,000 and $20,000.

4. *Monthly payment.* The payment is the key within the amortization table. You can use the payment amount to quickly figure out your total interest cost, for example. Multiply the monthly payment by the term (360 payments in 30 years, for example), and then subtract the amount borrowed. The balance remaining is your interest expense. You can also quickly determine whether buying a particular house will work out financially once you know about how much you will get in rent. If the rent is about $600 per month and your mortgage payment will be $900, it probably won't make a lot of sense to proceed.

Comparisons between mortgage amounts for different terms are also very instructive. For example, compare monthly payments for 15- and 30-year terms; and then compute the difference in interest between those two terms.

REDUCING YOUR INTEREST COST

It makes sense, considering the long-term cost of interest, to reduce this cost whenever possible. The less interest you pay, the lower the real cost of the investment property. As a real estate investor, you are fortunate. Most types of businesses cannot reduce costs simply by spending more money to reduce debt, but in real estate, you are faced with a special situation: It is the debt itself that defines cost, so by paying off that debt more rapidly than required by contract, you can improve investment performance—directly and dramatically.

The big advantage in real estate is that you can make additional payments on your mortgage whenever you wish to. Even a very small amount of additional principal payment each month has a compounding effect over the entire remaining balance of the contract. The rate of return on such an investment as paying an extra amount each month works to cancel out the compounded interest rate you are paying on your mortgage. Think of reduced cost as the equivalent of interest earned—because the end result is the same.

Example: You recently mortgaged a property for a 30-year term at 9 percent. Your loan was for $80,000 and your monthly payment is $643.70. If you increase your payment by $28 per month, you will pay off this loan five years sooner than scheduled.

Several methods can be employed for reducing interest expenses and paying off the loan more rapidly. At the origination point of your mortgage loan, you could commit to a shorter period. For example, you may contract for a 15-year term instead of a 30-year term. That would typically require higher monthly payments, but some lenders are willing to negotiate a lower interest rate if you are willing to repay over a shorter term—a distinct advantage that has the effect of creating additional savings for you.

On the downside, the higher payment required for the shorter-term loan could also disqualify you. Remember, the lender compares the monthly payment to your income level. If the payment is too high, you will be disqualified. In this case, try an alternate plan: Contract for the 30-year repayment term, but make actual payments at the level required to pay off the loan in 15 years. The big advantage in this is that if you run into a period of time when money is tight, you can always revert to the minimum required payment. When matters improve, you can again increase your payment. With this plan, you have complete flexibility.

The process of paying off your loan more rapidly than required by making additional payments to principal is called *mortgage acceleration*. This can save you thousands of dollars over the period of the loan. Remember, in a 30-year term at 8 or 9 percent, you will pay for that property two to three times over. So any acceleration you do early on compounds and has a significant effect throughout those years. Of course, you should make those extra payments only when you can afford to. Once you put additional money into your loan payments you cannot get it back out without refinancing or taking out another loan, or by selling the property. Mortgage acceleration is a form of forced savings, but it offers you no liquidity whatsoever—you cannot access that money once it is sent to the lender.

To illustrate how mortgage acceleration works over time, consider a mortgage of $100,000 at 7 percent. With a 30-year term, total interest comes to $139,512. If the same loan is repaid over 15 years, interest totals $61,789. You will save $77,723 by accelerating payments on this loan. The comparison is illustrated in Figure 4.4.

The loan balance for the shorter-term loan falls more rapidly because the payment is higher. It is designed to amortize, or pay off, this loan in one-half the

mortgage acceleration
a technique for reducing interest costs. By paying additional amounts to principal, the outstanding balance is reduced, so interest is reduced as well, having the effect of lowering the interest cost and speeding up the repayment term.

$100,000 loan, 7%

	Loan Balance	
Year	7% 30-Year	15-Year
5	$ 94,130	$77,410
10	85,810	45,290
15	74,020	0
20	57,300	
25	33,600	
Total interest	$139,512	$61,789

FIGURE 4.4 Mortgage acceleration.

time. Because principal is reduced more quickly, the overall interest is much lower, too. Remember, time equals higher costs. The longer it takes to repay, the more gradually the principal balance falls, and the more you will pay in interest.

Another way to look at the cost of interest is to figure out the rate of *equity buildup*. Figure 4.5 shows that with a 30-year loan, most of the term passes before even one-half of the loan is repaid. Nearly half of the principal is repaid during the last seven years. In comparison, with a 15-year term, equity buildup occurs much more rapidly.

You can accelerate your mortgage using a number of techniques, depending on what works best for your budget. For example, you can simply round up to the next even $100, or add an even $25 each month, or convert your annual tax refund into an additional principal payment. It all depends on your ability and preference.

If you are paying on an adjustable-rate mortgage, some special techniques might be considered. If you pay more at the beginning of the term while your rate is low, you will accelerate because you are reducing principal. So when the rate is raised, the principal balance will be lower. This means the higher interest rate will be calcu-

equity buildup
the process of reducing debt by accumulating equity in the property over a period of time. Without accelerating the payments, the rate of equity buildup with a long-term loan is very slow. The more extended the term, the more slowly equity builds up.

10% Loan 15-Year Term	10% Loan 30-Year Term
	5 year 3.4%
	10 years 9.1%
5 years 18.7%	15 years 18.3%
	20 years 33.6%
10 years 49.4%	
	25 years 58.7%
15 years 100%	30 years 100%

FIGURE 4.5 Equity buildup.

lated on a lower balance. In that respect, you accelerate today and end up saving the rate of return on the higher interest rate later. When the rate is raised, so is the required payment. Early acceleration will soften that increase, since the required payment will be calculated on the lower balance.

Some would argue against early acceleration (see next section). The argument can also be made that you should wait until the rate is raised to accelerate. The problem, of course, is that when the interest rate is raised, the minimum required payment is raised as well. This places more pressure on your budget, reducing your opportunity to accelerate after the rate has been raised.

Regardless of the rate you are paying, or will pay in the future, you are always going to realize the greatest advantage when you begin accelerating as early as possible. This is true whether the loan has a fixed or an adjustable rate. The important point to remember is that interest is computed each and every month on the current outstanding balance. So the more you accelerate, the more effect you have on each and every month's interest from that point forward.

You might not be able to accelerate at the beginning of the loan period, simply because your budget is too strained. But by watching the market over time, you can take advantage of lower rates and refinance in the future. That is also a form of acceleration. One way to accelerate is to refinance for a lower interest rate, but keep the original remaining term and make the same level of payments. For example, if you have 23 years remaining on your loan, refinance for 23 years. If you start the 30-year term over again, that only adds to your overall interest cost.

ARGUMENTS AGAINST ACCELERATION

The strongest argument against acceleration is that the money cannot be taken back. It's true that acceleration is extremely illiquid. If you put the money in a savings account instead, you can get it out easily with a trip to the bank. Increased equity cannot be accessed in that way. One solution is to ask your lender for a line of credit, resolving to use it only for emergencies, and to pay down the balance as quickly as possible if you do use it. You should always have a line of credit, or a cash reserve in a money market account or a savings account, before you begin an acceleration program.

In addition to the argument about the liquidity problem, six other arguments can be made against acceleration.

1. *You are better off paying all of your interest and getting the tax deduction.* Many people accept this argument, believing it is wise to get higher write-offs. But the numbers just don't work. It makes no sense to save taxes by spending more than the amount you save.

An illustration makes the point, no matter what tax rate you use. For example, let's assume that the combined federal and state tax rate you have to pay next year is 45 percent—not unlikely in many states. This means you have to pay 45 cents in tax for every dollar you earn after you pass your marginal tax bracket threshold. Now consider the mortgage payment you will be making. Suppose your monthly payment includes an average of about $500 in interest. By keeping the payments at the minimum level, without any acceleration, you reduce your taxes by 45 percent of the total interest paid. So your taxes are reduced by $225 per month just by paying on this mortgage ($500 × 45 percent). That seems pretty valuable.

To complete the comparison, let's say you can accelerate so that average monthly interest is lowered to $400. For example, on a mortgage with a current balance of $80,000 at 7.5 percent, monthly interest is $500. If you accelerate so that the balance is lowered to $64,000, interest falls to $400. That produces a monthly tax savings of $180 ($400 × 45 percent). While your tax savings is lowered from $225 to $180, so that you "lose" $45 per month, look at the savings in after-tax payments. Before acceleration, you were paying an after-tax interest amount of $275 ($500 less tax savings of $225). But after acceleration, you are paying only $220 ($400 less tax savings of $180). *You have reduced your after-tax interest payment by $55 per month.*

	Before Acceleration	After Acceleration	Difference
Average interest cost	$500	$400	$100
Less: tax savings	−225	−80	−45
After-tax interest cost	$275	$220	$ 55

2. *You should invest your "disposable income"* elsewhere and get a better rate of return.* If you have money available to reduce your mortgage balance and you don't need to increase an existing emergency reserve fund, acceleration is usually a good idea. It would be difficult to

---

*The term "disposable income" is one used by financial consultants to mean money you can afford to invest. However, it also has a casual connotation, seeming to imply that you can afford to throw it away. For this reason, we do not use this term to describe discretionary funds; it is included here only to paraphrase the argument.

prove otherwise by the numbers. The opportunity to make more money elsewhere at a higher rate would be rare, especially with a comparably low risk. Remember that interest rates tend to change on both sides of the investment equation at the same time. That is to say, when it is expensive to borrow because rates are high, it is also a good time to lend, for the same reasons. What you have to pay versus what you can earn are actually two sides of the same market. So when mortgage rates are relatively low, potential yields on other investments will be low as well. We have said that accelerating your mortgage yields a compound return equal to your mortgage rate. That is an extremely low-risk investment. In virtually every market, the only way to beat that yield somewhere else is to take much greater risks.

The risk element destroys the argument that "disposable income" should be invested elsewhere. To make a valid comparison between two choices, the risk level should be identical; otherwise, it is not a fair comparison. With real estate, you have direct control, and historically values hold well and tend to beat inflation. The investment is protected by homeowner's insurance. It provides rental cash every month that you use to pay down the debt. And finally, real estate provides you with immediate tax benefits. To find an investment of comparable benefit for greater yield than real estate would be quite a challenge. Such an investment does not exist.

3. *Acceleration is not necessary, since fixed-rate mortgages protect you from inflation.* This is a clever argument because the anti-inflation claim is true, but the point being made does not address the argument about whether acceleration is a prudent idea. Fixed-rate financing does protect you from inflation; that does not mean you should miss an opportunity to maximize your return. This argument is often put forward along with the claim that since tenants are paying your mortgage anyhow, it doesn't matter what you pay in interest. (See point 4, below.) Wouldn't you prefer a lower cost?

To look at the matter realistically, an investor has to realize that interest is compounded over the entire term of the loan. Acceleration reduces the cost and compounds the reduction each and every month.

4. *Acceleration is unnecessary because your tenants make your mortgage payments for you.* Investors generally are people who pride themselves on using their capital wisely. With a relatively small down payment, you can acquire one or more properties, hold for several years, and sell at a profit. Along the way, the debt is repaid by your tenants. And this is true.

However, acceleration still belongs in your arsenal of investment strategies. If the money is available to pay down your mortgage, you should do so unless you believe that you can beat the market by using that money elsewhere. For example, perhaps you would like to expand your real estate portfolio and are saving up for another down payment—a legitimate reason to hold off on acceleration. But remember that as wise as leverage may be, it makes no sense to employ leverage if all your capital gains are converted to interest or, putting it another way, to lender profits.

5. *Sophisticated investors never pay down a loan faster than they're required to.* While sophisticated investors understand leverage and know how to use it, that does not mean they miss an opportunity. If you have the chance to reduce the cost of property by accelerating your mortgage, if you have an emergency reserve fund, and, finally, if you believe that acceleration produces the best return on your money, then it makes sense. Understanding the subtlety of comparable risk and return is a sophisticated level of comprehension, and many investors forget to make that comparison.

Too often, investors are aware only that real estate has historically beaten inflation and has been a reliable investment, but they fail to realize that their profits are easily eroded in the form of interest over the long term. Beating inflation on its face is not good enough if leverage has the effect of taking up your profits.

6. *You should keep your tax benefits and invest elsewhere.* This is the least supportable argument against mortgage acceleration, but a favorite among some advisers. The argument goes something like this: Rather than giving up your tax benefits by reducing interest, you should use your capital to invest elsewhere. But, if you are paying on a 9 percent mortgage and earning only 6 percent somewhere else, you are losing 3 percent. Another flaw in this argument is that investment income you earn elsewhere will be taxable. That money would be better invested in mortgage acceleration.

The truth is, many financial advisers are against mortgage acceleration because it does not yield a commission. They would prefer that you pay a fee by selecting stocks or mutual funds, or other investments that will pay a commission to them. If you spend all your "disposable income" on mortgage acceleration, the financial planner will get nothing. This demonstrates the inherent conflict in people earning commissions to advise others how and where to invest their money.

A smart way to look at acceleration is as an investment in your own equity. You should recognize the real cost of buying property. It has less to do with listed price than with interest cost, so the more you reduce interest cost, the less you end up paying. With that in mind, acceleration is a real bargain in most cases.

HAVING TWO LOANS

Successful investors know their costs and track them over time. This is not always easy. For example, if you have two loans outstanding on one investment property and the rates are different, you need to know your average rate. This is important when considering whether to refinance. Let's say you are thinking of replacing two existing loans with a completely new loan. It could make sense if the average rate of your two loans is higher than the new rate.

In this instance, you need to figure out the *weighted average*. If loan balances are not the same, it will not be accurate to simply average two rates. The larger-balance loan has to be given proportionately more weight to get a true average.

Example: You have two outstanding mortgages on your investment property and you are considering refinancing. Your first mortgage balance is $85,000 and the interest

weighted average
the average interest rate of two loans, when both the outstanding loan amounts and the interest rates are different. The larger-balance loan is given proportionately more weight to reflect a true average interest rate.

rate is 9 percent. The second mortgage balance is $35,000 and the rate is 7 percent.

If the two balances were exactly identical, you could simply estimate the average of the two rates. (The average of 7 percent and 9 percent is 8 percent.) But because the loan balances are not the same, you need to calculate the weighted average. The formula for calculating weighted average is:

1. Express each loan as a fraction of the total, and multiply by the applicable interest rate. In this example, the total of the two loans is $120,000 ($85,000 plus $35,000):

   First Mortgage

   $$\frac{\$85,000}{\$120,000} \times 9\% = 6.37\%$$

   Second Mortgage

   $$\frac{\$35,000}{\$120,000} \times 7\% = 2.04\%$$

2. Add together the two weighted percentages to arrive at the true weighted average of the loans:

   $$6.37\% + 2.04\% = 8.41\%$$

In considering whether to refinance, you would compare this weighted average to the refinancing rates available. If an available rate is below 8.41%, refinancing might make sense.

CONCLUSION

A thorough analysis of your interest expense over the period of time in which you invest in property is not only useful and important, it could also determine whether you make money. It could lead you to conclude that reducing interest costs is the most important aspect of the real estate investment formula. It is important to select properties with the best potential for future appreciation, to put good tenants in those properties, and to maintain value through maintenance. However, a swing of $5000 to $10,000 in initial price is insignificant compared to the difference in true cost you can achieve through managing debt. Whether by refinancing or by acceleration, the ultimate profitability of real estate will be determined not by capital gains but by what you end up paying in interest.

Reducing costs for real estate is a long-term aspect of your investment program. However, one of the more immediate and important reasons that people choose to invest in real estate is for the annual tax benefits. No other investment offers legitimate tax shelters comparable to real estate. The next chapter explains how tax benefits work for you as a real estate investor.

Chapter 5

Tax Benefits
of Real Estate

B y actively managing your rental property, you are allowed to claim deductions for all of your rental expenses. So if you report a loss from operating rental properties, that loss reduces your overall tax liability. For example, if you also earn a salary, you might end up owing considerably less in taxes because you own rental property.

Before going on, an important note must be inserted. First, tax laws are likely to change at any time. The general rules and guidelines provided here should be used as a starting point in developing your tax strategy. Deductions for investment losses are also limited in a number of ways, so you will need to consult with your tax adviser to ensure that the deductions you claim on your tax return comply with current law and regulation.

The Taxpayer Relief Act of 1997 made significant changes to the law regarding treatment of the sale of primary residences. These changes do not apply to rental properties; however, they bring up some interesting strategies. Because you are allowed to switch a primary residence into a rental, and vice versa, some long-term planning could help you to legally avoid or defer taxes on gains (both on your primary residence and on rental property).

Real estate investors enjoy several benefits not available to others. Collectively, these benefits make real estate one of the best investments when tax liabilities are an important consideration. By designing a package of benefits for real estate investors, the Congress has recognized the many economic benefits that are derived from real estate investing, not only regionally but for the entire country.

These benefits are explained in more detail later in this chapter. By way of providing an overview, the following summarizes the main benefits:

✔ You can defer (put off) tax liability on the profit from selling investment property, often indefinitely; and by timing a sale carefully, you can also completely control when you recognize capital gains.

✔ Ordinary and reasonable expenses connected to real estate are deductible as investment expenses, including interest, property taxes, utilities, insurance, maintenance, supplies, legal fees, and others.

✔ You can claim depreciation of buildings and other improvements, which greatly increases your deductions and reduces tax liabilities.

✔ You can refinance property debt and take out cash—even if the amount taken out is higher than your original investment—without being taxed on the proceeds.

You will probably need professional tax help not only to ensure that you claim all the deductions to which you are entitled, but also to make sure you follow all of the rules. The federal income tax rules are complicated to the extent that most people are overwhelmed by the process of annual reporting. When you add special schedules for real estate, including calculations not usually performed, the task is even more daunting. As a real estate investor, you will need to fill out several schedules you would not use otherwise. A professional tax expert who knows the rules can help you comply, freeing up your time and energy to manage your invest-

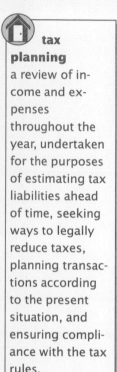

tax planning
a review of income and expenses throughout the year, undertaken for the purposes of estimating tax liabilities ahead of time, seeking ways to legally reduce taxes, planning transactions according to the present situation, and ensuring compliance with the tax rules.

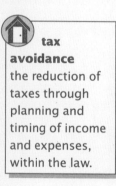

tax avoidance
the reduction of taxes through planning and timing of income and expenses, within the law.

ments, rather than worrying about paperwork and the federal tax code.

Don't overlook the importance of *tax planning*. Review your status throughout the year to anticipate future tax liabilities and identify actions you can take now to legally reduce taxes. It is perfectly legal to time decisions to reduce taxes, but if you wait until next April, it will be too late. A competent tax professional can help you by identifying the actions you can take today—or put off until tomorrow—that will help you to better plan and manage your tax liability.

AN OVERVIEW OF TAX STRATEGY

Planning ahead is a valuable and important investment strategy. It distinguishes the professional from all other investors. You can adopt the policy of preplanning and practice planning as a recurring action to improve your performance. If you are willing to devote a few hours per week in reviewing and anticipating what is happening with your personal taxes, you could save a lot of money by the end of the year. If you do not plan, you will lose the opportunity.

Smart investors see tax planning as a process in legal *tax avoidance*. By arranging your affairs in advance and timing income and expenses, you can defer tax liabilities to the future, and legally avoid paying some taxes this year. As a general rule, *tax deferral* is considered a smart practice. If you can put off a tax liability from this year until the future, you reduce current taxes, giving you more capital to invest today. By using and investing your capital well, you will help your equity to grow, so tax deferral makes sense. A series of tax laws in recent years has helped real estate investors to benefit more than ever from tax deferral. The Tax Reform Act of 1986 and the Taxpayer Relief Act of 1997 have both dramatically affected real estate investing, and have helped to make real estate truly the best legal tax shelter available. One expert identified the benefits of the 1986 tax reform law by explaining: "Deferral represents the heart of tax benefits in the post–Tax Reform Act of 1986 era. It's currently the only game in town."*

While the 1986 tax act pointed out the advantages in real estate, the 1997 law also had an important effect, especially for homeowners. While the press concentrated on the debate over a $500-per-child tax credit, the real news was missed. Congress exempted from federal tax the profit on selling a primary residence, up to $500,000. That means you could earn a profit of $500,000 without having to pay any taxes. The law does away with the need to defer tax liability, because the liability itself was eliminated. While this does not affect investment property, it raises an interesting possibility. The exclusion of tax is available for only your primary residence. So, you could convert a rental property to your *primary residence*, live there for two years or more, and then sell and legally avoid taxes.†

As you can see, the tax code requires a lot of planning and strategy. As the law is reformed, new strategies grow from the reforms themselves. It all comes down to the realization that paying taxes is *not* a productive or profitable use of money. Taxes do not go to work within the economy, and are not available for you. Tax increases do not create jobs; they eliminate them. Taxes do not make the economy strong; they threaten its health. Taxes are spending, and nothing else. So the less you pay in taxes, or the more you legally defer tax liabilities, the more capital you have to put to work in a positive way.

One argument against deferral is that tax rates might be much higher in the future. This cannot be known. They might also be much lower, and that argument has to be given as much merit. The point is, we can only plan based on what we know today and what we think the fu-

 tax deferral delaying tax liabilities until future years, often as a part of a long-term plan. This practice is especially beneficial when taxable income is expected to be lower in the future than it is today, so that delayed profits will be taxed at a lower rate.

primary residence the property in which you live, defined under tax rules for the purpose of excluding profits upon sale, as the house you lived in for at least two of the past five years.

---

*W. Todd McGrath, "The Value of Tax Benefits in Real Estate Investment," *Real Estate Review*, 1993, p. 57.
†Under the new law, you cannot escape tax on depreciation (a topic covered later in this chapter). If you converted an investment property to your primary residence and then sold it, you would have to pay some tax, based on the amount of depreciation previously claimed.

ture will hold. If we knew what was going to happen, planning would be easy.

Deferral is the most practical example of tax avoidance. This is entirely legal, as it represents nothing more than the prudent management of business matters. Why pay more in taxes than you are legally required to pay? As long as you report income and deductions according to the law, tax avoidance is acceptable and is one of the more important forms of money management.

Failing to report income, or reporting false expenses, are examples of *tax evasion*, which is illegal. This is not an acceptable form of money management, and it will land you in jail or in court, subjecting you to fines and other penalties—including having assets seized.

Example: An investor plans to sell an income property this year, and will realize about $50,000 in profit. By waiting a few months, this profit will be deferred until next year, when the investor's taxable income will be lower. This is an example of tax avoidance.

Example: An investor sells an investment property and does not report the profit on his tax return. He believes the exclusion will not be caught. This is an example of tax evasion.

Timing is important in tax planning. By delaying the sale of a property, you defer the tax liability to the future. Later in this chapter, we will show how gains from investment properties can be deferred indefinitely by using the tax laws to your advantage.

You can also affect your tax return by the timing of expenses. Most people pay taxes using the *cash method*, meaning that income is taxed and expenses are deducted in the year received or paid. For most individuals, this is the default method. For example, you pay taxes on all the income you receive this year; some additional income is owed to you, but not paid. And the same is true with expenses. You might owe money to someone else, but if you don't pay it in the current year, it isn't deducted until the year paid.

 tax evasion
falsifying a tax return, failing to provide complete information, or reporting untrue information on the return, for the purpose of illegally reducing tax liabilities.

 cash method
a method for reporting income and expenses at the time cash is exchanged. All income is reported in the year it is received, and all expenses are deducted in the year paid.

Some businesses use the alternative, the *accrual method*. While this method is more accurate because it matches income and expense to the proper year, it is also a more complex way to keep books. Under the accrual method, you account for income as it is earned and you keep track of expenses as they are incurred. The expression *earned income* means income that applies to the current month. Payment might not be received for a month, two months, or three months later; that doesn't matter. It is reported as being earned in the proper month. Matching earned income on the other side of the ledger is *incurred expense*, which is deducted in the "proper" month or year, meaning the time it was incurred or committed, and not the month the bill is paid.

You will probably use cash accounting for keeping your books, although you should be aware that interest is usually deducted in the proper (incurred) period regardless of the bookkeeping method you select.

Example: You own an investment property and in November, the annual premium for fire insurance comes due. You have the choice of paying for a full year or of making quarterly or monthly payments. If you pay the entire premium before December 31, you can claim the full amount as a deduction this year. If you were reporting under the accrual method, you would be allowed to deduct payments only in the years to which the premium applied.

According to tax regulations, cash-basis reporting allows you to deduct only what you actually spend in the current year. But if you pay business expenses using your credit card, that counts as cash—even if you don't pay the bill until January.

REAL ESTATE LOSSES AND YOUR TAXES

If you are like most real estate investors, you will have income from a full-time job, and property management will be a sideline for you. This is where real estate's tax benefits become valuable. For example, it is possible that you

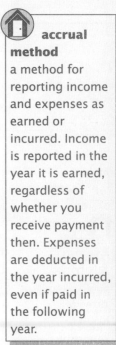

accrual method
a method for reporting income and expenses as earned or incurred. Income is reported in the year it is earned, regardless of whether you receive payment then. Expenses are deducted in the year incurred, even if paid in the following year.

earned income
income earned in a specific month or year, even though the actual payment might not be made until later.

incurred expense
expense that applies to a specific month or year, regardless of when payment is actually made.

will have a loss from real estate; but that loss reduces your overall income, so that your tax liability will be lowered as well. Because tax benefits are valuable, you will need to keep track of all the money you spend in managing property. You probably want to claim all of the deductions to which you are entitled. Allowable deductions for real estate investing include:

✔ *Interest.* The interest you pay on rental property mortgages is deductible as an investment expense, whereas interest you pay on your home mortgage is claimed as an itemized deduction.

✔ *Property taxes.* Taxes paid to your local government are also deductible as one of the expenses of doing business.

✔ *Insurance.* The premiums you pay for fire insurance and, if your lender requires it, mortgage insurance, are fully deductible for rental property.

✔ *Utilities.* The utilities you pay for your rentals are deductible.

✔ *Operating expenses.* The cost of supplies, maintenance, repairs, bookkeeping services, legal fees, landscaping, telephone, and any other expenses necessary to maintain your rental properties is deductible as an investment expense.

While an expense is deductible, a *capital expenditure* is not. These become the *basis* in the property. Examples include the building itself, flooring and roofing, materials and labor for an addition, well or septic systems, and other costs that add permanent value to the building. The test of expense versus *capitalization* is whether something adds permanent value (if it does, it is a capital asset) and whether it can be removed. (Generally speaking, a fixture is permanent and is capitalized, but removable items like drapes or throw rugs would be considered expenses.)

Expenses are generally paid by writing a check. But in the case of *depreciation*, a certain amount is claimed as an expense each year, for a specified period of time. Depreciation is a noncash expense because no check is writ-

 capital expenditure
money spent on improvements to rental property, including buildings and all permanent fixtures. These cannot be deducted as expenses, but are depreciated.

 basis
the cost of the building on your property, plus improvements and fixtures, which can be depreciated but not claimed as deductions. In computing the profit upon sale of investment property, land is included in basis; but land cannot be depreciated.

ten; it is claimed based on the original cost, whether financed or paid for in advance. To many, the idea of claiming an expense without actually paying out the money seems wrong; however, it is not only legal, but proper as well. The purpose of depreciation is to spread out the cost of acquiring property. You are not allowed to buy a property and claim a deduction in the year it is bought. Instead, it is capitalized and a small amount is claimed each year. The one exception: Land itself cannot be depreciated. So when you buy property, it has to be divided between land and improvements. Only the improvements can be depreciated. (The usual methods for dividing the property are based on the proportionate division used by your local tax collector or assessor, an appraiser's report, or values assigned for the purpose of buying fire insurance. Computing the breakdown is discussed in detail later in this chapter.)

capitalization setting up of capital expenditures as assets subject to depreciation. Capitalized assets are not deducted as expenses but are instead written off through depreciation over a period of years mandated by tax regulations.

HOW TO CLAIM DEPRECIATION

Depreciation is the expense claimed each year to write off a portion of a capital asset. You can claim this deduction over a number of years. Depreciation reduces your basis each year so that, when you sell the property, your basis will be lower than it was when you bought it. The more depreciation claimed, the lower the basis and the higher your taxable profit.

For residential real estate and improvements, you claim depreciation over 27½ years. All other property (nonresidential investment property) is depreciated over 31½ years.

Each asset is depreciated within guidelines established in tax regulations. The period of time is called a *recovery period*. Each type of asset has its own recovery period and each type can also be depreciated under a limited number of methods. Real estate—buildings and permanent improvements—are always depreciated using the *straight-line depreciation* method. That means the identical amount is deducted each year, with the exception of the first year, in which the amount is prorated. Some other

depreciation an annual expense representing part of a capital asset's basis. Depreciation is deducted as a noncash expense each year, and reduces the basis in the investment property as it is claimed as an expense.

recovery period
under depreciation rules, the number of years over which depreciation is claimed; within each recovery period, certain kinds of depreciation can be used.

straight-line depreciation
a form of depreciation in which an identical amount is deducted each year in the recovery period, until the entire basis has been fully depreciated.

accelerated depreciation
a form of depreciation allowing more deduction in the earlier years of the recovery period, with less depreciation claimed in the later years.

types of property, such as vehicles and office equipment, can be depreciated more rapidly than real estate, using *accelerated depreciation*. Under such a method, you are allowed to deduct more in the earlier recovery period years, and less later on.

An important point concerning depreciation is its relationship to leverage. Whether you put down a lot of money or very little, you calculate depreciation the same way—based on the price of the real estate and not on the amount of cash you put into the deal. The tax advantage is that depreciation is based on your basis, so the less capital you invest, the more value you get back from depreciation; that is to say, in comparing your cash investment to your tax advantage, a smaller amount of capital invested yields a greater dollar-for-dollar tax advantage.

For personal property (as distinguished from real property), you are allowed to depreciate under three different recovery periods: three, five, or seven years. (*Note:* Some extended, additional periods are also used, but usually for assets other than those related to real estate investing.) Each of the recovery periods allows the use of a modified form of accelerated depreciation (modified because it reverts to a form of straight-line depreciation in the last few years). The percentages applicable to these recovery periods are summarized in Table 5.1.

TABLE 5.1	Personal Property Depreciation		
	Recovery Period		
Year	Three Years	Five Years	Seven Years
1	33.33%	20.00%	14.29%
2	44.45	32.00	24.49
3	14.81	19.20	17.49
4	7.41	11.52	12.49
5		11.52	8.93
6		5.76	8.92
7			8.93
8			4.46

The percentages listed in the table are used each year to claim the depreciation. At the end of the period, the entire basis in the asset has been depreciated. Note that the period of depreciation requires one extra year to claim the last remaining part of the allowable depreciation. This is based on the method of depreciating assets that assumes property is bought halfway through the year on average. So for the first year, you get only six months' worth of depreciation—and that leaves a half year's worth at the end as well. This rule, called the *half-year convention*, assumes that, on average, assets acquired in any one year are bought and put into service at the halfway point of the year.

While the half-year convention usually applies to personal property, buildings and improvements are calculated during the first year using the *mid-month convention*. This means that the first year's depreciation is calculated depending on the month you acquire property; you are allowed to deduct a percentage of the per-year depreciation based on the month purchased. Because the mid-month convention is used, each month's percentage will reflect a percentage based on mid-month calculation, not on full-month calculation. For example, if you acquire property in January, you will be allowed to deduct 23/24ths of the calculation for that year (the full year less one-half month). And if you buy property in February, you will be allowed to deduct 21/24ths for the first year.

half-year convention
a rule often used in calculating depreciation of personal property, which assumes that on average, assets are purchased and placed into service halfway through the year. The first year's depreciation is allowed for only half the year, and a half-year's worth is left to take up at the end of the recovery period.

Example: You bought an investment property for $100,000 and closed during the month of April. The land is worth $45,000, so your basis for depreciation is $55,000. Since residential real estate can be depreciated over $27^{1}/_{2}$ years, the straight-line depreciation method for real estate yields depreciation of $2000 per year:

$$\frac{\$55,000}{27.5} = \$2000$$

But using the mid-month convention, your first-year depreciation will be only $1416.60. That represents 17/24ths of the first year's depreciation (the second half of

mid-month convention

a rule for calculating depreciation for buildings and improvements, which assumes that on average, assets are purchased and put into service halfway through the month in which they are purchased. The first year's depreciation is calculated from the mid-month forward, with the excess assigned to the final year of the depreciation term.

April plus the remaining eight months), which equals 70.83 percent of the full year:

$2000 \times .7083 = \$1416.60$

Table 5.2 summarizes the multiplier to use for each month for the first year you own property.

Your first task in calculating depreciation is to identify the basis of property. When you buy personal property, the basis is simply the amount spent. In the case of real estate, basis is not as straightforward. Because you cannot depreciate land, you have to first take out the land's value to arrive at basis for the purpose of depreciation.

Example: You own an investment property that you bought for $125,000. The land is valued at $30,000 and cannot be depreciated. The remaining $95,000 is the value of the building and improvements. Because it is a residential property, the depreciation term is $27\frac{1}{2}$ years. Annual depreciation will be $3454.55:

TABLE 5.2 Mid-Month Convention	
Month Placed in Service	Multiplying Factor
January	0.9583
February	0.8750
March	0.7917
April	0.7083
May	0.6250
June	0.5417
July	0.4583
August	0.3750
September	0.2917
October	0.2083
November	0.1250
December	0.0417

$$\frac{\$95,000}{27.5} = \$3454.55$$

The exception occurs in the first year, when depreciation is reduced according to the month in which the deal closes.

The amount that is subject to depreciation is called the basis. Current market value is never used, even when that value is considerably higher because you have owned the property for many years. For example, you might have paid $45,000 for property 15 years ago, and today it is worth $225,000. That value increase does not affect depreciation, which is always based on purchase price and not on current value.

To establish how much of your purchase represents land and how much represents building and improvements, you can use several methods. At the time you enter the deal, if it is financed, there will be an appraisal. The appraisal report breaks down the estimated value of the two components, which you can use for your own breakdown. A second method is to use the breakdown applied by your insurance company for the purpose of providing fire insurance. This also involves a calculated division, since there is no need to insure the land. And finally, the most popular method is to use the *assessed value* assigned by your local assessor for property tax purposes, from which you can figure out the portion of the total price representing buildings.

Example: You bought a property for $125,000, which is the current market value. However, your assessed value shows the property being worth $60,000. Your county assessor reported the breakdown as:

Land	$14,400
Improvements	45,600
Total	$60,000

To compute the breakdown and apply it to your actual purchase price, first calculate the percentage representing improvements:

assessed value

the value of property for the purpose of calculating and collecting property taxes. That value is broken down between land and buildings, and can be used to calculate depreciation basis.

ordinary income
income earned from salaries and wages, interest or dividends, self-employment, partnerships or trusts, rentals, and other sources not subject to capital gains tax.

capital gain or loss
a gain or loss resulting from holding investment property, which is subject to capital gains tax rather than tax on ordinary income. Capital gains and losses are reported on a special schedule as part of the federal income tax return.

$$\frac{\$45,600}{\$60,000} = 76\%$$

Next, apply that percentage to your actual purchase price:

$$\$125,000 \times 76\% = \$95,000$$

In this example, you would be allowed to depreciate $95,000 over 27½ years. The assessed value breakdown is frequently used because it is official and easily available. It is a common practice that has gained wide acceptance.

WHEN YOU SELL INVESTMENT PROPERTY

When you work for a salary, or when you receive interest on a savings account, income from rentals, and so forth, that income is called *ordinary income* for tax purposes and is taxed at the standard rates. However, when you buy rental property (or other investments) and later sell, the profit or loss is treated not as ordinary income, but as a *capital gain or loss*. You are limited in the amount of capital loss you can deduct each year. If you have a loss greater than that maximum, the difference can be carried over to future years.

When you report a capital gain, the net gain is taxed at a different rate than ordinary income. The rate may also vary based on how long you owned the asset. The rules for treatment of capital gains have been altered many times by Congress, and probably will be changed again in the future. The amount of gain is calculated starting with the *adjusted basis* of the property. This is the original cost, plus closing costs paid at the time of purchase, plus capital improvements, and minus all depreciation claimed.

The actual capital gain or loss is the difference between the *adjusted sales price* (sales price plus closing costs) and the adjusted basis. If the adjusted sales price is higher, there is a capital gain; if adjusted basis is higher, there is a capital loss.

ANNUAL TAX BENEFITS

For most investors, one of the major attractions of owning real estate is the annual tax benefits such ownership provides. The combined deductions for interest, property taxes, utilities, maintenance, and other expenses paid in cash, as well as depreciation, add up to an immediate and substantial tax shelter each and every year.

The profit or loss from operating real estate is not easy to identify compared to other businesses, where tax benefits do not have such immediate effect. For every real estate investor, *cash flow* is the real bottom line. Cash flow is the difference between money received and money paid out; it excludes depreciation, a noncash expense that is tax-deductible, but includes payment of principal on mortgages and any payments for capital assets, which are not tax-deductible. (For example, you have to buy a refrigerator for your rental property; that is a capital asset and not a tax-deductible monthly expense.) To determine your real tax-based profitability on real estate, you have to calculate your *after-tax cash flow*.

One of the risks in real estate is that you will pay out more money each month than you receive. This becomes especially difficult to manage if you have more than one property. The condition of paying more than you receive is called *negative cash flow*. Here is an example of negative cash flow:

Monthly rent income	$900
Less: operating expenses	−312
Net operating income	$588
Less: mortgage payment	−761
Negative cash flow	−$173

Without considering the effect of tax benefits, negative cash flow looks bleak. But when you modify this situation for the tax benefits—which vary from one person to another based on total income—the benefits and tax sheltering features of real estate become obvious.

 adjusted basis for the purpose of computing capital gains or losses, the original purchase price plus closing costs paid at the time of purchase, plus the cost value of improvements done while the property was held, less all depreciation claimed.

 adjusted sales price for the purpose of computing capital gains or losses, the sales price plus closing costs paid at the time of sale.

cash flow
the amount of money received from rental income each month, minus the amount paid out in mortgage payments, the purchase of capital assets, and payment of operating expenses. Cash flow is not the same as profit, since it includes nondeductible payments.

after-tax cash flow
cash flow with the tax benefits and savings taken into account. This number might be substantially different from pretax cash flow, especially when depreciation reduces tax liabilities.

Example: An investor owns a seven-unit apartment building. Results last year were: rental income, $35,800; operating expenses, $11,450; mortgage interest payments, $21,007. Thus, before taxes the operating taxable income was $3343. When taxes of $1100 and mortgage principal payments of $4255 were taken into account, the after-tax negative was $2012. However, operating expenses included $9300 in depreciation. As a noncash expense, this has to be added back to see the true picture, showing positive after-tax cash flow of $7288.

This analysis can be summarized another way:

Rental income	$35,800
Less: operating expenses	−11,450
Less: mortgage interest	−21,007
Taxable income	$ 3,343
Less: taxes	−1,100
Less: mortgage principal	−4,255
After-tax loss	$−2,012
Plus: depreciation	9,300
After-tax cash flow	$ 7,288

In this example, the owner will report a net loss for tax purposes of $5957—taxable income of $3343 less depreciation of $9300. That loss is likely to recur over several years in the future as well, since depreciation will not change but remains the same each year. At the same time, the true after-tax result shows *positive cash flow*.

To determine the extent of tax benefits you are likely to receive from investing in real estate, make a few assumptions about the kind of property you will buy, and apply those assumptions to your current income level.

Suppose that you can afford to buy a rental property for $100,000, and that $75,000 is the building's value. Annual depreciation would be approximately $2727 ($75,000 divided by 27½).

Next, determine the fair rents in your area. Study the For Rent ads in your local paper to estimate a reasonable rental level. You might decide, for example, to use $800 as the typical average rent for a three-bedroom, two-bath house. (Remember, rent levels vary significantly from one place to another; $800 is used to illustrate a point only.)

Next, estimate the likely mortgage payment and the breakdown between interest and principal (see Chapter 4). Also make estimates for property taxes, utilities, and insurance.

Prepare an estimated profit and loss summary for this property, taking all of these elements into account. You will probably report a tax loss when depreciation is included, even if you rent out the property for 12 full months. Rents should be sufficient to cover all or most of your mortgage payment (depending on how much down payment you made). But depreciation, a noncash expense, will create a tax loss in many cases even when you are experiencing positive cash flow.

Although the rental might generate negative cash flow from month to month, it is entirely possible that you will save more in taxes than you're paying out in cash. And even if the outcome is marginal, remember that you have control over a growing asset. As long as rental receipts pay for the majority of expenses, time is on your side. Eventually, as the market grows, your rents will increase while the mortgage payment remains at the same level. Typically, it takes 5 to 10 years for properties to season, so future cash flow is usually better than cash flow during the first few years.

The higher your down payment, the better your cash flow. That's because a lower mortgage requires a lower payment, so by investing more equity, you help reduce the strain on your monthly budget. In addition, when you reduce overall, long-term interest, that reduces the true cost of your investment, which increases your return.

Another attractive feature of real estate is that any borrowed money secured by real estate is not taxed. You only pay capital gains on the profit you earn upon sale. So if you refinance and are able to take out cash proceeds, you do not report that as income; it is borrowed money only.

Example: You bought an income property five years ago, paying $80,000. Your down payment was $20,000. The seller financed the balance of $60,000 with a 30-year,

negative cash flow the condition in which payments are greater than receipts.

positive cash flow a situation in which cash receipts are greater than cash payments.

fixed-rate loan. As of the beginning of this year, the loan balance was about $58,000. You can refinance the debt and get a new loan up to 70 percent of current market value. Market value is now $140,000, so you could finance $98,000, which is $40,000 more than what you owe on the mortgage you have now.

Outcomes like this are not rare. However, lenders may impose a policy that they will not allow cash to be taken out on refinancing of rental property; so be sure to check into this before paying a loan application fee. However, if you do find a lender willing to allow you to take out cash, you can do so without any tax consequences.

DEFERRAL RULES

The year-to-year benefits of owning real estate are very attractive. These benefits, by themselves, often spell the difference between negative and positive cash flow. Even more attractive is the fact that, with proper planning, you can defer capital gains taxes—in some cases indefinitely. All you need to do is replace one investment property with another of equal or greater value.

 deferred gain
a capital gain on investment property, put off until a future date. The property must be replaced within a time limit by another property costing as much as or more than the property that was sold.

This rule applies to all real estate held for investment, whether residential or nonresidential. A *deferred gain* simply means that the profit, while subject to tax, is not recognized until a future period. You will eventually pay a tax on the profit, but for the immediate future, all of your profits can be turned around and invested in more property.

This applies only to investment property. For your own home, the rules are easier to follow. You are not taxed on any of the profit you realize from selling your home, up to a maximum of $500,000 (per married couple) or $250,000 (for a single person). This applies to only your primary residence, which is a home you must have lived in for at least two out of the last five years. You can escape tax on gains on your primary residence as many times as you like, with one important restriction: You can claim such an exclusion no more often than every two years.

If you acquire rental property and use it that way for

several years, eventually moving to that house and making it your primary residence (meaning you have to live there at least two years), you could sell at a profit and escape tax on *most* of that profit. You will have to declare as profit the amount of depreciation claimed while the property was rented out. The Appendix includes the full language of Section 312 of the Taxpayer Relief Act of 1997, where this new section was added to the law.

The rules for deferring gains on rental properties are quite different. As a general rule, if you sell a rental property and make a profit, you are subject to capital gains. (Remember, "profit" is defined as your adjusted sale price minus adjusted basis, which includes adding back any depreciation claimed.) However, special rules apply allowing you to defer gains if you meet certain requirements.

Deferral for investment property is done by a *like-kind exchange*. That means that when you sell investment real estate, you need to buy new investment real estate in order to fall under this rule. So, you can replace residential with commercial, or industrial with residential—as long as it's still investment real estate.

Section 1031 of the Internal Revenue Code contains the rules for this kind of transaction, and the text of this code section is included in the Appendix. Because of the section in which these rules are found, like-kind exchanges often are called 1031 exchanges. Three special conditions need to be met for you to qualify for the deferral of gain under code section 1031:

1. *You usually have to work through an intermediary.* You need to set up the exchange transaction through an intermediary, often called a facilitator. This individual cannot be a relative or business partner, or your real estate agent, attorney, or employee. In other words, the facilitator has to be able to act as a neutral third party.

The intermediary collects and pays funds much like an escrow agent or attorney in a real estate deal, primarily to ensure strict following of the rule that, in a 1031 exchange, you are not allowed to exercise control over the funds involved. The money has to roll from one property to another without your taking control of it, even for a moment.

 like-kind exchange (also called a 1031 exchange, referencing the Internal Revenue Code section) an exchange of one investment property for another of the same type, with taxes deferred. In order to qualify, investment real estate has to be replaced with other investment real estate. As long as the new property is bought within 180 days of the sale and costs as much as or more than the old property, all of the gain is deferred. If the new property does not cost as much, the shortfall is taxed in the year of the sale.

2. *You have to identify your new property within 45 days after the close of the sale of the old property.* Identifying a property means finding a property that is for sale, and naming it as the "identified" property. The actual rules defining this process are quite complex. The intermediary you select to facilitate the 1031 exchange should be qualified and should understand the rules, so that you will be ensured of compliance. As pointless as these rules might seem, they must be followed or the deferral will not be allowed.

3. *You have to close the sale on the new property within 180 days from the close of your old property.* The actual closing on the new property has to occur within 180 days from the closing of the old property—no exceptions. If you miss this deadline, you lose the opportunity to qualify under section 1031, and that means you're liable for capital gains tax on the profits. In addition, you will still have to pay the facilitator for going through the steps up until this point.

CONVERTING BETWEEN RESIDENCE AND INVESTMENT PROPERTY

The idea of converting a primary residence to an investment property has always had a certain appeal. Under the pre-1997 rules, there was an incentive to convert residential to investment property. By doing so, you could sell and execute a 1031 exchange, thus deferring the gain. However, with the 1997 changes, it is no longer necessary. An entirely different incentive has been created: to convert investment property into residential, use it as a primary residence for at least two years, and then sell it tax-free (except that depreciation is taxed upon sale in that instance).

If you invest strictly in single-family properties, this is possible. However, you cannot convert a five-unit apartment building to your residence and qualify under the new rules. Some situations are not affected. But, for the many people who deal only in rental houses, the new rules present some long-term planning opportunities.

For example, some investors allow rental houses to go unpainted for a few years, planning to update when they're ready to sell. But now that primary residence gains are free of federal income tax, those same investors have a good incentive to move into their rental properties. It's much easier to complete cosmetic repairs while living in the house. These can include painting in and out, putting on a new roof, upgrading plumbing, installing new floors, and many other improvements designed to add value. This makes sense in anticipation of putting the property on the market.

The new tax rules have liberalized and simplified the requirements for homeowners. You need to live in a house for only two years to call it your primary residence. If you sell, the profit is not taxed (up to the limit of $500,000 for married couples and $250,000 for single people).

To be sure you qualify for the rules of deferral for investment properties, or simply to identify the amount of profit on income property, you need to be sure you're keeping accurate and complete books. For many people, bookkeeping is a little less desirable than root canal work. But by keeping it simple, you can also minimize the time commitment and the pain of having to keep records. The next chapter gives you some ideas for keeping an accurate but simple set of books.

Setting Up Your Books

In any business or investment enterprise, you need a recordkeeping system that ensures you claim and are able to prove every deduction to which you are entitled.

There are several reasons for keeping good records, including these four:

1. *It's required by law.* If you claim deductions against your income, the tax laws require that you keep records that are clear enough to prove your expenses.

2. *You will profit from good records.* By maintaining consistent and accurate records, you build a file that helps with future analysis. This can be extremely valuable information.

3. *Proper analysis depends on accurate records.* It can be very frustrating when you need to analyze records, only to discover that your books are not reliable.

4. *In the event of a tax audit, good records are vital.* An audit is nothing to worry about as long as you have accurate and complete records. You need to be able to prove every deduction you have claimed on your annual tax return.

USING PROFESSIONAL HELP

Your tax accountant should be available to help prepare your tax return unless you insist on doing it yourself. Once you become a serious real estate investor, you will discover that you face many special situations and questions not encountered in the typical tax return. For example, you might be required to file annual information returns if you pay interest to any individuals with whom you have a mortgage; you may need to calculate depreciation for a number of real property and personal property items, including different recovery period computations; you might be required to calculate capital gains or losses and factor these in with your other income; and you will be required to file several schedules that most people do not use every year.

Should you hire an accountant, a bookkeeper, or both? The answer depends on:

✔ The volume of transactions.

✔ The complexity of your overall tax situation.

✔ Your skill level and understanding of the tax rules.

All businesses deserve an individually tailored bookkeeping system. This is not a difficult thing to create. In fact, a tailored system is efficient because it addresses all of your needs. It should provide you exactly what you need and want, no more and no less. An example of tailoring is breaking down all expenses by property when you have two or more investment properties; this is necessary because you have to report that way on your annual tax return. Such considerations as departmentalization might not be as necessary or as informative in another kind of business. Six guidelines for tailoring your records are:

1. *Keep records as simple as possible.* Good records are simple records. A complicated set of books takes too much time and does not provide valuable information when you need it. The time required to maintain a com-

plicated set of books also means you will never have fully updated information.

2. *Identify exactly what you need and then design it.* Every business is different, and every set of books should reflect that. If you keep your own books, you will discover as time goes by what works and what does not work. If you use an outside service, work with the service provider to ensure that your recordkeeping system is effective and simple.

3. *Try to find a bookkeeper familiar with real estate bookkeeping.* If you use an outside service, you will get maximum benefit if the provider is already familiar with your requirements. A service specializing in real estate understands the tax requirements, types of expenses, depreciation rules, and other information needed to tailor your books perfectly.

4. *Listen to good advice, but design your system for your convenience, not someone else's.* Don't allow someone else to talk you out of getting what you want from your bookkeeping system. If the bookkeeper offers advice and there is a sound reason for it, take that advice. But often, such advice is for the convenience of the bookkeeper. Insist on the right to have final say about design ideas. If compromise leads to conflict, find a different service.

5. *Be sure you get answers from your books.* A set of books should inform, not confuse. It should enable you to see—with minimum work—whether you are making or losing money on your properties. The books should help you plan cash flow. If the books are just too complicated to understand, something is wrong. Find a different service, one that can simplify your life and your books.

6. *Modify the system according to changing needs.* No business remains the same for long. What works in your books today could be out of date within a few months. Be willing to constantly modify and update as changing demands require. For example, when you have only one rental, the expense records can be fairly simple. But when you add a second property, you need to keep expense records for each one. That complicates everything. As you grow and your mix of investments changes, you need to keep up by upgrading your recordkeeping system.

DESIGN SUGGESTIONS

Even if you start out on a very small scale as a real estate investor, you can set up your books to anticipate future expansion of your base. You can attempt to design your books to allow for growth in the number of properties you own, as well as in the volume of transactions.

Set up your accounts in the sequence you will be required to report on your federal income tax return. This makes sense, not only because it conforms to the sequence, but also because it is easy to trace information from the tax return back to the ledger. Real estate income and expense are reported on Schedule E, Supplemental Income and Loss. While the design of tax forms changes from time to time, Schedule E has followed the same sequence of account listings for several years. The form includes the following 15 account categories:

1. *Advertising.* This includes ads you place to rent properties, or to buy and sell properties. It might also include ads you place for related purposes, such as locating used appliances, a handyman, a plumber, or an electrician.

2. *Auto and travel.* You are allowed to deduct automobile expenses to the extent that you use your car for rental-related business. That includes driving to properties to view them, keeping an eye on rentals after you have bought them, picking up supplies, and any other use of the automobile made necessary by your real estate investments. You need to keep a log of the mileage, since that is the basis for a deduction. Two methods are used. First is the proportionate actual expense basis (gas, maintenance, parking fees, tires, license and registration, and depreciation); second is the per-mile allowance, in which you are allowed to deduct a specified amount per mile of business use of your automobile. When it comes to claiming a deduction for business use of your automobile, recordkeeping is essential.

Travel is included in this category. Travel is deductible under the same terms; it has to be related specifically to your investments. For example, if you own property in a different city, travel to take care of buying and selling or managing tenants and the property is deductible. A situation where this might come up would be if you convert a property to a rental and move to a different region.

3. *Cleaning and maintenance.* The cost of cleaning property is deductible. For example, after a tenant leaves, you need to clean the carpets and drapes, so you hire a cleaning service. That is deductible. Or, you rent a rug shampoo machine and do the work yourself. The cost of renting the machine is deductible, but you cannot claim a deduction for your own labor.

4. *Commissions.* Payments to real estate agents or others at the close of property you sell are deductible as business expenses; or, if you use a buyer's agent, commissions paid to the buyer's agent are deductible.

5. *Insurance.* Insurance premiums for rental properties are deductible. As a general rule, you will purchase a policy protecting the buildings and providing liability insurance, but excluding tenants' possessions. In addition, some lenders will require that you pay for mortgage insurance or default insurance; the premiums for those policies are also deductible as an investment expense. If you use a vehicle exclusively related to your real estate investments, the insurance you pay for that vehicle is also deductible. For example, some landlords buy a used truck, knowing that they will need to make frequent trips to the landfill, or to move construction material and furnishings from one rental to another.

6. *Legal and other professional fees.* Payments to professional advisers are deductible as long as the discussion concerns your real estate investments, tax planning and tax preparation relating to real estate, or rental matters such as evictions.

7. *Management fees.* Many investors hire a company to deal with tenants—locating and screening, collecting rents, making mortgage payments, and authorizing needed repairs. Such payments to a management company are deductible.

8. *Mortgage interest paid to banks.* A distinction is made between interest paid to institutions and interest paid privately (see next classification). The amount you claim here should correspond to the amount the lender reports to the government at the end of each year. The lender will send a copy of its information summary to you.

9. *Other interest.* This category is for all interest you pay to private parties. For example, if you buy a house and the seller carries a mortgage, you report the interest here. You are also required in this situation to file an information report of your own, called a form 1099, in which you advise the Internal Revenue Service of the amount of interest you paid, as well as the recipient's name, address, and Social Security number. You *must* file this report each year; and the amount you claim as a deduction in this category has to correspond with the amount you report.

10. *Repairs.* Repairs to rental properties are deductible as long as they do not constitute permanent improvements (which are depreciated over $27^1/_2$ years). Typical repairs include work performed to fix broken systems such as plumbing and electrical.

11. *Supplies.* You can deduct the expense of items you buy to make minor repairs and perform maintenance. These include paint, hardware, small furnishings, lightbulbs, and smoke alarms, for example.

12. *Taxes.* Property taxes are fully deductible as current expenses. In addition, other taxes may apply, such as excise taxes charged on sale of property.

13. *Utilities.* Some utilities are paid for by tenants, but others are usually paid for by landlords, such as sewer and water in multiple-unit buildings. Any utilities you pay for, including utilities for periods between tenants, are deductible.

14. *Other.* Some expenses will not fit into the classifications included on the IRS forms. It is always wise to break down miscellaneous expenses into groups, so that you don't report one lump sum without further explanation. Some typical categories here include licenses and fees, landscaping, office expenses, or telephone.

15. *Depreciation.* All of the previously listed expenses involve payments in cash. Depreciation is calculated based on original basis, as previously explained.

The one-line entry reported on Schedule E is also detailed on a different form, 4562, called Depreciation and Amortization.

In setting up your books to correspond to the 15 Schedule E accounts, it is also a good idea to break down each category according to the property. This is essential because, under federal reporting rules, you are required to break down your reported income and expenses by property. When your books correspond to this requirement, it makes your recordkeeping and reporting task much easier.

To better understand the rules concerning reporting and recordkeeping, you can telephone the Internal Revenue Service at 1-800-TAX FORM (1-800-829-3676) and ask for copies of the following free publications:

Form	Title
1	Your Rights as a Taxpayer
334	Tax Guide for Small Business
463	Travel, Entertainment, and Gift Expenses
523	Selling Your Home
527	Residential Rental Property
534	Depreciation
535	Business Expenses
536	Net Operating Losses
537	Installment Sales
538	Accounting Periods and Methods
544	Sales and Other Dispositions of Assets
550	Investment Income and Expenses
551	Basis of Assets
587	Business Use of Your Home
910	Guide to Free Tax Services
917	Business Use of a Car
925	Passive Activity and At-Risk Rules
936	Home Mortgage Interest Deduction
946	How to Begin Depreciating Your Property

Publications can be ordered on the Internet. Contact the Internal Revenue Service at their Web site, http://www. irs.ustreas.gov. You can also write for forms by contacting the appropriate IRS Distribution Center for your state:

If You Are Located In	*Write for Forms To*
Alaska, Arizona, California, Colorado, Hawaii, Idaho, Kansas, Montana, Nevada, New Mexico, Oklahoma, Oregon, Utah, Washington, Wyoming	Western Area Distribution Center Rancho Cordova, CA 95743-0001
Alabama, Arkansas, Illinois, Indiana, Iowa, Kentucky, Louisiana, Michigan, Minnesota, Mississippi, Missouri, Nebraska, North Dakota, Ohio, South Dakota, Tennessee, Texas, Wisconsin	Central Area Distribution Center P.O. Box 8903 Bloomington, IL 61702-8903
Connecticut, Delaware, District of Columbia, Florida, Georgia, Maine, Maryland, Massachusetts, New Hampshire, New Jersey, New York, North Carolina, Pennsylvania, Rhode Island, South Carolina, Vermont, Virginia, West Virginia	Eastern Area Distribution Center P.O. Box 85074 Richmond, VA 23261-5074

MULTIPLE PROPERTIES

When you own two or more properties, you will need to report income and expenses separately for each property. The Schedule E tax form has room for three properties. If you have more than three to report, you have a choice: File more than one Schedule E, or attach a supplementary schedule for each property. The latter is the preferred method, since each property is then clearly distinguished one from the other. All supplementary schedules can then be reported in one total and referred to the details in the attachments. All supplementary schedules should be clearly labeled and include the following information:

✔ Your name.

✔ Your Social Security number.

✔ The tax year.

✔ The form to which the schedule is attached (Schedule E).

✔ The street address and city of the rental property.

When you are dealing with several properties, you need to keep highly detailed account records. As we said before, the tax form is broken down by categories. But in your own records, you need to keep separate account records for each property. This is achieved by setting up a *subsidiary record* for each property. Each category—income and all expenses previously described—is subdivided within the ledger account, so that every property can be reported individually. It is a good idea to keep these records throughout the year. Otherwise, you will need to go through the entire year's records at tax time and break out each and every expense.

Some expenses cannot be assigned specifically to any one property. Examples include general advertising not specific to any one property, office expenses, telephone, certain landscaping expenses, legal fees, accounting, and insurance on a business truck or automobile. In such cases, the expense has to be broken down for each rental property and allocated in some manner. The most reliable and consistent way is to break down unassigned (or, indirect) expenses based on the proportionate share of rental income.

Example: An investor owned three properties. Last year, rental income was:

Property 1	$ 9,250
Property 2	8,115
Property 3	10,735
Total	$28,100

subsidiary record
a record for breaking down an expense by property. The expense account within the general ledger is broken into several subsidiary accounts, one for each property, so that expenses can be tracked not only by expense classification, but also by property.

The investor had several expenses that could not be assigned directly to any one property. These included legal fees of $200. The best way to break down this expense is to first determine the percentage of the total represented by each property:

Property 1: $\dfrac{\$9,250}{\$28,100} = 33\%$

Property 2: $\dfrac{\$8,115}{\$28,100} = 29\%$

Property 3: $\dfrac{\$10,735}{\$28,100} = 38\%$

Next, apply these percentages to the indirect expense, in this case $200. Each property is then assigned the dollar amount according to the breakdown:

Property 1: $200 × 33% = $66.00

Property 2: $200 × 29% = $58.00

Property 3: $200 × 38% = $76.00

These allocations should be done at the end of the year, for two very good reasons. First, you cannot know the percentage breakdown until the end of the year. Second, it would be unnecessarily tedious to break down every indirect expense throughout the year. While you are recording transactions during the year, include one subsidiary account for each property and an additional one for unassigned expenses. Then do your breakdown as part of the year-end process in preparation for completing your tax return.

Keep accurate records of your allocations. You need to be able to demonstrate precisely how you broke each expense down between properties, and how your assumptions were consistent. If you don't keep records, you might not recall in the future how you arrived at your breakdown. A complete record also helps remind you next year how you break out indirect expenses, making your closing process easier.

A subsidiary record for multiple properties serves a purpose beyond tax compliance. It also helps you to keep

general ledger
the document for recording monthly transactions and summarizing the breakdown between total expense and subsidiary records.

balance sheet
a statement listing all assets, liabilities, and net worth of a business or individual. Assets (things you own) minus liabilities (amounts you owe to others) equals net worth, or equity. The balance sheet lists the dollar value in these three classifications as of a specified date.

track of profit and loss on each property. In your *general ledger*, keep track of all income and expense with subsidiary record breakdowns.

Typically, a general ledger is set up to show each month's activity in summary and by account. For example, the general ledger for legal and other professional fees would look like this (assuming a balance forward of $100):

Legal and Other Professional Fees

Date	Charges	Credits	Balance
			100.00
3/31	200.00		300.00

This typical general ledger account can be expanded to include a subsidiary record for each property. In this situation, each entry is recorded as a general entry, to be broken down at the end of the year (rather than for each transaction). For example, applying the percentages developed above and assuming three properties, the account would be divided among three properties. The percentages would be 33, 29, and 38 percent:

**Legal and Other Professional Fees:
Subsidiary Record**

Property 1	Property 2	Property 3	Total
99.00	87.00	114.00	300.00

All entries to the subsidiary record have to be identical to the total amount entered into the account. For example, the total in the above example is $300. The combined subsidiary record total has to agree with the total in the general ledger account.

FINANCIAL STATEMENTS

We usually think of financial statements for corporations and not for individuals. Accountants deal with the preparation and interpretation of financial information and the statement is a summary of such matters. As a real estate investor, you cannot be expected to become an expert in the analysis of financial statements; but there are a few things you need to know.

You need to be able to convey basic information to a lender in order to get financing. This means you have to be able to explain what you own, what you owe, and what you are worth; and to summarize your income, expenses, and profits in a clear, concise, and accurate manner. Every time you buy property or refinance property you already own, the lender will expect to see the information that is reported on a financial statement.

There are two primary types of financial statements. First is the *balance sheet*. This statement lists all of the information as of a specified date showing what you are worth. It includes every *asset* and every *liability* you have as of a specified date—the date of the balance sheet. When you subtract liabilities from assets, the amount left over is your *net worth*.

The second type of financial statement is the *income statement*. Also called a "profit and loss statement," this is a summary of income, expenses, and profits earned over a period of time. Expenses are subtracted from income, and the remaining number is profit (if positive) or loss (if negative). While the balance sheet is stationary—reporting balances of assets, liabilities, and net worth as of a fixed date—the income statement is dynamic. It reports activity of sales, expenses, and resulting profits over a period of time. By practice, the ending date of the income statement's reported period should correspond with the date of the balance sheet. For example, if the balance sheet reports balances as of December 31, then the income statement reports activity for the year ending on that same date.

The information you report on federal tax Schedule E is a summary of the same information as is on an income statement. The two financial statements show the current status as well as the summary of operations. Following is an abbreviated version of what each financial statement shows:

asset
a property owned by the individual or business; something of value. Real estate, for example, is an asset. Its gross value is recorded on a balance sheet as an asset, and the balance of the mortgage owed is listed as a liability.

liability
the amount of debt owed by a company or individual as of a specified date. Liabilities are listed on the balance sheet to offset assets. For example, current mortgage balances are liabilities against real estate assets.

net worth
equity; capital;
the net value of a
business or investment portfolio. Net worth is
the difference
between assets
(the value of
things you own)
minus liabilities
(amounts you
owe to others).

income statement
a statement that
summarizes the
income,
expenses, and
profits for a period of time,
often one full
year, for a corporation or for an
investment portfolio.

Balance Sheet: Assets − Liabilities = Net worth

Income Statement: Income − Expenses = Profit (or loss)

When you, as an individual, approach a lender to request approval of a loan, you face two problems. First, you have to apply for a loan as an individual. This means you will be asked to integrate personal information with investment information. The value of your home, offset by your home mortgage, plus other assets and liabilities, will be mixed in with investment values and liabilities— even though the nature of these things is not the same. The second problem is that the lender will probably count *all* of your investment expenses, while discounting your rental income. This is done on the assumption that you will have some vacancies during the year. Regardless of whether you actually experience any vacancies, the lender will probably reduce your rental income by 10 percent (the equivalent of about seven weeks' rent) just to be conservative. The consequence of this is to reduce your cash flow from investment income, making it harder for you to meet the qualification standards for a loan.

Lenders ask you to complete a loan application. While you list everything on the schedule, you should keep personal and business assets separate and label them clearly so that the lender can see the distinction. The current value of real estate is listed as an asset (and if more than one property is involved, you will be asked to complete a separate schedule for each), while the current balances of mortgages are listed as liabilities. The lender's standard form is designed for the reporting needs of the average wage earner, and is poorly designed for reporting real estate investments. So you will need to mix your personal residence with your investment assets and liabilities. As undesirable as this is, to the lender it makes no difference.

The whole purpose in taking information and comparing debt payments to income is to ensure that you can qualify for a loan. Most people are aware of the importance of good credit, and the lender will get a credit report to see whether you make payments on time and to find out if you have ever defaulted on a debt. But the other side of the evaluation process is to determine whether you are *bankable,* meaning that the comparison made by the bank between your debt payments and your income is within the guidelines that the lender uses.

Many of your recordkeeping requirements will vary according to the volume of transactions, number of properties you own, type of properties, and your strategy (for example, if you buy fixer-uppers and spend a lot of money versus simply renting out a property). If you need help designing or modifying your system, work with a professional bookkeeper or accountant to try out alternative ideas. Strive to keep the system simple enough to spend as little time as possible recording numbers but detailed enough to meet all of the requirements of law, reporting needs for lenders, and documentation needs for income tax reporting.

 bankable
a term describing a person's ability to qualify for loans with conventional lenders. To be bankable, the ratio of debt to income has to be low enough to meet the lender's standards.

Chapter

Managing Your Investment

As a real estate investor, you need to decide how much control you will have in managing your property. Control is a two-edged sword. Being fully in control means you make all decisions on your own; but it also means you deal with tenants and related problems without any insulation. If you want to have as little involvement as possible, you are probably going to be better off investing in a real estate investment trust (REIT) or in a pool of mortgages, and avoiding direct ownership of real estate. (See Chapter 12.) Another option is to hire a property management company (see page 210).

Direct control is a powerful advantage. You cannot have direct control when you own shares of stock or put your money in a mutual fund, a savings account, or a mortgage pool. Direct control means that to some extent—and often to a great extent—your decisions will affect future market value. Sometimes matters as simple as mowing the lawn, painting the outside of the house, or repairing an old gate can have a significant effect on the property's market value. Direct control also means that you have to be involved in the day-to-day management of the property.

You can hire professionals to help you with some of the management aspects of owning real estate. Many are involved as a matter of course, including insurance agents, bankers, appraisers, contractors, and accountants. Just as the president of a corporation depends on the board of directors, corporate officers, and managers to run the company, you have a lot of professional help available, if you need it. The important point here is that as a direct owner, you have a definite advantage. However, the range of decisions you will face can be overwhelming, so don't overlook the importance of getting help from other experts if and when you need it.

WHEN TO BUY

Generally, it makes sense to buy real estate when the following five conditions prevail:

1. *You are financially able to buy*. It is advisable to approach any investment decision realistically. You might have plans to invest in real estate; but if you don't have down payment money, or if lenders will not grant you credit, then there is no point in spending time looking for property.

Make sure that you are financially able to buy. In Chapter 3, the recommendation was given to prequalify with a lender. It makes sense to know not only that you can get financing, but also how much financing the lender is willing to grant to you. This determination is made strictly by formula, based on your income and, of course, credit history.

2. *It is a buyer's market*. The best time to buy is when you have maximum advantage in the market—when there is an abundance of properties for sale, and too few buyers to take up the inventory. In these conditions, you are likely to find real bargains.

Do your own *local* investigation to find out whether you are in a buyer's market. Don't depend on stories you read in nationally published magazines or newspapers. In real estate, markets are strictly regional, and what is going on in one area—or even in several areas—is not necessarily an indication of what is happening in your area. This is true for housing prices as well as for supply and demand, both for property and for rentals. One expert has observed the regional nature of real estate: "High rental costs have more to do with local overall costs of living than they do with the supply of rental houses."*

Another factor making local markets more important than national trends is the difference in living standards between large cities and small towns. In 92 percent of large metropolitan areas, the cost of living is higher than the national average, and one of the biggest contributing factors is high housing costs.† So depending on where you live, you need to compare local housing costs with averages to get an idea of current market conditions. A good source for information about prices in your area is the regional office of the Department of Housing and Urban Development, which tracks fair market rents by county. Or, check the HUD Web site (http://www. huduser.org).

3. *You believe that the cycle is at its bottom.* All investors have to estimate the place in the cycle at any given time. Whenever you consider buying, one of the first questions should be, What is the state of the market? Putting it another way, Where are we in the current cycle? Most people are keenly aware of stock market cycles, because the market is constantly being studied and reported on in the press. That is not the case with real estate, for which the cycle is more slow-moving and less exciting. In looking back, cycles are clear to see. In looking ahead, the future is more difficult to predict.

Even though the pace of real estate cycles is slower, you need to perform the same kind of analysis as a stock market investor. You need to know the market indicators—number of properties on the market, time required for the average sale, spread between asked price and sale price, number of new housing starts, number of sales in the past year, recent population sta-

*Phillip T. Kolbe, Ph.D., "Real Estate Markets Are Local," *Real Estate Appraiser*, August 1992, p. 45.
†Berna Miller, "Beating the High Cost of Living," *American Demographics* Marketing Tools home page, June 1997.

tistics, and so forth. All of these reveal the condition of the market. By being aware of these indicators, collectively and over time, you will be able to spot cycle points and estimate cycle bottoms.

4. *There is a demand for rental units.* As pointed out earlier, the demand among buyers for investment properties is not the same as renters' demand for rental units. The two forms of demand might appear contradictory when, in fact, the timing is off, so that demand in one indicator lags behind the other. As a real estate investor, you need to be aware of several supply and demand cycles, there being three major ones: The best known is the buyer/seller cycle. In addition, there is the cycle of money supply, which is reflected in lender policies and current interest rates. And third is the supply/demand cycle among rental units (supply) and renters (demand).

The demand for rental units should be high enough that you won't have a chronic problem finding suitable tenants. If you suffer excessive vacancies, you will run into cash flow problems early on, and the market rent levels might be lowered as a consequence of low demand.

5. *The amount of rent is adequate to provide you with the cash flow you need.* Be sure that the property you are thinking of buying will yield enough rent to cover all or most of your expenses. This is not to say you have to ensure that rents are always higher than your expenses; but you should be comfortable with the level, even if the advantage is found in tax benefits and not in month-to-month cash flow. If you spend so much for the house that your monthly payments are far above rental receipts, any future profits will be drained away in negative cash flow. You need to find houses you can afford, for which rental income will justify the investment.

When purchase prices are high and rents are low, it could be only a temporary problem. It could also indicate that in your community, it does not make sense to invest in rental properties at this moment. You need to wait out the market or look somewhere else. In some cases, looking at a vastly different economic market in a nearby community gives you the advantage you seek to find the right time (or place) to buy.

WHEN TO SELL

· You should plan to sell in these three conditions:

1. *You want to sell.* Investors are constantly tempted. Resisting temptation and exercising patience—in other words, following a sensible plan rather than responding to the allure of momentary greed—is a difficult strategy, but it pays off. For example, if you buy stock because you believe it has long-term potential to produce profits and pay dividends, selling after a quick price run-up is contrary to the investment goal. The same holds true in real estate. Don't sell unless selling fits into your plan. However, when you want to sell because your goal has ripened, that should be the main indicator that it's time to do so. For example, you bought a house to fund a child's college education. A decade later, the child is ready to go off to college. That's the time to cash in your profits and fund the college education.

2. *It's a seller's market.* In a buyer's market, sellers have to compete with one another for a limited number of buyers; in a seller's market, the opposite is true. As a seller in such a market, you have the luxury of getting offers from a number of people who want to buy. In a very hot market, there could even be a bidding war, with offers coming in *above* your asked price.

If you can afford to wait out the market, the cycle will eventually come around, and a seller's market will materialize. You can afford to wait as long as you don't have to sell, and as long as you are satisfied with the tax benefits and cash flow you are getting from the property.

3. *You believe that the cycle is at or near the top.* Tops of cycles are no easier to identify than are bottoms of cycles. Anyone who has played the stock market knows how deceptive indicators can be, and knows that false signals look like the real thing. The same applies to real estate. Developing cyclical indicators are only obvious in hindsight.

If your analysis tells you that the top of the cycle is at hand, and if you are ready to sell, this is probably the best point you will find at which to sell.

WHEN TO WAIT

You should hold onto your property and wait when the following four situations exist:

1. *You are not certain whether the timing is right to sell.* Uncertainty about a cycle is one symptom of being involved with any investment. Experience and knowledge about how to read indicators help, but there are no sure ways always to know what is going on.

Eventually, every investor faces the decision to sell or to wait. If you are simply not ready to sell, then you should not react to cyclical indicators. We often hear that stock market analysts give out a "sell signal," meaning they are announcing that people should sell a particular stock. But how do they know what investors' goals might be? Perhaps some investors want to hold that stock as a long-term investment. Using the same argument, you should wait to sell if you are unsure about the timing, or if the time is not right given your long-term goals.

2. *You would sell in the right conditions, but you are willing to wait.* Many investors find themselves perpetually in the status of being willing to sell, if the right offer comes along. This describes a large percentage of real estate investors. Cycles do not always time themselves for your convenience, of course, so you often need to exercise patience and wait for conditions to bring buyers to you.

3. *Cash flow is acceptable for the moment.* Why sell under pressure if you do not need to? While the prospect of selling is attractive, you might do better by waiting a few months to see if conditions change in your favor. This is especially advisable if rental income is paying your mortgage for you, and you are enjoying tax benefits in the meantime.

4. *You don't have any specific plans for the proceeds if and when you do sell.* Some investors think they are obligated to sell whenever a profit opportunity presents itself. That is poor planning, because it means the "plan" is to react to circumstances beyond your control rather than to create circumstances that you desire. You often have several choices as a real estate investor: sell, refinance, expand, or wait and see. If you have no immediate plans for your capital, and there is no pressing need to use that money elsewhere, you might be better off to wait and take no action today.

It is a better idea for investors *not* to act when they are not certain, than to act. Waiting often clarifies matters, whereas acting on impulse could be costly. It would be nice if the real estate cycle would conform exactly to your plan and timetable; but it does not. While the three most important principles in real estate are location, location, and location, perhaps we should also recognize numbers four, five, and six in importance: timing, timing, and timing.

NEIGHBORHOOD CONDITIONS AFFECTING VALUE

Location is of absolute importance to value in real estate, both today and in the future. Start checking out different neighborhoods to gain a sense of what properties are worth in different parts of town. In very little time, you will become an expert on estimating fair values for property simply by driving around and comparing open houses to each other.

You will notice that location plays perhaps the greatest role in determining value. That will be apparent. However, several other conditions will also affect value in the neighborhood. These include:

1. *Changing crime level.* There is a direct correlation between crime trends and housing values. When crime is on the rise, families move away and more properties go on the market, increasing the supply and reducing overall values of other homes. When a previously crime-ridden area changes in a positive way, the area becomes more desirable. People start fixing up their properties and more people want to move in. This creates new demand and prices rise.

As an investor, you have limited resources beyond

supporting law enforcement and forming neighborhood watch programs to help control crime. Being aware of which neighborhoods are going through transitions—in either direction—will help you to select properties wisely and to maximize the potential for growth in market value.

2. *Construction activity.* When you see an increase in new home construction activity, that is usually a positive sign, especially if you already own property in the area. Construction is a symptom of growing demand. That also indicates that property values are on the upswing. It is unusual for builders and developers to undertake a high volume of construction in weak markets; the opposite is true. If you want to spot potentially positive neighborhood conditions, construction activity is one very visible sign.

3. *Improvement and remodeling activity.* Closely related to construction of new housing is a volume of activity in improvements and remodeling. That, too, is a sign of increasing property values. People tend to invest more money in their homes when those homes are rising in value, for the same reasons that homeowners do not invest when property values are falling. High levels of remodeling also might be a sign of turnover from an older generation to a younger one. That is a positive trend because new owners coming into the area mean revitalization, which is also good for property values.

4. *Physical appearance.* Neighborhoods vary in their general appearance—for good reason. Every neighborhood has its own character, and the impression defines that neighborhood as well as property values. Appearance includes the details such as lawn maintenance and condition of homes—roofs, paint jobs, and other cosmetics. It also extends to whether the streets have sidewalks, night lighting, proper signaling at intersections, and so forth. It is the combined impression of homeowner maintenance of individual properties and local government maintenance overall.

5. *Change in zoning.* When zoning is changed in an area, the result can be dramatic changes in land values. If the zoning change is bad for residential neighborhoods, that will be reflected in declining housing values. For example, if the county puts a road through the neighbor-

hood and changes a previously residential street to
mixed commercial use, you may expect the residential
value of homes on that and nearby streets to fall. The
neighborhood loses its value as a residential site. (It is
interesting to note, however, that the potential commercial values on such a street may be far greater than the
previous residential values. A zoning change often involves devastating one land use interest while delivering
profits to another.)

Before buying property, get a copy of the neighborhood plan from your local planning department and find
out what plans are in the works. If your government is
planning big changes in the area you are considering,
you should find out what those changes will mean before you buy.

6. *Level of enforcement of existing zoning laws.* Some
cities and counties are very strict about establishing zoning rules and enforcing them. They scrupulously prevent
encroachment of one land use upon the zoning of another. However, in some areas, the zoning is more loosely
defined and means much less, and the local government
may not have the budget, the will, or the inclination to
strictly enforce the rules. If your area allows mixed-use
zoning, that could be a poor sign for future market values—depending on what the mixed zone has in it and
how it operates. Some people miss the old neighborhoods
with corner stores and service stations, versus today's
highly planned shopping malls surrounded by carefully
mapped out residential-only developments. An old-style
charm could add a lot of appeal. But if mixed-use zoning
is abused, residential uses can suffer, resulting in lower
market values.

7. *Changing demographics.* A stable neighborhood
can change very suddenly, due to unexpected shifts in the
population, job market, and other outside influences. For
example, if your town has one major employer and that
plant closes down, all of those jobs will be lost, too. That
will have an immediate effect on residential values, because families will be forced to move to wherever the jobs
are. When a new employer comes to an area, that can
have the effect of causing a rapid increase in housing

prices, a reflection of demand. Study the current demographics for important indicators, employment and population being foremost.

PROPERTY CONDITIONS
THAT AFFECT VALUE

The physical condition of property has the most obvious and visible effect on value. Often, little things that could easily be fixed are left unfixed to the detriment of that property's market value. Both today's price and the rate of equity growth in the future are affected directly by what you see when you look at that house.

Conditions of the property are directly within your control. Four aspects include:

1. *Cosmetic conditions of land and building.* Anything that affects only the appearance of your property may be called "cosmetic" in nature. The two most obvious cosmetic conditions are the paint job and landscaping.

You enhance property value by keeping the property fresh and new-looking, repainting as needed. If you do not paint when needed, property value is held down. The choice of colors matters, too. Selection of an unconventional color, tends to detract from value. The more bizarre the color the more reduction. Cosmetic nonconformity can restrict your market because, even though the problem is easily solved by repainting, buyers tend to think in terms of what they see and less in terms of what could be changed. While it might cost about $2000 to have your house repainted, a nonconforming color choice might reduce value by $5000 or more.

Dark-colored houses tend to make negative impressions and to look smaller than they are. Even a well-maintained paint job with too dark a color might lead to lower offers simply because of the impression such color choices make. To get an idea of what is popular on the market today, drive through newly built subdivisions and observe what color choices are being used. For the most part, developers tend to use neutrals—white, off-white, gray, and similar colors, thus allowing a lot of latitude in trim colors, landscaping coordination, and selection of draperies, for example.

Landscaping advertises the house and sets a tone. A well maintained area makes a very positive impression, while a poorly maintained yard takes away value. The problems are easy to fix in terms of both time and money. The house looks old and shabby when the yard is neglected, but a couple of days' work can make a lot of difference. A carefully planned, well cared-for yard makes a modest house look more impressive.

2. *Level of deferred maintenance.* Some properties have deferred maintenance of a low level, and those conditions are easily cured. Other forms of deferred maintenance may require thousands of dollars to fix. You need to be able to tell the difference before making an offer on a property. Examples of expensive deferred maintenance include:

✔ Extensive painting, landscaping, and other cosmetic deficiencies that add up to a lot of work.

✔ The need for upgraded plumbing and electrical systems in older homes.

✔ Leaking roofs and rotted-out gutter systems.

✔ Obsolete and inefficient heating and cooling systems.

✔ The need to upgrade windows to energy-efficient replacements.

These types of repairs will cost money, in comparison to minor work you can perform on your own for little expense and without the need to hire outside professional help. Houses usually need a round of repairs every seven to eight years. So if you buy a property that is six years old, you should expect to go through a repair cycle fairly soon thereafter. You might want to reflect that in an offer you make on the property, perhaps based on an inspection report (see Chapter 9). After 15 to 20 years, you should expect another, more extensive maintenance round, this time probably involving a new roof, upgrade or replacement of heating and cooling systems, and replacement of appliances.

Repair and renovation is big business. In 1996, Americans spent $119.1 billion to upgrade and renovate their properties. Of that total, 78 percent of the work was performed by hired professionals.*

3. *Quality of improvements.* Property values are affected by the quality of workmanship, both in the original construction and in subsequent repairs and upgrades. So important is this consideration that some lenders will not grant home improvement loans to homeowners planning to perform their own work. The risk is that the job won't be finished, or the quality will be so poor that the homeowner will end up having to hire a professional to fix the mistakes—which means the lender may hand over the money only to discover later that more money is needed to complete the job.

Unless you are a contractor or highly skilled in home improvement, you should plan to work with a professional contractor to complete major renovations. You should also be sure that all the proper permits are taken out, work is inspected, and that the quality of the work passes the local code requirements.

4. *Type of improvements.* Some improvements add more value than others. Keep this in mind and check remodeling industry surveys now and then. The most popular improvements are new or upgraded kitchens and baths, followed by windows, room additions, sun rooms, and other interior work. A recent survey also shows that most homeowners perform remodeling work within 18 months of purchase.†

Improvements that tend not to add value include swimming pools, greenhouses, and highly specialized rooms without broad appeal. As an investor (as opposed to a homeowner), you should be especially sensitive to

---

*U.S. Bureau of the Census, cited by the National Association of the Remodeling Industry Web site (http://www.nari.org), 1997.
†National Association of the Remodeling Industry Web site (http://www.nari.org), 1997.

creating functional living space rather than customized, expensive features most people don't want or need.

Additions of bedrooms and family rooms tend to add value over the long term, but probably not within the first five years after completion of work. The delay is an estimate based on the principle that all real estate needs to season, including improvements. The delay is not hard and fast; it is only an estimate based on price averages. That means that improvements need time to become valued on the market. They also may reflect the problems of nonconformity (discussed next), so that features that exceed average features of other homes in the area will not appreciate as rapidly as you might wish.

THE DANGER OF OVERIMPROVEMENT

To truly understand price movement in real estate, you should be aware of the concept of conformity (defined in Chapter 2). The nonconforming or overimproved house presents some considerations for you, as a likely investor, that should be in your mind when comparing potential investment properties. These four considerations are:

1. *Your offer should reflect the problem of nonconformity.* The nonconforming house presents a marketing problem. You want to be careful not to pay for features that will not add value to that house in the future. The market will limit the return on a nonconforming house. When you are a buyer, try to think like a seller. What problems is this seller having in marketing the property? And what will that mean to *me* when it becomes my turn to be the seller?

2. *If you pay a higher price for extra improvements, you might not necessarily be able to command more rent.* Market demand dictates the range of rents you can charge. So, if you pay extra to get special features in a house, that does not mean you will be able to charge more rent. Those special features may even limit your market. For example, families with small children might not want a house with a swimming pool.

3. *You might never be able to get your money back.* In some situations, what you pay in premium for improvements might never be recaptured in a future sale. And when you are the owner, the money you invest to upgrade is subject to the same risk. You might not be able to overcome the limitations imposed by the market when the house is nonconforming.

4. *Nonconforming houses might be difficult to sell.* In a slow market, it is difficult to sell any house. But a nonconforming house will go right to the bottom of the list. Those extra features are not positives when you want to sell, because buyers perceive that the house's price reflects the unneeded extras.

MANAGING IN A BUYER'S MARKET

Of course, you want to sell in a seller's market. Every investor enjoys having many buyers trying to outbid one another and running up the price. In a seller's market, anyone can sell and make a profit.

It's more challenging to produce profits when the supply and demand relationship is turned upside down. In a buyer's market, you have to compete with an excess of sellers. Without enough buyers to go around, prices fall and sellers have to make concessions to close the sale. The problems associated with a buyer's market invariably translate to lower profits. Five ideas to help you to sell in a buyer's market are:

1. *Consider carrying a second mortgage.* Even though you might prefer to get all of your equity at closing, you might have to delay receiving a part of it. To make your deal more attractive than the deals being offered by other sellers, consider carrying a mortgage. While this delays your getting all of your proceeds, it does produce interest income. In calling this a "second" mortgage, we assume that the buyer will finance the majority of the purchase price through a conventional lender. Invariably, such a lender will insist on being in first position (meaning it gets paid first in the event of a default); so the second mortgage is an alternative available to you to help the buyer close the deal, but you will be in line behind the other lender.

Another advantage in carrying a mortgage is that you might qualify to treat part of your gain as an installment sale. That means the gain is taxed only as it is received. So when you are getting repaid gradually over a number of years, the profit—and the tax—is spread out over time. Whether you qualify to treat this situation as an installment sale depends on how the deal is put together, so you should talk to your tax adviser.

If you recognize the need to carry a mortgage in order to close the deal, but you still want to get your money out, there is yet another way to go. You can get through the deal and then sell your contract to someone else. When this occurs, you will be expected to accept a discount. For example, let's say you carry a $30,000 second mortgage. After the deal is closed, you look for someone to buy the contract. Commonly, pension management companies like to buy up second mortgages at a discount so their clients can invest pension funds. Other types of companies look for deals like this, too. You might be asked to take a discount. For example, if the deal offered to you is a 30 percent discount and you accept, you will get $21,000 to sell the note.

Some real estate investors believe that carrying a note facilitates a sale in a slow market, and also helps defer a part of the tax bite. This is also a form of diversification, with some of your capital invested in equity (ownership of real estate) and part invested in debt (lending money through the second mortgage).

2. *Reduce your price.* Some sellers resist the suggestion that they need to reduce their price. To be realistic, market value reflects the lowest price a seller is willing to accept and the highest price a buyer is willing to pay. Therefore, if no buyers put in offers at the original asked price, then you are above the market, at least for the moment. A reduction in price might be necessary. Some buyers automatically assume that the listed price is always set high to allow room for negotiation. This might be true, but you need to be able to assess realistically the price you're asking, not as it relates to other prices on the market, but in terms of how many offers you get (if any), and how far they are below your asked price.

In setting a price, also be aware that a property can have several different "prices." A quick-sale price (bargain price) will be lower than a firm price. If you are firm, that means you're willing to wait indefinitely for a full-price offer. At times, the price might be negotiable against the cost value of work that needs to be done. Sellers might be willing to negotiate for a lower price in exchange for buyers assuming responsibility for deferred maintenance, for example.

3. *Offer to pay the buyer's closing costs.* One concession that carries a lot of appeal is an offer to pay the buyer's closing costs. Some might call this a gimmick because, compared to the seller's costs, the buyer pays very little at closing (other than the costs of getting financing). Still, the idea gets attention and has a certain attraction that many buyers can't resist. It certainly makes your property more alluring than a comparable property that could require several hundred dollars more at closing.

Such an offer can be made as part of negotiations as well. For example, you might offer to pay the buyer's closing costs in exchange for a full-price offer. While this creates an outcome identical to accepting a lower price without paying costs for the buyer, this idea might have greater appeal to someone who considers oneself to be a bargain hunter. This is more of a marketing and negotiating strategy than an economic one.

4. *Offer to fix defects as part of the deal.* You might be planning to paint the house or put on a new roof as part of preparing for the sale. In a buyer's market, you can offer to perform that work for free as part of the contract negotiation. This enables you to argue price with greater leverage, since you are making concessions to the buyer.

5. *Offer to include personal property.* If the house includes furnishings, you can also offer to include some (or all) as free property with the deal. You might be able to avoid moving and storing unneeded furniture by using it to close a deal. Some types of items, like built-in systems, pool tables, hot tubs, and other luxuries are especially appealing to new buyers. You can also offer to include appliances that were not originally part of the deal.

You face an uphill struggle in a buyer's market. When the real estate market is extremely slow, you might even have to delay your decision to sell, preferring instead to refinance to get out cash. You may want to adopt a wait-and-see attitude, waiting for the market to improve.

HAZARD INSURANCE

Besides managing your real estate well and timing purchases and sales, you also need to protect your investment. When you have a mortgage, your lender will require you to cover insurance protection, because a catastrophic loss would be more of a risk to the lender than to you.

If you own your home, you already know quite a bit about hazard insurance (commonly called fire or homeowner's insurance). Most homeowners first hear about this insurance when they discover it's in their closing costs or premiums are added onto their monthly mortgage payments. So first-time buyers rarely have the chance or the inclination to shop around for the best deal on this form of insurance.

You do have choices. One of the more important clauses to have included is an automatic inflation guard, including extra protection for specific types of losses. As a landlord, you do not need to buy insurance for the personal property tenants have, although you do need minimum coverage for furnishings you own and for appliances. This is usually included automatically with the typical landlord's hazard insurance policy.

If you convert your personal residence to a rental, be sure to contact your broker and change your coverage. You will save money by eliminating insurance for personal property. Also be sure you have adequate personal property coverage in your new home. For example, you might switch your home and a rental. When you change insurance coverage, you have to make the personal property premium adjustment on both of the properties.

 basic insurance (also called HO-1) a form of hazard insurance offering only minimal coverage. Only 11 named perils are covered.

Types of Hazard Insurance

There are seven policy forms:

1. *HO-1.* The *basic insurance* policy protects you against 11 named perils. These are for losses caused by:

1. Fire or lightning.
2. Loss of property removed from premises due to fire or other peril.
3. Windstorm or hail.
4. Explosion.
5. Riot and civil commotion.
6. Aircraft.
7. Vehicle.
8. Smoke.
9. Vandalism and malicious mischief.
10. Theft.
11. Breakage of glass constituting a part of the building.

2. *HO-2.* The *broad insurance* policy provides coverage for 18 named perils, also known as extended coverage. The extended coverage includes the 11 named perils offered with basic insurance, plus coverage for losses caused by:

12. Falling object.
13. Weight of ice, snow, or sleet.
14. Collapse of building or building part.
15. Sudden and accidental tearing, cracking, burning, or bulging of a steam or hot water heating system or domestic appliance.
16. Accidental discharge, leakage, or overflow from plumbing, heating, or air conditioning.
17. Freezing of plumbing, heating, or air-conditioning system, or household appliance.
18. Sudden and accidental injury from artificially generated current to electrical appliance, fixtures, or wiring.

broad insurance
(also called HO-2) a form of hazard insurance offering protection for 18 named perils.

all-risk insurance
(also called HO-3) a form of hazard insurance offering protection against all losses to the dwelling except any named exclusions; and for 18 named perils on personal property.

renter's insurance
(also called HO-4) a form of hazard insurance offering protection against losses to personal property only, with no coverage for losses to buildings.

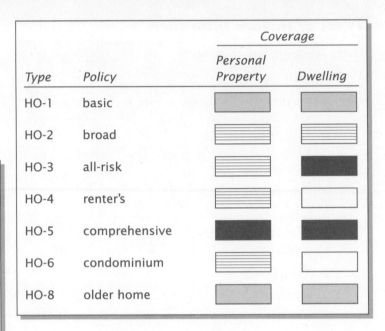

Type	Policy	Coverage	
		Personal Property	Dwelling
HO-1	basic		
HO-2	broad		
HO-3	all-risk		
HO-4	renter's		
HO-5	comprehensive		
HO-6	condominium		
HO-8	older home		

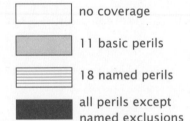

no coverage

11 basic perils

18 named perils

all perils except named exclusions

FIGURE 7.1   Homeowner's insurance.

comprehensive insurance
(also called HO-5) a form of hazard insurance offering protection against all losses except named exclusions, on both dwellings and personal property.

condominium insurance
(also called HO-6) a form of hazard insurance offering protection against losses to personal property and structural losses within the unit, but excluding losses to the outside of buildings and to common areas.

   3. *HO-3*. This is called *all-risk insurance* coverage. It includes coverage on all dwelling losses except any named exclusions, and coverage on personal property losses to the extent of the 18 named perils.
   4. *HO-4*. The *renter's insurance* policy, designed specifically for renters, protects only personal property, and excludes the building itself, which is the owner's responsibility.
   5. *HO-5*. This is the *comprehensive insurance* form. It covers all losses to both personal property and the dwelling, except named exclusions.
   6. *HO-6*. The *condominium insurance* policy is designed for the specific insurance needs of owners of con-

dos and co-ops. In those situations, the owner is responsible for personal property and for that part of the dwelling on the inside; but not for the outside of the building or for common areas (parking lots, clubhouses, swimming pool areas, etc.). Coverage includes the 18 named perils for personal property and dwelling coverage for only the inside of units.

7. *HO-8.* The *older home insurance* policy is a form of insurance against losses, but only provides for serviceable replacement, and not for a duplication of materials or workmanship such as are often found in older homes.

Figure 7.1 summarizes the coverage provided by each of the policy forms.

Maintaining and protecting your property requires study and analysis. Because you control your property directly, you can affect its market value. The next chapter explains the analytical techniques you can use to evaluate your real estate portfolio.

 older home insurance (also called HO-8) a form of hazard insurance designed to replace losses to serviceable condition, but not to duplicate quality of workmanship or materials.

Chapter

Analyzing the Market

How much return do you expect to earn each year as a real estate investor? How do you calculate your return? How much is a particular property worth? These seemingly basic questions can actually be complex, and not as easy to answer as you might think.

Many investors, when asked these questions, will admit that they haven't thought about it, or that they simply don't know. Yet, you should be interested in knowing how to judge your own investment results and how to judge the overall market. Otherwise, how can you determine whether you are succeeding?

Valuation of real estate, not being determined in an auction marketplace like the stock market, is also not valued by any authoritative source. It is true that appraisers decide market value, but that is a reactive science. That is to say, an appraiser will tell a lender whether a home's appraised value is close enough to the offered price to justify lending money. If the lender wants to make the loan, there is every reason to believe that the appraisal will support that decision most of the time. Real estate values are driven by the market, as they should be. Buyers and sellers establish value, not bankers, brokers, and appraisers. While the players (buyers, sellers, lenders, etc.) depend on appraised value, remember that it is the buyer and seller who ultimately dictate what the market price should be. An investor who is familiar with the area will know immediately whether an asked price is high or low, meaning the experienced investor knows when to make a lower offer or when to grab a bargain. This knowledge grows from awareness of relative values in the area and in the region, the current supply and demand level, the availability of financing, condition of the property (including the degree of visible deferred maintenance), age of the property, and many, many other factors, both tangible and intuitive. In other words investors are able to spot value and it does not take much practice to acquire the ability to arrive at a reasonable ballpark estimate of a property's potential value.

Pricing is not set in isolation, or with any single factor in mind. It is interesting that people who have never owned real estate tend to think that prices are set by sellers, often without just cause, and that's what you have to pay if you want the house. But more experienced investors and homeowners know that price is the result of a complex series of supply and demand features. Prices depend on much more than the property-related or market-related features. The real elements of price include determination of value, which is difficult to define. Value includes:

✔ Potential rental value.
✔ Current supply and demand levels.
✔ Building activity.
✔ Employment level.
✔ Crime levels and trends.
✔ Construction quality.
✔ Weather.
✔ Convenience.
✔ Popularity of the area.
✔ Perception of likely future value.

POPULAR METHODS FOR SETTING VALUE

Investment property values are set differently from home values. This is especially true for multiple-unit buildings such as duplexes and apartments. Investment property values are determined by the dollar value of rents earned or, putting it another way, are based on how well that property generates income. The method includes an adjustment for an assumed vacancy level, a contingency applied even when recent history shows that no vacancies have occurred.

Basing value on gross rental income (adjusted for the vacancy factor), is common practice for multiple-unit buildings, but not for single-family housing. Even if you invest in a single-family house and use it as a rental property, an appraiser is probably going to judge its value based on the same methods used for owner-occupied housing—using comparable values of houses in the same area or similar areas rather than calculating value based on the income you generate. This makes sense. A potential buyer will not necessarily use that house as a rental, whereas the buyer of an apartment building will definitely rent out the units. From the appraiser's point of view, a single-family house has value as an owner-occupied property, regardless of how it is actually being used today.

Two calculations are commonly used for setting value on income property. The first is the *gross rent multiplier (GRM)*, a factor developed by dividing sales price of an investment property by monthly rents.

Example: An appraiser is setting the value on a three-unit investment property you want to sell. You earn $1500 per month in rent. Using three comparable properties that sold recently, the appraiser develops gross rent multipliers (GRMs) for each. The sales prices are divided by monthly rents to arrive at the GRMs:

Property	Sales Price	Rent	GRM
1	$180,000	$1,400	128.6
2	172,000	1,350	127.4
3	194,000	1,550	125.2

gross rent multiplier (GRM)

a calculation used by appraisers to set value for income property. Sales prices of recently sold properties are divided by monthly rents. The result is the gross rent multiplier. An appraiser performs this calculation for several comparable properties, and then applies the average GRM to the rents received on the property being appraised. This produces an estimate of market value.

Next, the appraiser calculates the average GRM of the three comparable properties, by adding the three GRMs together and dividing by three:*

$$\frac{128.6 + 127.4 + 125.2}{3} = 127.1$$

Rents on the subject property are $1500 per month. To develop an estimate of value under this method, the appraiser multiplies monthly gross rents by the average GRM:

$$\$1500 \times 127.1 = \$190,650$$

This estimate indicates that the appraised value for this investment property is $190,650. Of course, the appraiser might modify this estimate for other reasons; however, this example shows how GRM is used to arrive at estimated value for income property. The formula for GRM can be summarized as:

$$\frac{\text{Sales price}}{\text{Monthly rent}} = \text{GRM}$$

For example:

$$\frac{\$125,000}{\$800} = 156.25$$

The second method used by appraisers is called the *cap rate*. The cap (capitalization) rate is a test that compares rent levels to purchase price. To calculate, divide the annual net income by the purchase price.

Example: A property is on the market for $785,000 and annual net income is $68,000. To calculate cap rate, divide income by price:

*This example assumes the appraiser gives equal value to each of the comparables being used. In practice, though, the appraiser might give greater or lesser weight to some of the properties, resulting in a weighted average.

 cap rate
a percentage rate of return, short for "capitalization rate." This is used both to estimate value and to determine whether rents are in line with market rents, based on the purchase price. Properties may be compared by applying a standard cap rate for the region to several different properties, as a test of acceptability of the profit level from a particular property.

$$\frac{\$68,000}{\$785,000} = 8.66\%$$

This provides a general means for comparison. For example, if the standard cap rate in your area is 10 percent, that would indicate the property is worth only $680,000, and not the asked price of $785,000. On the other hand, if the area's standard cap rate is 8 percent, then, based on the cap rate, the property should be marketed for $850,000—and the asked price of $785,000 is a bargain. (Other factors could influence the price: the buyer's original basis, anxiety for a fast sale, deferred maintenance, location, etc.).

DETERMINING MARKET VALUE

Many things can influence the asked price. Investors should not review formula answers in isolation, depending only on GRM and cap rate. Remember, the price paid for property reflects the price that seller and buyer both accept, regardless of what appraisers say. Among the factors influencing price are the following five considerations:

1. *How anxious is the seller?* A seller might be very anxious to sell. Some sales involve moving to another part of the country and buying a new house, a deadline for starting a new job and getting children started in school, and the desire to close out business in town and go elsewhere. The degree of seller anxiety affects the price: the higher the anxiety, the more bargaining room. The quick-sale price is the bargain price a seller will accept in exchange for a fast close. On the opposite extreme is the firm price, the price a seller believes to be fair; a firm-price seller will not accept offers below that price and is willing to wait.

2. *What is the current supply and demand?* If sellers have to compete with a large number of other sellers, higher-priced property moves slowly, if at all. In such markets, bargains are necessary to get a sale. A motivated seller (translation: anxious seller) might have to take a substantial discount to get a sale in a slow market.

3. *How does the price compare with prices of similar properties in the area?* Just about all sellers realize that market value depends largely on how other, similar properties are priced and, to a greater degree, the price for which they sell. Properties priced above those levels simply do not sell for the asked price.

4. *What is the condition of the property?* Properties often have several different prices at any given time. Deferred maintenance levels dictate various pricing adjustments. There may be an "as is" price and an "if fixed" price. In other words, if the buyer will have to fix the problems, that will require a price reduction. If the seller accepts responsibility to fix defects, that supports the asked price. Being aware that there are various prices depending on these points helps you to identify value in the market, and to negotiate accordingly.

5. *Is financing available?* For many people, financing is the most important part of the deal—more important than price itself. Even in a market with plenty of bargains, there is no point trying to get a deal if there is no financing available. It becomes a problem for buyer and seller alike. The unavailability of funds (or at least, the unavailability of funds at a practical cost) means there is no real market unless sellers are willing to carry mortgages and buyers can bring a large sum of cash to the table—not always practical or possible.

The true meaning of "market value" is important both to buyer and to seller. Given that there are numerous definitions of price, you should be able to identify the price you are hearing. For example, a real estate agent may inform you that "the seller is motivated," or "the seller will look at all offers." These are messages that the price is negotiable.

Another way to judge whether you can make an offer below asked price is to evaluate the differences between asked prices and final sales prices in the recent market. This information is readily available from your local Multiple Listing Service (MLS), local brokers, or local banks. This difference between asked and sales price is called the *spread.* As the spread widens, the indication points to a

spread
the percentage difference between an asked price of a property and the price at which it sold. As a tool for judging conditions of the market, the recent average spread and the trend in spreads indicate the relative strength or weakness in prices.

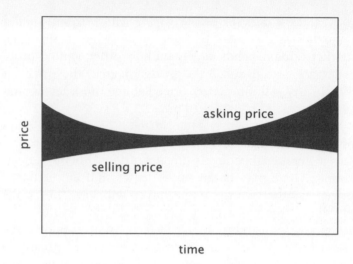

FIGURE 8.1 Spread.

growing buyer's market; as it narrows, the indication is that a seller's market is developing. The relationship between asking price and selling price is summarized in Figure 8.1.

The spread shows only the relationship between what the seller wanted and what the buyer paid. Another indicator to watch is the trend in price itself. A drop in prices means that the market is getting weaker. Or does it? Analysis is not simple enough on the surface to be able to clearly recognize the real meaning behind a trend. Cycles do not move decisively in a straight line or pattern, but are characterized by starts, stops, and reversals. Cycles are hard to predict because of the false indicators.

ANALYSIS OF CASH FLOW

To this point in the chapter, we have discussed the study of real estate as buyer or seller. You will also need to develop a means for analysis as a holder of property. This usually means tracking cash flow and vacancy rates, both for properties you own and for the market in general. Remember that cash flow is the amount of money left over

when operating expenses and loan payments are subtracted from rent income:

Rent income, one year	$47,500
Less: operating expenses	– 9,019
Less: loan payments	–32,684
Cash flow	$ 5,797

Cash flow is not the same as profit, especially profit
for tax purposes. To calculate profit for taxes, you exclude
principal payments, but you include depreciation. So the
outcome of profit is quite different from that of cash flow:

	Cash Flow	*Profit for* *Taxes*
Rent income, one year	$47,500	$ 47,500
Less: operating expenses	–9,019	–9,019
Less: interest payments	–31,919	–31,919
Less: principal payments	– 765	
Less: depreciation		–4,654
Net total	$ 5,797	$ 1,908

When net cash flow is negative (the amounts you are
paying out exceed what you're bringing in) the situation
appears bleak. However, to make the analysis fair, you
also need to calculate the tax benefits. You might be realizing an after-tax positive cash flow.

Example: You receive $32,500 per year in rental income,
and you pay out $34,000 ($1500 more than received) in
mortgage payments and operating expenses. But, with depreciation deductions, your annual tax liability is reduced
by $2200. This creates a pretax negative cash flow but an
after-tax positive cash flow:

Rental income, one year	$32,500
Less: payments and expenses	–34,000
Pretax cash flow	$–1,500
Plus: tax savings	+2,200
After-tax cash flow	$ 700

Your cash flow is strongly affected by vacancies. In explaining vacancy rates in Chapter 2, we showed only one of the three versions of calculation—that of the number of vacant units (e.g., an apartment complex with 25 units and an average of 3 units vacant at any given time translates to a vacancy rate of 12 percent). Two additional methods of computing vacancy rates can be important for analysis of cash flow: vacancies in terms of dollar amount, and vacancies in terms of time.

For cash flow analysis, the dollar amount method is probably the most useful. For example, the lost income due to a vacancy of three months may be $2100. If maximum annual rent is $20,000, that means your vacancy rate is 10.5 percent.

Vacancies can also be assessed in terms of time vacant. For example, if you experience vacancies for 1.5 months on average each year, that translates to a 12.5 percent vacancy rate.

The methods of calculating vacancies are summarized in the following examples:

Units

$$\frac{3 \text{ (vacant units)}}{25 \text{ (total units)}} = 12\%$$

Dollar Amount

$$\frac{\$2100 \text{ (lost income)}}{\$20,000 \text{ (maximum income)}} = 10.5\%$$

Time

$$\frac{1.5 \text{ (months vacant)}}{12 \text{ (months)}} = 12.5\%$$

 occupancy rate
(1) the opposite of vacancy rate: the number of units occupied, divided by total units; (2) in multiple-unit buildings, the total rentable area divided by the total area of the building.

It may be preferable to discuss the *occupancy rate* rather than vacancy rate. Lenders use vacancy rates by rental unit to evaluate a borrower's ability to repay a loan; and prudent investors have to allow for the contingency of vacancies in planning. However, from a seller's point of view, occupancy rate is a more positive form of expressing the statistics about a rental. Rather than admitting that you have suffered an average 12 percent vacancy rate, doesn't it sound better to boast of a consistent 88 percent occupancy rate? As a borrower, you can tell the lender how well occupied your property is, rather than discussing the negative flip side of vacancies.

Occupancy rates are expressed in terms of the number of units in an apartment complex, and in terms of time for other investments. If a building includes a lot of common areas, such as laundry rooms, hallways, stairways, and foyers, occupancy rate is also used to express the rentable area as a percentage of the building's total area.

The two versions of occupancy rate are illustrated in this example:

Units

$$\frac{22 \text{ (occupied units)}}{25 \text{ (total units)}} = 88\%$$

Area

$$\frac{37,490 \text{ sq. ft. (rentable area)}}{46,000 \text{ sq. ft.(total area)}} = 81.5\%$$

Cash flow is related directly to occupancy (or vacancy), and can be used to estimate *breakeven* percentage. That is, in a particular building, what percentage of maximum rent is required in order to break even? This is an excellent monitoring analysis to perform, because you know your cash flow "line in the sand" with this information, which helps you to set goals and monitor your investment. The amount of rent you must actually receive in order to cover your payments each month represents the breakeven percentage. To arrive at breakeven, perform the following calculation:

 breakeven the rent required to cover all monthly payments and operating expenses, expressed as a percentage of maximum rent.

$$\frac{\$30,875 \text{ (expenses)}}{\$38,000 \text{ (maximum rent)}} = 81.25\%$$

Breakeven is used to illustrate the worst-case scenario for a lender. It is intended to show that a property will produce positive cash flow. In the example above, we calculated that breakeven was at 81.25 percent. That means that 81.25 percent of maximum rent has to be collected just to cover expenses and payments, and that anything above that level is positive cash flow. When this illustration is compared to historical occupancy rates at or above 90 percent, the lender will be reassured.

Breakeven, occupancy, and vacancy analyses are most often used for investments in multiple-unit buildings. However, the same principles apply to all real estate, including single-family housing. For houses, lenders tend to use standard vacancy factors to assume future rental income, and will tend to qualify a borrower on the basis of comparing assumed discounted rent levels to required monthly payments.

CALCULATING RETURN AND YIELD

In all markets, investors want to find the most realistic and accurate way to calculate profit. This is not an easy task. Many different methods can be used and, unless you are certain about what you are trying to find, you could end up not properly identifying the correct result.

The more important consideration is: *Whatever method you use to determine profits, use it consistently. Your information is reliable only if you apply the same formula in every situation.*

It is neither fair nor accurate to use one method in one case and not in another. Once you have studied the many ways to analyze profit, pick the one that reveals what you need to know, and stay with that method. Some investors want to know their annual profit, which means net profit after expenses are deducted from income. Net profit is then divided by gross income to arrive at the percentage of return. This method is the one used most commonly in business. You have heard that last year, a certain company reported profits of 8 percent. That means profit equals 8 percent of sales.

In real estate, the net return method is not necessarily an accurate measure of profit. The method does not include a study of cash flow, nor does it say anything about the benefit of reducing personal income taxes. In real estate, year-to-year profit is not usually the goal. Rather, you usually seek to cover expenses through rental income while enjoying yearly tax benefits; and ultimately, you realize a capital gain after holding a rental property for several years. With that in mind, the net return calculation is relatively meaningless.

It is doubtful that you would want to measure your success by studying only the net return. For example, what value is a 12 percent annual return if you also suffer from negative cash flow? The net return is more of a merchandising measurement than an investment measurement.

Example: You receive $9600 per year on your rental property, and the cost of interest, insurance, and property taxes is $8448. Your net return is $1152, or 12 percent. This does not take into account tax benefits or nondeductible payments.

You also pay an average of $200 per month to principal on the note, or $2400 per year; and $500 per year on average for capital improvements. Your negative cash flow is $1748 per year:

Rental income	$ 9,600
Less: operating expenses	–8,448
Net return, 12%	$ 1,152
Less: principal payments	$–2,400
Less: capital improvements	–500
Negative cash flow	$–1,748

A pure study of only profits is further complicated by your own income tax situation. One of the values in measuring profits is not only to compare them from one year to another, but to compare your results to the results of others doing the same thing. Publicly listed corporations are compared within one industry in an unending stream of analytical reports. In real estate, however, this does not work, because so much of the real benefit has to do with income tax benefits. So, if you live in a state without an income tax and your federal tax is paid at the lowest tax rate, it would not be accurate to compare your after-tax return to that of someone who pays a state income tax and a high rate in federal taxes.

Example: A real estate investor earns a high salary that places the family in an effective tax bracket of 37 percent (federal and state, combined). Based on this, deductions from real estate losses are worth 37 cents per dollar of loss, due to tax savings. A few years later, the family's effective rate jumps because the spouse takes a job, and now the effective combined tax rate is 44 percent. This increases the tax benefits of real estate investments substantially.

This example points out the problem, even for one investor. Your year-to-year comparisons on an after-tax basis are not the result of real estate investing, but are affected more by your individual tax bracket. Consequently, it is not fair to make after-tax comparisons of your investments as long as your status changes from one year to the next. Deductible real estate losses may even have the effect of reducing your overall tax bracket (federal, state, or both). The difference this might make on your overall tax liability can be significant.

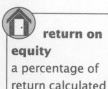

return on equity
a percentage of return calculated by dividing annual net income by equity.

For all of these reasons, attempting to calculate net return is troubling and not really reliable as an indicator of success. A more revealing indicator is the *return on equity*. This is a calculation of net income as a percentage not of income, but of the equity you have invested in the property. In other words, it reveals how your money is working for you, an appropriate investment measurement. For purposes of consistency, expect to use the net income amount before taxes are calculated. The yearly variation in your tax liability will otherwise distort the return on equity.

Example: Your annual net income from investments is $6290. (This excludes depreciation, since we want the calculation to be based on cash income and cash expenses. Depreciation is a noncash expense.) Your total original investment was $85,000, which represents the value of the property you purchased. The return on equity is 7.4 percent:

$$\frac{\$6290 \text{ (annual net income)}}{\$85,000 \text{ (equity)}} = 7.4\%$$

This calculation is much clearer than net return, because it shows the results based on the amount invested. However, even this calculation has problems. For example, let's say that you paid $85,000 for the property, but only included a down payment of $15,000. In that case, shouldn't "return on equity" be much higher? After all, the only real invested amount is the down payment; the rest is leveraged.

The answer is that you should use the purchase price of property, for three reasons:

1. *Consistency*. You may have two or more properties with various levels of down payment. Using actual money invested distorts the real return. What you need to calculate is the yield you get on the property, as a means for comparing its price to its net income.

2. *Accuracy*. A higher or lower down payment has no effect on the degree of return you will get from a particular property. However, the purchase price does tend to dictate return. The appropriate measurement is how return on equity differs from two different properties in similar price ranges.

3. *Meaningful result*. You should perform a particular calculation only if it provides you with some kind of insight. If you compare annual net profit to the amount of down payment, that information has no real value. It reveals nothing about your talent for selecting properties, your management skills, or demand for rentals. Comparing net profit to the purchase price of the property, however, is highly revealing—especially if you buy several homes within one price range but results vary considerably. That is the situation in which analysis reveals useful information to you.

While this calculation is called return on equity, it is more accurately a return on the total value of the investment. The fact that you leveraged a part of the purchase price does not matter, except that more highly leveraged properties will yield a lower rate of return (due to higher interest expenses). A variation on the return on equity calculation may include the amount of principal reduction each year. The argument favoring this method is that your real income from real estate investments consists of profits plus cash flow that is used to reduce principal. This adds to your real equity; as a result, this method is called *equity return*. This is calculated by adding cash income to principal reduction for the year and then dividing the result by the purchase price. The formula:

$$\frac{\text{Cash income} + \text{Principal reduction}}{\text{Purchase price}}$$

Example: Last year, your cash-based net income from investment activity was $5980. However, you also paid down your mortgage balance by $1752. Your original purchase price for the property was $82,000. Your equity return is 9.4 percent:

$$\frac{\$5980 + \$1752}{\$82,000} = 9.4\%$$

Another method for judging your investment results is called *equity dividend rate*. This calculation uses cash flow rather than profits and excludes depreciation. The investment level should be adjusted by adding in any capital expenditures, such as improvements, that have been paid since buying the property. The formula is:

$$\frac{\text{Cash flow}}{\text{Investment}}$$

Example: An investor had cash flow last year of $3915, which included reduction for some capital improvements made during the year. Also deducted from this amount

equity return

a percentage of return calculated by adding cash income to principal reduction and then dividing the result by the investment base (purchase price).

equity dividend rate

a calculation comparing cash flow with the investment amount. The rate includes all investment in the property—original purchase level plus all capital expenditures.

was the reduction of principal on the mortgage loan. Depreciation has been excluded from these values. The total investment in the property, including capital improvements and without deducting depreciation, is $45,000. The equity dividend rate is 8.7 percent:

$$\frac{\$3,915}{\$45,000} = 8.7\%$$

A simplified form of analysis is called *yield*. This is a comparison between annual net income (pretax) and the cost of the property. This is the most straightforward of the available calculations, and it can be performed from year to year consistently. It is also a useful calculation for comparing one property to another. The formula:

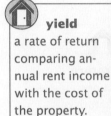

yield
a rate of return comparing annual rent income with the cost of the property.

$$\frac{\$10,695 \text{ (annual net income)}}{\$115,000 \text{ (purchase price)}} = 9.3\%$$

The problem with the yield calculation is that it can become distorted. Different down payments affect income because lower mortgage amounts translate to lower costs. For example, you could own two properties both purchased for $115,000; on one the down payment was $11,500, on the other, $34,500. In the latter case, income will be higher because interest will be lower, assuming that all else is equal.

None of these calculations produces perfect or consistent outcomes. However, each offers something of value to help you monitor your investments.

PROFIT UPON SALE

The final version of profit in real estate can be calculated only when you finally sell the investment. This is called *total return*. This is the most accurate, comprehensive, and reliable measurement, but it can only be performed at the end of the holding period. The calculation takes into account all of the elements involved: annual income, tax benefits, and capital gain.

total return
a rate of return including a calculation of capital gain, net rental income, and tax benefits received during the holding period; expressed in terms of average annual rate of return.

Example: You sold an investment property last year and realized a net sale price of $169,500. The adjusted purchase price 12 years ago was $110,000 (adjusted for depreciation claimed during the 12 years), so your capital gain was $59,500. Over that same period, your net rental income was $22,500 and you calculated that your overall tax benefits (reduction in tax liabilities resulting from holding real estate) were $5200. Total profit based on these calculations was $87,200 over the 12 years, or 79.3 percent return. Divided by the 12-year holding period, annual average return was 6.6 percent. This example is summarized below:

Sale price	$169,500
Less: purchase price	−110,000
Capital gain	$ 59,500
Net rental income	22,500
Tax benefits	5,200
Total profit	$ 87,200
Total return	79.3%
Years held	12
Annual return	6.6%

Annualizing the return is important for purposes of comparison. For example, this property was held for 12 years. You might realize an identical overall return on a property held for only eight years, in which case the annual return would be nearly 10 percent. The advantage of total return is that it combines all forms of return, including tax benefits, and expresses the full outcome on an average annual basis.

Chapter 9

Working with Professionals

Real estate investors have available an array of professionals, ready to help them manage the complexities of the business. Few other investments are accompanied by such a variety of specialized resources.

The need for many different professionals arises from the complexities of buying and selling real estate. Many aspects are involved: legal, valuation and appraisal, financing, movement of funds, inspections, and even locating property and negotiating the transaction. These matters make real estate investment a field requiring professional help.

REAL ESTATE AGENTS

The expert you'll deal with the most, at least at first, is the real estate *agent*. Agents deal with both sellers and buyers, and need to understand contract law, financing, appraisal standards, inspection criteria, and the real estate cycle. Although operating within a complex legal environment, the agent is not allowed to give legal advice.

The majority of real estate agents are members of the National Association of Realtors (NAR), and may earn the designation *Realtor*, which is a trademark designation given only to NAR members who have been tested and

agent
an individual representing the interests of another person (the principal) in contract law. In real estate, the agent is a sales associate acting in the role of either listing or selling agent. The principal is the seller of that property.

realtor

a trademark name of the National Association of Realtors (NAR). Members using this title agree to conduct themselves according to a Realtors' Code of Ethics, and are subject to the rules of the association.

broker

the individual responsible for matching a buyer's offer to a seller's listing, usually working through agents employed as salespersons by the brokerage firm. The broker is responsible for all of the actions and statements of these agents.

qualified in the basics of real estate, and who agree to abide by the Realtors' Code of Ethics.

This only means that the individual with this designation has taken a basic test and has agreed to a set of standards. It is a starting point only. The real qualification to provide professional service is based on experience and knowledge, which cannot be gained by studying for a test.

In most real estate transactions, the agent works for the seller. Because the seller pays the commission and actually enters into a listing contract with the agent's *broker*, the agent is clearly responsible to that seller. However, the real estate contract is an odd arrangement, because that same agent also has obligations to the buyer. Both sides have interests that the agent is required to protect.

When buyers approach agents, either at open houses, on the telephone, or in their offices, they should be aware of the agent's role. They are retained by sellers to find buyers and, because that seller will be compensating the agent, the agent's loyalty and self-interest has to favor the seller's interests. With the Multiple Listing Service in use, all listings by member brokerage firms are listed in one place. When someone brings a buyer to the deal, that agent is entitled to part of the seller-paid commission. In practice, under the MLS system, all member agents are potentially working in the role as agents for the seller.

An agent who gets a listing directly acts in the role of *listing agent*. The listing agent is always entitled to a portion of the overall commission, even when a different agent finds the buyer. Similarly, the *selling agent* is entitled to part of the commission even when not also the listing agent.

Although all commission arrangements are negotiable, including the commission rate itself, the usual arrangement is easily explained. In cases where a sale occurs above a specified amount, such as $100,000, a reduced rate might be applied. For example, the deal might specify that a 6 percent commission will be paid on the first $100,000 and a 3 percent commission on the balance.

If a contract conforms to the standard 6 or 7 percent commission rate, the breakdown usually involves a 50-50 division between listing agent and selling agent. Within a brokerage firm, the commission is further divided, a common arrangement being 50-50 between agent and broker. For example, suppose the commission is a straight 6 percent, and the listing agent and selling agent work for different firms. Under the typical arrangement, the 6 percent commission would be broken down into four payments:

✔ 1.5 percent to the selling agent.

✔ 1.5 percent to the selling agent's broker.

✔ 1.5 percent to the listing agent.

✔ 1.5 percent to the listing agent's broker.

If selling agent and listing agent work for the same firm, as is often the case, the broker gets half of the total, and the other half is divided between the two agents. However, in some firms, agents work on 100 percent commission. They pay a flat fee to the broker to cover the office's operating expenses, but they keep all their commissions.

The agent performs services beyond simply matching up buyers and sellers, although that is ultimately the entire purpose in the activity. The agent also works with the seller to try to set a realistic price for the property. While the seller has the right to ask any price he or she wants, it makes sense to listen to the advice of an experienced agent who understands the market and establishing market value.

The agent is able to inform the seller about likely market value by finding comparable recent sales. The agent is in a position to know the market well. Indeed, if a seller's agent is not an expert about the market, then a different agent should be used. The Multiple Listing Service is also available to every agent, and provides a wealth of information about pricing, neighborhoods, and volume of sales activity. Most areas have an automated MLS service so that searches can be tailored in any way desired: by price range, street, neighborhood, or even to include selection of special features (such as acreage, fireplaces, dens, swimming pools, number of rooms, financing terms, etc.). This information can be of great value to the seller, and the agent should be able to answer all questions intelligently to explain exactly what the competition looks like.

listing agent
the agent who enters into a listing contract with a seller, agreeing to find a buyer and to represent that seller's interests in negotiating a contract. The listing agent is always entitled to a commission, even when a different agent finds a buyer.

selling agent
the agent who locates the buyer and brings an offer to the seller. The selling agent is an agent of the seller and is entitled to a commission if the deal goes through.

THE REAL ESTATE CONTRACT

The agent's job is to present the seller with written offers from potential buyers. Agents offer value to sellers because they represent a network—not only of potential buyers, but also of other agents. Collectively, an inventory of properties is available to buyers, and of equal value, the market itself, consisting of buyers and other agents, is available to every seller. This exposure works within the *agency* system, which operates and controls the actions of real estate agents, and defines their duties and responsibilities. Agency is also a section of law concerning the relationship between agents and their customers.

Agents have to be completely familiar with the concepts of contract law, since the most important moments in their routine come when they sit down with buyers and draw up an offer, and when they present and explain the terms of that offer to the seller. Without being able to perform these functions, the agent cannot get a deal closed. The agent should be aware of all the elements a contract must contain. These include the following seven conditions:

1. *The real estate contract must be in writing.* Under the terms of contract law generally, verbal contracts are enforceable, although they present some obvious problems—such as agreeing about exactly what the agreement stated. There are important exceptions, and real estate is one of them. A real estate contract that is not made in writing is not a legal contract. So even the initial offer itself cannot be considered unless and until it is made in writing.

2. *The terms of the contract must be within the law.* The law recognizes and enforces contracts only if they are legal. So if any terms of the contract are outside the law, then at the very least that part of the contract is void; and depending on which part is outside the law, the entire contract might be void. For example, if one party agrees to sell a property he or she doesn't actually own, that same party cannot enforce the section of the contract requiring a down payment from the other side.

3. *The people entering the contract have to be able to do so legally.* Everyone who enters into a contract has to

agency
an area of law concerning one person's actions undertaken on behalf of another. Agents assume duties and responsibilities according to a contract, and perform under specific guidelines.

consideration
the reward, benefit, or payment given by one person to another as part of the contract, with equal consideration being provided by the other side. A payment is consideration for property; turning over title to that property is consideration exchanged for the payment.

be able to make a contract according to the law. This excludes minors and people who are mentally incompetent. Legally, these people do not have the legal ability to make agreements, so their contracts simply do not exist. In some forms of contract, both parties also have to be U.S. citizens.

4. *The contract has to provide something of value for both sides.* A contract is not enforceable unless it includes equal *consideration*. In a real estate contract, the usual forms of consideration begin with an agreed-upon price in exchange for the title to the property. These may be modified for other agreements, such as performance of needed work, payment of closing costs, or carrying part of the financing. If the buyer does not produce the agreed-upon down payment or does not qualify for financing, then the contract fails. Consideration by both sides is required for the contract to remain in force.

5. *The contract requires certain acts or concessions by both sides.* A contract requires that both sides follow the terms of the contract specifying *performance*. Sellers must relinquish title and perform other work they agree to in the contract. Buyers have to produce the purchase price through down payment and financing, and perform other actions to which they agree.

Performance is often elaborated on and spelled out through a series of contract provisions required by one side and agreed to by the other. These are referred to as *contingencies*. A contingency that buyers qualify for financing is virtually automatic in most real estate contracts; another common contingency is that the offer becomes effective only if and when the buyer completes the sale of a presently owned home. A real estate contract that does not include some contingencies is unusual.

6. *There must be a general agreement between the parties as to the terms and conditions of the deal.* In law, a contract can exist only if and when both sides have actually agreed on the same terms and conditions. This is called a *meeting of minds*. A contract does not exist until a meeting of minds has occurred. For example, if you are in the negotiation phase and you have not agreed to a price—even if some of the details are agreed—there is not yet a meet-

performance
an action required as part of the contract. If one side fails to perform, the contract is breached. Examples of performance include paying a down payment, obtaining financing by a deadline, performing repair work, or transferring title.

contingencies
terms in a contract qualifying the agreement by stating that for the deal to go forward, one side or the other agrees to meet certain conditions. Typical contingencies include qualifying for financing and completion of inspections.

meeting of minds

an agreement to terms, when both sides in the contract know what the agreement states. Without a meeting of minds there is no contract. In a real estate contract, one side agrees to sell a property and the other agrees to purchase that property. However, if they have not agreed on the price, there is not a meeting of minds.

offer

the proposed terms of a contract in real estate. The offer is put forward and must be accepted by the other side before a contract can exist.

ing of minds. Nothing in the works is binding as a contract until both sides believe there is an agreement.

7. *There must be a series of proposed terms, and the other side must agree to those terms.* A contract comes into existence only when the conditions have been reviewed by both sides. One party cannot draw up the terms and impose it on the other without discussion and agreement. This process begins when one side makes an *offer*, which is a proposal of terms to be included in the contract: price, contingencies, work that each side will perform, closing costs each side will pay, and so forth. The offer does not create a contract; it merely begins the process. In order to create a contract, there must first be an *acceptance*.

In practice, offer and acceptance are not always straightforward. One side makes an offer, and the other side may modify the terms and present a counteroffer. That process could go back and forth several times before acceptance occurs. To begin the process of seriously negotiating offers and counteroffers, the initial offer is normally accompanied by an *earnest money deposit*. This is a check or promissory note to be held in trust pending the creation of a contract; it demonstrates that the buyer is making the offer in earnest. If the buyer's offer is accepted and that buyer later fails to honor the contract, the earnest money deposit is forfeited.

These general rules of contract law are clear and specific. Even with a written contract, though, disagreements can and do come up. Both sides may recall and interpret the terms of the agreement in a dissimilar way. However, without the guidelines specified in contract law, it would be virtually impossible to transact real estate in an orderly manner.

INSPECTORS

Once a buyer's offer is accepted by the seller, several additional steps will have to occur. First, the buyer will need to get a commitment from a lender to provide financing, and the contract will include a deadline for completing this step. The seller typically agrees to the completion of inspections and an appraisal, which will be required for financing; in some cases, the seller agrees to perform work to fix defects in the property.

One of the first steps is to call for a pest inspection. This is a requirement for borrowing as a matter of course in most areas, and a good idea at any rate. Real estate agents often recommend that sellers make an appointment for a pest inspection at the time of accepting an offer. Some even suggest getting the inspection completed before offers are received. That eliminates one of the unknown elements about transacting property.

The pest inspector looks for defects or damage caused by termites, beetles, ants, and other pests. Depending on the climate in your region, different pests might be expected to show up. For example, in warmer climates, termites are a chronic problem; in cooler regions, they are unheard of, but ants and beetles present problems. The inspector writes a report, usually including a diagram of the property, itemizing any problems discovered, and listing the actions required to fix those problems. Many of these include removal of debris, improving ventilation, spraying to prevent infestation, or replacing damaged wood.

The lender will require that all defects found by the pest inspector be fixed before financing will be approved. The seller may pay to fix the defects or negotiate something with the buyer. If the buyer agrees to share the costs or to modify the price, the deal goes forward. If the two sides cannot agree at this point, the deal could fall through. The negotiation depends on the extent of the damage and the cost involved in fixing those problems.

Lenders may also ask for specialized inspections. On older homes, for example, the lender might insist on checking plumbing, electrical, and heating systems and the foundation. Or a general structural or home inspection might be required, to be performed by a contractor or a licensed home inspector. The lender might also ask for a general inspection with special emphasis placed on looking at particular systems or areas of the property.

Whether you are acting in the role of seller or buyer, you should always insist that a home inspection be per-

acceptance agreement to the terms presented in an offer. Offer and acceptance must exist before a contract can come into being.

earnest money deposit a deposit, made by check or promissory note, presented by the proposed buyer at the time an offer is made. If the buyer's offer is accepted and the contract is later breached, the earnest money deposit may be forfeited.

formed by an objective, qualified professional. That means that the person doing the inspection should not also be in the business of receiving money to fix the problems. A qualified home inspector is one who cannot perform repair work, and will not even refer you to a contractor. That is the only way you can depend on getting a fair and objective inspection report.

APPRAISERS

 appraisal the process of estimating current market value of a property, based on the value of comparable properties that sold recently, income generated by a property, the estimated cost required to replace a property of similar size and quality, or a combination of these methods.

Lenders require an *appraisal* of the property to be performed by an qualified appraiser. This person should know what conditions affect value, and should know how to find comparable properties to decide what properties are worth. You might not have a say about which appraiser is selected; but to the extent that you are allowed to participate in the process of selection, you should ask that the appraisal be performed by someone who has a qualifying license and has been tested, and who has enough experience to know how to do this job well.

An appraisal is a qualified opinion, based on a thorough inspection of the property and a comparison with recently sold properties in the same area or in areas with similar features and characteristics. Lenders depend on well-documented appraisals that explain exactly how the opinion about value was developed.

You have read in previous chapters about some of the concepts that appraisers work with every day. Conformity is the similarity of features among properties in the same area. A nonconforming property's market value is restricted to some degree by the average value of conforming properties in the same neighborhood. This is an important premise for appraisers. If a particular neighborhood is characterized by three-bedroom, two-bath homes of 2000 square feet, a 5000-foot property with six bedrooms and three baths is clearly nonconforming. That means that, for appraisal purposes, the potential maximum market value of the nonconforming property is held back by the very fact that it does not conform with other properties in the same area.

Appraisal is by no means an exact science. The property being appraised, also called the *subject property*, is valued by the appraiser, but that value is not the final word; it is only an estimate. Certainly, an experienced appraiser's opinion should be given weight, but the real decision about value goes back to the basic supply and demand rule: Value is the amount agreed on by buyer and seller.

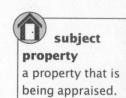

subject property
a property that is being appraised.

Another important point to remember about appraisal is that the appraiser is paid by the client. But who is the client? It may be the lender, a developer, a homeowner, or a buyer; the appraisal may be done for any of these. (In the case of the lender, the appraisal cost is passed on to the buyer in most cases, but the lender is considered the client.) The appraiser always needs to define who the client is before determining value because, to be realistic, the identity of the client may affect value. For example, if a seller pays for an appraisal before an offer is made, a lender might want to get its own appraisal, being aware that a seller-paid appraisal might not be as conservative as the lender would like. (With this in mind, it is not always a smart step to get an appraisal ahead of time.) On the other hand, if a divorcing spouse hires an appraiser to convince the adversarial attorney that the occupied property is not all that valuable, the appraisal might be fairly low. Appraisers have a broad range of discretion in valuing property, depending on the comparable properties they use, and on how much weight they give to one or more of those comparable properties.

The appraisal will tend to vary in its conclusion based on the client. You may see vastly different appraisals when the appraisal is of concern for foreclosure, divorce, a lender's risk evaluation, a seller's estimate, or estate valuation. Each of the clients involved in these matters has a different motive and perspective. The appraiser's opinion about value may be affected by whose interests are involved.

The appraiser's conclusion might also be influenced by the appraiser's status. While some appraisers are outside consultants, others are employed by the lending institution. As a general rule, if the lender is inclined to grant a loan, the appraisal will conclude that the property is worth at least as much as the agreed-upon price. If the lender wants a conservative appraisal in order to justify asking for a higher down payment, that may also influence the way the appraisal is prepared. These observations are not offered by way of claiming that appraisal is dishonest. However, the range of discretion is so broad, and methods available can be construed in so many different ways, that appraisal is often more of a ritual than an objective study of market value.

This problem was explained by two experts in the field:

> Telling the public that appraisers do not have precise answers makes appraisers no less professional—just the opposite. Prospectuses for stock issues are often replete with warnings about what might happen. Appraisals should be recognized for what they are, not what appraisers or others want them to be.*

It is a disservice to the market and those involved with it, as well as to the appraisal industry, if appraisers are placed in the position of being required to set market value of property as an absolute, final authority. There may be a number of fair market values, reasons for selling, and other factors that are not reflected in appraisal.

For income properties, the appraisal method is not the same as the method used for single-family housing. Because value is based on income, this method is in many respects more precise and less likely to be manipulated. When someone wants to buy a house to use as a primary residence, the appraiser is concerned with such questions as:

✔ Does this property fit with other properties in the neighborhood?

✔ Is the purchase price in line with comparable properties?

✔ Does the condition of the house support the price level?

market comparison approach
an appraisal method based on values of similar homes in the same neighborhood or in similar neighborhoods that have sold in the recent past.

income approach
an appraisal method establishing market value on the basis of current and potential income that can be generated from the property.

*Joe R. Roberts, MAI, and Eric Roberts, MAI, "The Myth about Appraisals," *Appraisal Journal*, April 1991, p. 216.

On behalf of the lender, the appraiser needs to determine whether the property is valuable enough so that the lender's risk in granting a loan will be justified. But when the appraiser values income property, the basic assumptions are completely different. Here, the appraiser needs to identify *potential* profits that can be generated from the property. That is the basis for establishing appraised value.

In Chapter 8, some of the tools used by appraisers in valuing income properties were introduced: gross rent multiplier and cap rate. These are the essential calculations the appraiser uses for income properties. However, with all properties, appraisers can combine and use three different approaches; and here is where the appraisal itself can be manipulated to come out to any number the appraiser wants to find. This is because the appraiser might give more weight to one method over the other. In some cases, 100 percent weight will be given to one method and zero weight to another, even though both methods are used. Furthermore, in finding comparable properties, the appraiser can weight (upward or downward) the comparable property's value for any number of reasons. The only possible conclusion is that the appraisal process demonstrates the skill of the appraiser at justifying a conclusion, while not always applying objective scientific method in the way that conclusion was reached.

The three commonly used methods for appraisal are:

1. *A study of the market.* This is the method best known and understood by most homeowners and investors in single-family homes. The *market comparison approach* involves comparing the subject property to other properties with similar features and located in the same area or in similar areas, that sold recently (usually within the past year). Obviously, the more recent the comparable sales, the better that comparison should be. The concept of conformity comes into use with this method; to the degree that the subject property and the comparable property are not the same, the appraiser will add or subtract value in an attempt to estimate the comparable value as closely as possible.

 alternative income approach
a variation on the income approach of appraisal, under which gross rent multipliers are calculated for comparable properties, and the average is used to calculate value on the subject property.

 cost approach
an appraisal method that establishes value based on what it would cost to acquire a similar or identical property, given values of land as well as replacement or reproduction value of improvements.

2. *Valuation based on potential income.* This method assumes that value—especially when it involves multiple-unit property—should be based on potential for generating income to the investor. With the *income approach* the appraiser uses the gross rent multiplier and an assumed cap rate—based on local standards and averages—to arrive at fair market value. Maximum gross rents are discounted for yet another assumption, the vacancy factor. Operating expenses are also subtracted, and the net result is then divided by the cap rate. The following example illustrates this process:

Rental income	$135,000
Less: 9% vacancies	−12,150
Effective gross income	$122,850
Less: operating expenses	−68,000
Net income	$ 54,850
Cap rate	8%

$$\frac{\$54,850}{8\%} = \$685,625$$

The *alternative income approach* involves calculating gross rent multipliers on comparable properties, and then using the average to calculate value.

3. *Appraisal based on cost.* Under this method, the appraiser attempts to identify what it would cost to acquire an identical property of the same value as the subject property. The *cost approach* involves determining the actual current value of the property based not on other property values, but on what it would actually take to duplicate the property through purchase or construction. There are four steps in this appraisal method:

1. Land is appraised based on current land prices, assuming that the land in question is properly zoned and will be put to its highest and best use.

2. The cost to construct a similar or identical building is calculated, based on current construction costs.

3. The assumed cost value is reduced to reflect levels of obsolescence in the subject property.

physical obsolescence
a form of obsolescence resulting from physical condition or features, such as investment property that cannot be fully utilized at a profit due to expensive internal systems resulting in high utility costs or recurring high maintenance, and a decline in potential rental value that results from those conditions.

locational obsolescence
a form of obsolescence caused by changes in zoning and uses of buildings, including property designed for purposes for which a market no longer exists.

4. Finally, the net values of land and building are added together, and estimates for obsolescence are subtracted. The result is the appraised value based on use of the cost approach.

In using the cost method, an appraiser considers three different forms of obsolescence, and may apply any or all of them. First is *physical obsolescence*. These are features that reduce income potential and increase operating expenses, including high utility costs and recurring maintenance. Second is *locational obsolescence*, which includes property located in an inappropriate zone. A home in the middle of a commercial district is one example. Locational obsolescence also refers to property designed for a purpose for which there is no longer a market. The third kind is *functional obsolescence*. This occurs whenever a building cannot be used for its intended design, or when the design makes its use too costly or inefficient.

The various adjustments to value reflected in calculations for obsolescence allow the appraiser to explain why cost value is adjusted downward. A subject property with any of these forms of obsolescence would not command a market value that would be realized if those problems did not exist.

Another variable in the cost calculation is the fact that there are actually two variations in the calculation of cost itself. The *replacement cost* is what the appraiser estimates it would cost to duplicate the building as it stands today, but based on current material and labor costs. That means that hand-designed woodwork or in-laid floors are not allowed for; but that a functional replacement would be provided. Replacement cost is normally expressed in terms of a dollar value per square foot. Another option, sometimes applied to older homes, is *reproduction cost*. This is the estimated cost required to produce an exact duplicate of a property, including the same quality of workmanship and materials. As an appraisal method, reproduction cost recognizes the value of exceptional quality often found only in older properties.

 functional obsolescence a form of obsolescence arising from changes in systems and uses of the building, rendering that building impractical or out of date.

 replacement cost the cost required to replace a building to the same functional condition and purpose that it serves today, based on the current cost of material and labor, but not necessarily to duplicate the same quality of workmanship using materials of identical quality as the original.

reproduction cost
the estimated cost to replace an existing building using the same quality of workmanship and materials as in the original.

escrow
the process of completing contractually required steps, such as obtaining financing, completing inspection work, paying and transferring funds, and recording changes in title, and of checking and clearing title to the property to ensure that all liens have been identified and are satisfied by closing.

THE ATTORNEY OR ESCROW AGENT

During the period of time between acceptance of an offer and actual closing, a series of transactions occur based on both sides fulfilling their sides of the contract. The process is referred to as *escrow*. During this period, several actions have to occur: Buyer and seller have to complete their financial obligations to the other party; inspection work must be completed and approved; contingencies must be satisfied; and title to the property is thoroughly checked, liens identified, and provisions made for satisfying those liens.

In some states, an attorney manages the details and transactions of escrow and holds funds pending completion of required actions, to be paid out later. The attorney also ensures proper and clear title to the property and examines the title record. In other states, all of these functions are completed by a *title company*. Whichever system is used, the escrow agent collects the required money from either side, makes required payments, and ensures that both sides abide by the terms of the real estate contract.

Several important elements of completing the real estate transaction have to be executed during the escrow period. The eight steps are:

1. *Satisfactory compliance with all terms of the contract.* The attorney or escrow agent provides service to both buyer and seller, acting as a neutral conduit for funds and paperwork during the escrow period. This means assuming responsibility for ensuring that the terms of the contract are met and that conditions of closing are satisfied by deadlines. For example, the appraisal has to be completed and a report prepared and sent to the lender with enough time to go through the financing approval process.

2. *Final approval of financing, including completion of all steps required by the lender.* The lender needs some time to complete its review of the application, including a review of the inspection and appraisal reports and a credit check. If payments must be made to the lender as part of this review process, the escrow agent has to collect funds from the buyer and remit payment to the lender.

3. *Collection of money and documents due from buyer and seller, and proper payment to all lien holders, real estate firms, inspection companies, and the seller.* Buyers are required to deposit funds to cover their closing costs and the down payment. Numerous documents have to be transferred in escrow: *reconveyances* of previous mortgages, inspection reports, and deeds to be recorded and transferred. The inspection companies also have to be paid on completion of their work. At closing, all current lien holders have to be paid in full, commissions are paid to the proper agencies, and remaining proceeds are forwarded to the seller.

Sellers are not usually asked to deposit money. Their closing costs are deducted from sale proceeds. When investment property is involved, tenant security and rental deposits are transferred in escrow from seller to buyer, and ongoing leases or rental agreements are transferred as well.

4. *Release of any funds held back.* Some real estate contracts call for holdback funds for various reasons. For example, a buyer might require the seller to complete work that cannot be completed until after closing. Rather than hold up the entire deal, both sides agree to a holdback, to be released on completion of the work. Depending on the agreement, released funds are paid directly to the seller, or to a company performing the work.

5. *Reporting to the IRS and other agencies as required by law.* Transfers of income property result in capital gains, and while homeowners are not required to pay taxes on the first $500,000 of their primary residence, escrow transfers of funds upon sale require a report to the IRS. Other agencies at the state level might impose similar reporting requirements above a specified dollar amount. The escrow agent is responsible for completing these information returns and for filing them.

6. *Completion of title search and issuance of a title insurance policy.* The attorney or escrow agent performs several important functions regarding the title (ownership) of the property. First, it is necessary to identify the property being sold by way of a *legal description*. This descrip-

title company
a company specializing in establishing title to real property, including identification of all existing liens on property. The title company issues a title insurance policy insuring that all liens have been disclosed at the time of closing.

reconveyances
documents filed at closing on the payment of a lien or mortgage, acknowledging that the debt has been satisfied.

legal description
a description of property identifying location and boundaries as well as lot size, as recorded on plot maps.

clear title
a title held without disputes concerning ownership or liens against the property; all liens are agreed to, identified, and not in dispute.

title insurance policy
a special form of insurance issued by a title company to insure the buyer against any undiscovered liens on the property. The coverage is paid by a single premium during escrow, and remains in force as long as the buyer owns the property.

tion has to match with the legal description included on the tax parcel account and the street address of the property, ensuring that (1) the seller holds proper title and is legally able to sell the property. This is an important test, because in order to validate the sale, it is first necessary to determine that the seller holds *clear title* without dispute; and (2) if the seller has more than one property, everyone is in agreement as to which one is actually being sold. The attorney or a title company inspects the title records to ensure that all liens on the property are clearly identified at the time of closing so that the buyer does not discover after the sale that someone has a claim on the property. By identifying these liens, arrangements can be made to pay for them from sale proceeds before closing occurs. The title company issues a *title insurance policy* that promises to pay any undiscovered liens that might arise after the sale. Title insurance is not transferable.

7. *Computation of expenses owed partly by buyer and partly by seller as of the closing date, and issuance of a closing report.* Some expenses are owed partly by each side, and have to be divided on some basis, usually the number of days involved on either side of closing. This is called *proration* of the liability. This is nothing but a division of liability between seller and buyer. The seller is responsible for the portion of the liability through closing date; and the buyer is responsible for the portion applying after closing date.

Property tax liability is a common example. If the tax applies from January 1 through June 30 (180 days), and closing date is on the 112th day, a proration must be made between seller and buyer. The seller is responsible for 112/180ths of the total bill, and the buyer is responsible for 68/180ths. If the seller prepaid the tax, the buyer will have to reimburse the seller's share of the total. The same rules apply to utilities, interest, community dues in a condominium or cooperative development, and rental income if the property is a rental. Proration is illustrated in Figure 9.1.

The attorney or escrow agent also prepares closing statements for both sides, which include a full accounting of all transactions involved: the sale price, lender fees, lien

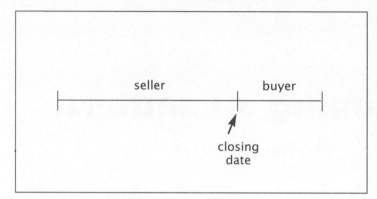

FIGURE 9.1 Proration.

proration
a division of liabilities at the time of closing between buyer and seller, usually based on the number of days before and after closing date over which the liability applies. Proration is used for interest, taxes, assessments, and utilities, as well as rental income if the property is rented out. The seller is responsible for prorations up to and including the date of closing; the buyer is responsible for the portion of the expense applied to the period after closing.

payments, title insurance premiums, escrow fees, real estate commission, inspection fees paid, net cash required at closing (from the buyer), and net proceeds to be paid (to the seller).

8. *Recording the transfer of title to property and recording deeds and mortgages.* The escrow agent or attorney takes one final step: recording all of the legal documents involved in the transaction. These include recording the transfer of title, recording of deeds and mortgages, and any other special forms and documents required by your local government. The new lien (mortgage) is also recorded. The escrow agent or attorney should also ensure that all previous liens and mortgages are reconveyed at the time of closing.

Becoming a Landlord

Tenants are your customers. Through rent, they pay the underlying expenses that allow you to build equity in your properties. To succeed as an investor, you need to know your customers' needs and match those needs with your housing "product." When the match is a good one, everyone gets what they need and the relationship works, sometimes for many years and other times for only a few months.

You will discover that there are important demographic differences among tenants, and between tenants and landlords as well. The most obvious differences are economic, with tenants tending to be younger than landlords and having lower earning power, for example. Other differences include attitude toward the property, opinions about ownership of property itself and about capitalism, and even perceptions about how the relationship between landlord and tenant works. By way of example, tenants often are surprised on being informed that landlords have a mortgage payment to make. They tend to see the relationship from their point of view only, meaning that they have to hand over a large chunk of money each month to the landlord—and that's where it ends.

These differences have to be explored. As a landlord, you will become aware of the different types of tenants you will attract for a property. The tenant pool is dictated not only by the amount of rent, but also by the neighborhood and the type of property. Some neighborhoods are characterized by young families with small children, where properties have fenced yards. In such a neighborhood, most properties also tend to be owner-occupied. If you have a rental there, you will probably be able to charge decent rents compared to other neighborhoods. Tenants will tend to be middle-management or executive-level people recently transferred to your community; they may be looking for a home to buy within 6 to 12 months.

In another neighborhood, the typical property might be multiple-unit, larger, with many more rentals than owner-occupied housing. It may be a student neighborhood near a large university, for example, or tenants might be younger families on the low end of the earning scale or single parents on assistance programs. Internal systems—plumbing, electrical, heating—will tend to be older; yards will not be fenced; and landscaping will be designed for very low maintenance. Rents will be lower as well, with many properties designed for shared rental arrangements.

While these are broad generalizations, they do exist. You should know that different properties receive different levels of rent, attract different kinds of tenants, and have other important attributes. For example, if you have a property near a university and rent primarily to students, you have to expect your tenant to move in June, and a new match of applicants to arrive in September. This does not mean you will have three months of vacancy; but it will be more difficult to find tenants in the summer months.

Before buying property, you should define the kind of tenant you believe you would like, and look for properties in the neighborhoods most likely to fit those needs. No specific market is necessarily better or worse in every case; it depends on what kind of emphasis you want in the properties you will buy and hold for several years.

DEMOGRAPHICS OF TENANTS

The statistical facts about tenants, compared with those who buy properties as homeowners or as investors, make the point: There are differences. Nationally, average income among homeowners is about double the income of average tenants. For homeowners, housing costs represent 20 percent of the monthly budget; for tenants, housing consumes 30 percent. This disparity has much to do with age and income differences. About 35 percent of homeowners are in the peak earnings age range (45 to 64), compared with only 18 percent of renters. And only about one-third of renters are married, compared with two-thirds of homeowners.*

These statistics reveal the important differences between renters and owners. By implication, it also defines the likely demographic facts about serious investors: They will tend to be older than their tenants, earn more money, and have settled down in a permanent residence. Renters, in comparison, will tend to be less settled, earn less, and be less stable in their work and personal lives. For you as a landlord, this means that tenants tend to move more than you would, so turnover is going to be a fact of life when you have rental property.

People move when they get better jobs and, in fact, even without a job; they may move simply because they have lost a job, with the idea of finding better economic conditions elsewhere. They will also move when they find cheaper rent, or when it's time for them to buy their own home. Often, the very best tenants you will find are also the least likely to stay for very long. They will want to buy their own home. For example, someone transferred to town will rent for a brief time—long enough to make sure the job will work out and to become familiar with the community. At that point, this tenant will want to buy a home; being a renter is only part of the transition. While you would enjoy keeping a tenant who pays the rent on time, cares for your property, and shares many of your values, you are more likely to have entirely different types of tenants.

Single-family houses, although the most desirable rentals, are vulnerable to high turnover just like apart-

*James W. Hughes, "Homeowners: Winners and Losers," *American Demographics*, June 1991, p. 38.

ments, for one important reason. Rent levels compete with mortgage payments in the same housing range, but without providing any tax benefits to the renter. The sophisticated renter who understands these comparisons and would benefit from tax breaks will have not only the incentive to buy property as soon as possible, but also the income and credit history to easily qualify for a loan.

Single-family housing used for rental property is also susceptible to changing economic conditions, like all rentals. In tough economic times, higher-level rents tend to turn over more readily than cheaper apartment units; and as families are forced to cut costs, moving to smaller, cheaper living conditions is one immediate step that many are forced to take. So regardless of the kind of property you buy, your tenants and the local economy dictate the strength of rental demand and even the dollar amount representing fair market rent.

To cope as a landlord, both psychologically and financially, you will need to be realistic about the problem of turnover. Even if you do not lose any actual rent, turnover itself takes time and costs money—in cleaning, advertising, checking references, and so forth. If you have to deal with turnover every month or two, it becomes a time burden, perhaps becoming the biggest demand on your time as an investor. Prospective tenants should be thoroughly screened and all references checked. These steps minimize turnover and also reduce your risk of skips, evictions, and wear and tear on your property. Don't expect the average tenant to exercise the same level of care or sense of responsibility that you do. Remember the demographics of renters, and always remember that renters are not owners. You cannot expect a tenant to share your perspective about investing in real estate. The few who do will no doubt be buying their own property within a few months.

The importance of checking references cannot be emphasized too greatly. Be wary of any prospective tenants who cannot supply references or whose references are restricted only to their parents or employers. These are signs that, while there may be past landlords, the prospective tenants do *not* want you to speak with them, usually for very good reasons. Hopefully, you will be able to choose from among several viable candidates, so you should always go with those whose references can be checked, and do check out well.

THE LANDLORD'S DILEMMA

One of the hardest aspects of dealing with tenants—especially very young ones—is their tendency to view the landlord as a surrogate parent or authority figure. Tenants do often assume—without actually thinking about it—that landlords own the property free and clear, and are quite rich. From their point of view, they are handing over cash and you are taking it each month. Tenants do not think ahead to the fact that you have to pay your own mortgage. So when you apply strict rules about getting the rent in a timely manner, tenants may think you are being unreasonable. Some tenant education is then in order, if only to help them to see the bigger picture more realistically.

Tenants probably will not understand the fact that, as a beginning investor, you have to pay your mortgage, keep the property in good repair, and pay other operating expenses as they arise—while living with the risk that the rent might not come in next month. Even so, the purpose in trying to educate your tenants should not be to win sympathy or to help them adopt your point of view. The purpose is only to expand their understanding of the overall situation, to help them learn that there is more at stake than just whether they can make the rent this month. Younger tenants lack the life experience to see the bigger picture without help, or to analyze situations from another person's point of view. Your explaining these matters to tenants might have the effect of making them more responsible and more aware.

As landlord, you will experience what the Shakespearean character Jaques described: "And one man in his time plays many parts."* You will be called on to be a police officer, rule maker, enforcer, social worker, house-

*William Shakespeare, *As You Like It*, Act II, Sc. 7.

keeper, and parent. You may also be vilified as the evil, greedy landlord and become the target for tenants' frustrations at their own personal problems. It's difficult not to be offended when you call the tenant on the telephone and the child who answer calls loudly, "Dad, it's the stupid landlord!"—or something worse.

Landlording is indeed the human relations side of real estate investing. When you invest in the stock market, you only have to deal with a stockbroker and other investors. But in real estate, there is no insulation between you and the infinite variety of human nature.

A mature, responsible, honest tenant is delightful, and such tenants can be found. But you should realize that it is easier to find an immature, irresponsible, dishonest tenant. You will save yourself time and money by screening applicants with extreme care.

Your landlording task will be greatly simplified if you invest a small amount of time at the beginning of the process. That is the key. Look for danger signals, and simply do not rent to people—no matter how personable—who exhibit those signals. Some of the great con artists in your town may eventually want to rent your property. Watch out for:

- ✔ Unwillingness or refusal to fill out a written application.
- ✔ Inability to remember current or former landlord's name or phone number, or refusal to supply that information.
- ✔ Lack of landlord references or references who cannot be contacted.
- ✔ Using parents or employers as references, but no landlords.
- ✔ No bank account.
- ✔ No job or a claim to be self-employed for the past few months only, with exceptionally high income.
- ✔ An attempt to negotiate for lower rent or to barter a portion of the rent in exchange for services (a sign the prospective tenant cannot afford the place).
- ✔ A request to pay the security deposit in installments.

✔ A family obviously too large for the place you are renting.

✔ Overly aggressive pressure to move in earlier than you'd like.

Some of these points are self-explanatory, but a few require special explanation. When a prospective tenant cannot supply you with landlord references, that could be a sign that they have been evicted or have a dispute with their landlord—obvious danger signals. In checking landlord references, also be aware that the current landlord might have a strong incentive to provide you with a positive reference because of the need to get rid of the deadbeat tenant. The most important reference to check is the landlord previous to the current one.

The lack of a bank account is a very strong negative indicator. Most people naturally operate out of a checking account, even those who have just moved to town. You should be suspicious of people who want to pay their rent in cash, and you will discover that such people tend to be chronically late with payments or short part of the rent. Having a bank account is a good sign, indicating that the person is operating within the system and is able to keep an account going without bouncing checks all over town.

You can recognize the signs that people can't afford the rent you are asking: Their families are too big for the house, they want to reduce the rent, or they want to barter part of the rent. All of these are unacceptable. You should never negotiate with people about rent levels once you are satisfied that the rent is reasonable. And you should never, never do business with tenants. Bartering rent for work or exchanging rent for some service is a mistake that will backfire on you. It is impossible to reverse the agreement, and you give all of the advantages to the tenant: If the work they perform is unsatisfactory, you have no recourse.

One of the more subtle signs to watch out for is the complete con. The person pulling it probably is being evicted and needs to find another place immediately, but you will be told there are no current references because the applicant has been living with mother. Calling a person's mother to check is a waste of time; mothers never give negative reports about their own children. The prospective tenant will pressure you for permission to move in immediately, and will express great enthusiasm for fixing up the place, doing some inside decorating, ambitiously working in the yard, and other similar expressions of ambition, all designed to fool you into thinking you have found the perfect tenant. In truth, though, the individual will probably be late with the rent every month, never work in the yard or fix up the house, and adopt a nasty attitude toward you immediately upon moving in.

All of the danger signals should warn you about problems of affordability, personality, or other qualifications. Remember: People do not willingly look for a new place to live when they are out of work and out of money. Anyone who does not have the funds to pay a full month's rent and the required deposits is probably in trouble with the current landlord and will probably end up being a problem for you as well. You might not be getting the full story, and you probably are not getting the real story either.

Without exception, do not enter into an agreement with someone who cannot give you present and prior landlord references. Everyone has to have lived somewhere, and you should not take the risk of renting to someone who has been a problem tenant. Anyone who has not been a problem tenant will gladly provide you with references. Also, you should make it a practice not to rent to a first-time tenant, someone who claims to have been living with parents and to be looking for one's own place for the first time. Being a responsible tenant is something people learn as part of a process, and that process is expensive for landlords. Let someone else (e.g., a full-time landlord who has had more practice) provide this "life experience."

Set a policy and enforce it: No renting without complete references. No exceptions. That will help you avoid many, many problems. You should know that there is a form of adverse selection in the tenant market, meaning that many people looking for a place to rent have problems where they live now. And many of those problems are caused by the tenants. So in the range of applicants you will interview, there will tend to be many people to whom you would rather not rent.

Another policy you should enforce without fail: Always get a written application. Simply stating this rule screens out many deadbeat tenants. When they hear that you need them to fill out an application, many people don't even show up. Figure 10.1 is a sample application form you can use to capture information you need to have. Design a form that works for you or modify this form for your own needs.

Be sure to require Social Security number and driver's license number or other identification. If anyone is unable to supply you with this basic information, don't waste any further time. Having this information helps you qualify people, because virtually everyone needs to be able to present basic identification. In addition, if you go so far as to require a credit check from applicants, you will need identification numbers to get the report. Many people do not check credit on the theory that good credit does not necessarily make a good tenant, any more than bad credit necessarily defines a bad tenant. But one of the pieces of information you can discover in most areas by running a credit check is whether the applicant has ever been evicted or had a judgment against him or her for unpaid rent. This is valuable information.

The rental application form offers a number of useful features, including the following nine important items of information:

1. *Proper identification.* Be suspicious if an applicant will not provide you with the basic identification numbers and name of a local bank where he or she has an account. If an applicant does not want to provide you with that much detail, you may want to concentrate on other applicants.

2. *Name and phone number.* Always request both home and work numbers, to enable you to reach your tenants during day or evening. Plan to verify employment and earnings by telephoning employers and asking if the information is correct.

Property address _____

Name _____

Social Security no. _____   Driver's license no. _____

Bank _____

Telephone: Home _____   Work _____   Message _____

Present home address _____

  How long at this address? _____   Rent _____
  Reason for moving _____

  Owner or manager's name _____   Phone _____

Previous home address _____

  How long at this address? _____   Rent _____

  Reason for moving _____

  Owner or manager's name _____   Phone _____

Nearest relative

  Name/address _____   Phone _____

Person to contact in an emergency

  Name/address _____   Phone _____

Have you ever been evicted?   Yes ____   No ____

Names and relationships of all persons to live in the dwelling:
(Each adult coapplicant must fill out a separate application form)

Any pets? (Describe) _____

Do you own a waterbed?   Yes ____   No ____

Occupation _____   Monthly income _____

Employer _____

Work address _____

Telephone _____   How long with this employer? _____

Signed _____   Date _____

FIGURE 10.1   Rental application.

3. *Present home address, length of time there, and current landlord's name and phone number.* Do not allow anyone to skip this information, without exception. Always check current references to verify that the tenant is living there. Ask if rent has been paid on time, and if the tenant keeps the property and grounds clean and is cooperative.

4. *Previous home address, length of time there, and previous landlord's name and phone number.* The previous information is more important than current information. Make sure you can contact the previous landlord, and ask the same questions. The previous landlord has no incentive to mislead you about the individual applying for your vacancy. Ask:

✔ Was rent always paid on time? If late, how late and what reasons were given?

✔ Was the person tidy?

✔ Was the vacated property left clean?

✔ Would you recommend the individual? If not, why not?

5. *Name and phone number of nearest relative and person to contact in case of an emergency.* You need this information for your files, for several reasons. If a tenant skips out on you, it is useful to have a relative's name. If a tenant breaks the law or takes property from your rental when vacating, you can put law enforcement officials in touch with relatives to track down the ex-tenant. In addition, you might become suspicious if the applicant is unable to provide you with the names and phone numbers of relatives or friends.

6. *Name and relationship of every person who will live at the address.* You will need to screen families or groups too large for the property. While you cannot legally discriminate against people with children, you do have the right not to rent to a seven-member family when all you have is a studio apartment. If you later discover that there are more people living at the property than were listed on the application, you can enforce your restriction on having too many people there. This information is also reported on the rental contract form explained later in this chapter.

7. *Description of pets, if any.* Depending on the kind of property involved, pets might be allowed, or they might eliminate a tenant. This question also depends on the kind of pet. While an indoor, neutered cat presents few obvious problems, a large outside dog is distinctly a problem in a dense neighborhood; and even an indoor dog will cause wear and tear on carpets. You might allow pets but require additional security deposits; or you might decide—like most landlords—to strictly forbid cats and dogs. Be aware of the need to establish rules and enforce them. Some tenants will acquire pets after moving in, and this is a problem. If you have failed to specifically forbid pets and if you don't have enough of a security deposit, those pets could cost hundreds of dollars when the tenant moves out. This concern is not limited to carpet-related problems. A large outside dog can completely ruin a lawn in a short time, for example. The problems can be serious, not to mention the noise disturbance to all of your tenant's neighbors.

8. *Occupation.* You should be very interested in knowing whether the tenant is employed. Always verify dates of employment and salary that are reported to you on the application. Insist on getting the work telephone number. Be realistic, because some would-be tenants are not very realistic. If they make such a small amount of money that rent will represent half their take-home pay, they simply cannot afford to rent your property. By accepting such an applicant, you invite trouble.

A special problem arises with applicants claiming to be self-employed. Certainly, the status itself is not the problem, but verifying the information is virtually impossible. Many self-employed people exaggerate their income level; some unemployed people will describe themselves as self-employed in order to get through your screening process. Some suggestions when dealing with applicants who are self-employed:

✔ Ask for a business card. A legitimate self-employed person will normally have a business card, a letterhead, and a company identity.

✔ Ask for customer references, and check them out. Make sure there is an actual business, which requires customers.

✔ Ask for identification of not only a personal bank account, but a business account as well. Most legitimate business owners maintain completely separate records for personal and business transactions.

If the applicant in unable to provide these to you, chances are high that he or she is not really self-employed. It is not enough for you as a landlord to accept a tenant on the basis of a hobby or on the basis that the person is thinking of starting a business.

9. *Signature.* Insist that applicants sign the application form. The application should be thought of as part of the rental agreement, since you will enter that agreement based on what is claimed on the application.

The application is handy in several ways. As you check out references, jot notes on the form itself. If you run into problems later on, you can refer back to the original application to support your arguments or to identify inconsistencies.

The best screening device of all is the tenant who refuses to fill out an application. Many landlords don't even have an application blank and don't check references, so they tend to have the worst experiences with tenants. They end up, by default, getting those tenants that more cautious landlords reject. (Unfortunately, even when you check references thoroughly, you may still end up with some tenant problems.) The application documents information and eliminates some problems, increasing your chances for having good relationships with your tenants.

THE STATEMENT OF CONDITION

With the preceding section in mind, you certainly need to write down all of the current conditions in the property. Remember your argument: *The property is rented in current condition and that condition is reflected in the level of rent. If the tenant wants those conditions improved, the tenant also has to be willing to pay higher rent.*

The statement of condition is a valuable form for the landlord. It is used to write down exactly what condition the property is in, so that if arguments or disagreements come up later, you can refer to the form, signed by tenant and landlord. So dirty carpets, worn-out appliances, broken windows, or walls in need of paint can all be resolved—and responsibility assigned—based on what the statement of condition says. Such a document is required in many states. It is a good device for protecting yourself, and you can also use the form to provide a receipt for the security deposit you accept at the time you enter a rental agreement. A typical security deposit receipt, inventory, and statement of condition form is shown in Figure 10.2.

You should fill out this form completely, indicating the condition of all appliances, flooring, paint, windows, and window coverings, and listing all fixtures, furniture, appliances, yard tools, and other property you provide to the tenant. If there is a disagreement later on as to the condition of anything on the property, the statement of condition protects you and decides the argument.

At the time you sign a rental agreement with a new tenant, also fill out the security deposit receipt, inventory, and statement of condition form. Give a signed copy to the tenant, who is to document any discovered defects and return the form to you within a few days. Keep the original. If the tenant does find any additional defects you did not note on the form, inspect the condition for yourself and then initial the change on the copy returned to you.

Example: A landlord had a tenant sign the statement of condition. A month later, the tenant presented a list of requests to the landlord, generally complaining about the condition of the house—outdated systems, drafty conditions, out-of-style kitchen, and other similar problems. The tenant also stated that the walls needed painting and that the carpeting was worn and smelled. The landlord referred the tenant to the statement of condition, which

A security deposit in the amount of $_____ has been collected for the property at _____ from _____ in the form of ____ cash ____ check ____ money order. This is a security/cleaning deposit and will not substitute for adequate notice provisions or rent shortfalls.

The following furnishings and/or items were present at the time of rental and are to remain on the property in like condition:

Appliances (list)   Condition

Heating system:

Windows and window coverings:

Floors, rugs:

Condition of walls:

Newly painted?

Furnishings included (list on back and initial):

Garbage cans and recycling bins, number and type:

Hoses and garden tools, number and type:

Outbuildings, type and use agreement:

Keys and locks, number and type:

Other noted items (property is in clean, move-in condition unless otherwise noted):

Signed _____, Owner, _____ Date

Tenant stipulates agreement with this assessment. Any reevaluation must be delivered to landlord in writing within 10 days after possession.

Signed _____, Tenant, _____ Date

FIGURE 10.2 Security deposit receipt, inventory, and statement of condition.

specified that walls and carpets were in good condition only one month earlier. As to the other matters, the landlord responded that the age and condition of the house were reflected in the relatively low rent.

Don't overlook the need tenants have to establish themselves in their new home. One way that tenants try to establish their territory is by trying to get concessions from the landlord, and some of those requests are unreasonable. Good tenants do accept reasonable answers from landlords, even if the list of requests and demands is not filled. Most tenants eventually settle in and stop making demands.

DEPOSIT POLICIES

Every landlord faces the problem of deciding how much of a security deposit to request from tenants, and whether to ask for a deposit for additional rent. If you ask for too much, you narrow the field of prospective tenants; if you ask too little, you expose yourself to too much risk. Three guidelines are:

1. *Don't waive the deposit requirement, and avoid accepting payments of deposits over time.* Landlords hear every imaginable sob story, often even before money changes hands. You may be impressed with the references and the tenant, but when it comes time to collect a deposit, you may be asked to waive it, or to give the tenant a few days to get the money, or to allow payment in installments. These are danger signals. You will have problems with this tenant in the future, perhaps every month when the rent is due. The deposit gives you some leverage, especially when you collect both first *and* last month's rent. Establish a firm policy that the full deposit—including cleaning and security deposits and advance rent—has to be paid in full up front, before anything else occurs.

The purpose of the deposit is to ensure that the tenant has some financial stake in caring for your property. Any of these requests is a sign that the would-be tenant has problems planning financially, so how is the individual going to be able to make rent payments on time?

2. *Set the amount of the security deposit based on rent and other special circumstances.* The security deposit should be set according to the level of rent, plus extra deposits you require for smokers or for people with pets. You may set the security deposit as being equal to one-half of a month's rent, or equal to a full month's rent, for example—and then add additional deposits for situations that could lead to special cleaning problems later. If you also collect the last month's rent in the form of a deposit, you have some security against a tenant being late with the rent. In a case where you need to evict a tenant, having the last month's rent gives you leverage and gives the tenant every incentive to cooperate with you.

A large deposit restricts your potential tenant pool but also disqualifies many marginal or deadbeat applicants. In contrast, more liberal policies broaden your tenant pool but also expose you to risk. The policies you set depend to some degree on the strength of the tenant/rental market.

3. *Establish the deposit to protect against both damages and unpaid rents.* Laws vary from one state to another, but you should be aware that you probably cannot apply cleaning deposits against unpaid rent, at least not automatically. You may need to distinguish two separate deposits. One is intended to defray the costs of cleaning up after tenants if you need to; the other protects you against lost income when tenants do not pay their rent. Some tenants look on moving as an opportunity to leave a lot of junk for the landlord to dispose of, which is time-consuming and expensive. If you collect only a half month's rent and a tenant does not pay next month, you do not have enough deposit to cover all your costs. It will probably take at least one month to evict the tenant, which means a half month's rent is lost; and if you need to clean up after that tenant, that means more expense and lost time.

Some landlords expect to receive first and last month's rent in addition to a cleaning deposit. While this might place a large burden on a would-be tenant, it might be the only way to protect yourself from large losses. A lot depends on the type of property, its location, and the kind of tenants you attract to that property. While first-and-last policies are common to leases, a month-to-month agreement is more flexible, often requiring only first month's rent and a cleaning deposit.

If the initial period is less than one full month, prorate the first month's payment. For example, if you rent to someone on the sixth of the month and the month has 30 days, your first month's rent should equal 24/30ths of the full amount.

THE RENTAL AGREEMENT

When you find the tenant you want, you will enter into a contract, also called the rental agreement. Some people think that only a lease has to be in writing, but for very good reasons, *all* contracts should be put in writing. Even a month-to-month rental agreement must be in writing, so that any future disputes concerning the terms of the agreement can be resolved by referring to the contract. You can be sure of one thing: As a landlord, you *will* have disagreements with tenants. A sample of a one-page rental agreement for a month-to-month rental is shown in Figure 10.3.

The full rental contract includes more than the one-page rental agreement. It should be specified at the bottom ("Other agreements that are part of this rental agreement include") that the agreement extends to the original application, the statement of condition, and any additional forms—agreements regarding pets and so forth. List all addenda attached to the agreement, and be sure that the tenant receives a copy of all paperwork.

The agreement in Figure 10.3 covers the basic requirements. However, you should make certain that the contract you use conforms with the laws and regulations in your community. Some comments on specific clauses:

1. *Identification.* Be sure to date the agreement as of the effective date of the contract. Identify owner and ten-

Agreement between (owner) _____ and (tenant)
_____ for rent of a dwelling located at
_____ to begin (date) _____ . The
tenant agrees to pay rent for this dwelling on a month-to-month basis, in the amount of
$_____ per month, payable in advance on the ____ day of every calendar month, to
the owner or the agent. The first month's rent for this dwelling is $_____ and the
security/cleaning deposit on this dwelling is $_____ payable in advance and
refundable if the tenant leaves the dwelling reasonably clean and undamaged. Tenant is
responsible for payment of all utilities except _____
_____ .

The tenant agrees to give ____ days notice in writing before moving, and is responsible
for payment of rent through the end of the notice period. The owner will refund all
deposits due within ____ days after the tenant has moved out and returned keys, and
upon satisfactory walk-through inspection by the owner.
   Only the following persons are allowed to live in this dwelling: _____
_____ .

Without the owner's written consent, no other persons may live in the dwelling and no
pets are allowed except by written permission. The dwelling may not be sublet or used
for business purposes. This agreement has no holdover rights.
   The tenant agrees to:

1. Not disturb other people's peace and quiet by making loud noises or disturbances or
   playing music or broadcast programs at unreasonable hours.

2. Keep yard, porch, garbage, and common areas clean and well maintained.

3. Not paint or alter the dwelling without the owner's written permission.

4. Park motor vehicles in assigned spaces or areas, and to keep spaces clean; to limit
   the number of vehicles parked at the premises to _____ ; to keep all vehicles at the
   premises currently registered; and to not repair motor vehicles on the premises if
   repairs will take longer than one day.

5. Allow the owners or other agents to inspect the dwelling, make repairs, and show it
   to prospective tenants or buyers with reasonable notice.

6. Pay rent by check or money order made payable to the owner and mailed to the
   owner at the address below.

7. Not change locks without the owner's prior written permission; and upon changing
   locks, to provide two sets of new keys to the owner.

8. Pay for repairs for all damages they, their children, or their guests cause; if such
   repairs are paid for by the owner, the cost of such repairs shall be added to the
   following month's rent to replenish the security deposit.

Violation of any part of this agreement or nonpayment of rent when due shall be cause
for eviction. The tenant acknowledges that he or she has read this agreement and agrees
to its terms, and has been given a copy. Other agreements that are part of this rental
agreement include _____

Owner _____ Date _____

Owner's address _____ Phone _____

Tenant _____ Date _____ Phone _____

FIGURE 10.3 Rental agreement.

ant, as well as the street address of the property—essential information that is often overlooked.

2. *Rent and deposits.* The first paragraph specifies that this is a month-to-month contract, and the amount and due date of the rent. The last sentence of this paragraph states that the tenant is responsible for all utilities except as otherwise noted. If you will pay for water and sewer, for example, write in the specific information in the blank at the end of the paragraph.

3. *Required moving notice.* This paragraph specifies that the tenant agrees to give adequate notice. Required periods will vary from one state to another. A tenant who moves without providing you with adequate notice is responsible for rent through the notice period, and will have to pay rent unless you find a new tenant before that period expires. The landlord agrees to refund deposits within a specified number of days *after* the tenant has moved out. This provides you with time to inspect the premises and ensure that all required utilities are paid up (especially those that, if not paid, become your responsibility). Upon inspection—especially if the tenant has given you problems and has skipped out—you might find hidden trash, abandoned furniture, or broken fixtures on the premises.

4. *The people who will be living at the site.* You need to be able to enforce the requirement that only those people listed on the agreement have permission to occupy the property, not only for reasons of space limitation, but also so that you have control. If nontenants complain about conditions on the property, you want to be able to respond that you have no agreement with them and that they have no legal tenant rights. You want to restrict your contact and response to only those people with whom you have a rental contract.

Directly under the space provided to write in the names of all residents, the contract states that no other people are allowed to live on the premises. This limitation is important in order to maintain control. Some tenants will later allow friends to move in to help defray rent or, in some instances, they may have intended all along to have more people live there with them. You want to avoid the situation in which your original tenant—with whom you have a contract—has moved out, leaving other people living there with whom you do *not* have a contract.

5. *Other terms.* Most of the additional eight clauses and terms listed are self-explanatory, and are included to prevent some conditions from arising and causing you problems with the tenants.

6. *Violations.* The last paragraph cautions that if any terms of the agreement are violated, the result could be eviction. This section also provides space to list other documents that are part of the agreement. Write in the names of those documents, making sure that all of the documents are signed by you and by the tenant. Be sure to include the original rental application.

7. *Signatures and your address.* You and the tenant must sign the form. A contract does not exist until both sides sign. You also need to give the tenant a photocopy. Never give an original to the tenant and expect the tenant to make copies. Also be sure *your* address is filled in so that the tenant knows where to mail the rent.

PROPERTY MANAGEMENT FIRMS

Some real estate investors find dealing with tenants to be too exasperating. One alternative is to hire a property management firm, insulating yourself from the problems of dealing directly with other people.

Property management firms often are operated by real estate firms, but not always. They provide services such as paying all property-related bills, preparing monthly financial summaries for you, and dealing with all tenant-related matters, including locating and screening tenants, collecting and depositing rent, and evicting them when necessary. They also assume responsibility for responding to tenant complaints, getting repairs completed, and all other related matters.

For these services, the property manager is entitled to a fee, usually a percentage of rents collected. These fees average 10 percent. The biggest drawback of hiring a property management firm is that, since fees are based on rents collected, there is no real incentive for the property manager to hold down your expenses. So when a relatively minor repair comes up that you might fix yourself, the property manager might simply call a contractor.

Consider any alternative to dealing with tenants yourself if and when a tenant becomes a problem. But be aware that no one—not even a professional property management company—is going to have the same level of care and concern for your investment property as you do.

If you want to be a real estate investor but you cannot cope with tenants, another possibility you might consider is the fixer-upper market. The next chapter shows how you can invest in real estate without dealing with other people, and combine the investment with your own home by moving into a property.

The Fixer-Upper Market

When the idea of getting into real estate investing comes up, some people respond by saying, "I don't want to have to deal with tenants." This response is completely understandable, because the human relations side of real estate *is* where most of the complexity occurs. In comparison, finding the right financing, making monthly payments, maintaining the property, and planning for the next 30 years are not as difficult. However, there is a solution that enables you to invest in real estate without dealing with tenants.

A *fixer-upper* is any property currently valued lower than its full potential market value, because it is in disrepair, either cosmetically or structurally. Investors are often attracted to such properties when sellers are willing to carry financing because conventional lenders will not finance the properties due to structural flaws, such as inadequate foundations. Another reason for the attraction, though, is that fixer-upper property often can be brought up to full value in a short period of time and with very little money—especially if the problems are only cosmetic.

To some people, even minor cosmetic improvements are unacceptable. Homeowners comprise the largest segment of the market, and often potential buyers expect a property to be in perfect condition or they will not consider making an offer on it. This is where you have the advantage. Because the fixer-upper market is limited to

fixer-upper
a property requiring repairs, either cosmetic or structural, in order for it to gain its full potential market value.

those willing to do the work and who have the vision to see a property's potential, it is almost always a buyer's market, even during otherwise robust times. The lower purchase price such properties command is where the opportunity comes in; you can quickly gain equity in the property and put it back on the market to earn a profit.

TYPES OF FIXER-UPPERS

Finding a talented worker is a real plus. It's fair to estimate that this resource is going to be essential in order for you to work in the fixer-upper market, unless you are extremely handy yourself. Beyond that, you also need to decide which types of fixer-upper work you are able, qualified, and willing to do. Four broad categories you should be aware of are:

1. *Cosmetic.* Some properties simply need to be cleaned, repainted, and fixed up. The yard may need mowing, too. These are inexpensive chores that take a little time but almost no money to accomplish. In such a situation, a little effort goes a long way toward increasing market value. Appearance affects price. When a property that needs a lot of cosmetic work goes on the market, you might be able to get in at a real bargain price.

2. *Discount.* A second level of fixer-upper is the property marketed with some deferred maintenance that involves a particular problem. For example, a property might be in good shape, except that the roof has to be replaced. The cost of this repair can be estimated very precisely. So, when negotiating a price, you can have a good idea of how much you want to discount from the asked price.

3. *Major repair.* A third type of fixer-upper is the property needing a major repair. Such a property should be priced to reflect that, as you will need to put money into materials and labor. You still need to accurately estimate the total cost of repairs, because you need to keep potential market value in mind as well as know what it will cost to get there.

4. *Do-it-yourself.* A fourth fixer-upper is the most extreme case, a property in which the cost of repairs is so high that potential market value won't cover that cost. This property is "totaled" in the same way that a severely damaged car is totaled when repairs are greater than current value. For most people, demolishing this house and replacing it is the only viable alternative. The one exception is when an investor is willing to do *all* of the work, so that labor costs are deducted from the estimated repair cost. This requires that you work to build value through *sweat equity*, which is your own labor. Buying such a property might be worthwhile if the price is right *and* attractive financing is also available.

All four classifications are broadly called fixer-uppers, and the only way to tell which kind you are considering is to look at each such property in person. When advertised in the newspaper, fixer-uppers often are described in several ways: handyman's delight, handyman's special, bring your hammer, needs a little TLC (tender loving care), and rustic are a few of the favorite "best spin" phrases and words used to describe what might be either falling-down shacks or good houses with a lot of cosmetic deferred maintenance.

Most investors recognize that maintaining property is the best way to build equity and to preserve it. You may enter the fixer-upper market assuming that all the work has to be performed right away. But consider these four alternatives:

1. *You don't have to begin repairs right away.* If relatively minor defects have been there for several years, there is no particular urgency about fixing them right away. You can afford to wait a few months without worrying about more serious damage resulting. Be aware, though, that some types of deferred maintenance can cause greater damage and cannot wait.

2. *You could buy a fixer-upper and* not *correct its flaws.* You can simply not undertake the work required to fix defects. Ultimately, this means the property will not increase in market value, at least not to its full po-

---

sweat equity

equity that comes from the owner's labor rather than from growing market demand or reduction of a loan's balance; equity you develop from working on a fixer-upper yourself.

tential. Most investors appreciate the value of building equity at a greater rate than money is being spent, and have a motive to keep their property in the best possible shape.

The decision to not fix deferred maintenance problems is troubling, not only for you as an investor in terms of property market value, but also for the whole neighborhood. A socially responsible investor should not allow real estate to remain in a state of decline, if only out of consideration for the neighbors. Poorly maintained property brings down everyone's property value, and it is irresponsible to allow such conditions to persist.

3. *Wait out the market, conditions permitting.* In some very fast-moving markets, it is possible to simply hold a property for a few months to realize a profit. Real estate speculators do just that, and are not interested in repairing defects unless that is part of getting ready for a sale. In a hot market, property values will climb quickly enough that you could make a profit without fixing deferred maintenance problems.

As an investor, you need to decide whether waiting makes sense. In real estate, timing counts and, if you buy properties purely to speculate in a fast-moving market, planning to resell without doing any repairs might make sense.

4. *Put off work indefinitely if the property is habitable.* You can combine fixer-upper investing with landlording in some instances. Repairs can be deferred, assuming they do not pose a danger or extreme discomfort to your tenants. Not all deferred maintenance is critical. Some outdated properties, especially in areas with a lot of older housing stock, might be the rule rather than the exception. Examples: outdated design elements, older internal systems that work but are not modern, and exterior in need of a new paint job.

If you do combine fixer-upper investing with landlording, you will probably not get full market rental value. However, if tenants ask you to upgrade the property, you can remind them that their level of rent reflects the condition of the property.

LOCATING BARGAIN PROPERTIES

Not all markets present fixer-upper buying opportunities. All markets contain some fixer-upper properties, but prices might simply be too high to justify the work involved.

When you live in one of the top price markets, you will have greater difficulty finding fixer-upper properties in an affordable price range. In higher-priced markets, it is difficult to find properties that are supported by current rental levels; the same kinds of limitations reduce opportunities for the fixer-upper market.

Your first step in determining whether to go into the fixer-upper market is to assess market conditions in your area. A high-priced fixer-upper will demand a considerably higher down payment than a typical house in a lower-priced area, making it more difficult to obtain financing. Additionally, if the property qualifies as a fixer-upper, there is also the possibility that the condition itself will prevent you from obtaining conventional financing.

If it takes every cent you can scrape together to make a down payment, how will you be able to afford repairs? Unless the problems are strictly cosmetic, you won't be able to build enough equity to make the purchase worthwhile.

But, if you can put together a deal at a price you like, for a relatively low down payment, you stand a good chance of realizing a profit. Your market competition will be limited. Most people looking at houses are seeking a home for their family, and would not want to buy a fixer-upper unless they are forced to by financial restrictions. With a small pool of potential buyers, fixer-upper property prices may be more depressed than the market as a whole, further adding to the potential for profits.

THE CASH FLOW RISK

One of the biggest problems in getting into the fixer-upper market is what happens to your cash flow. Without income from tenants, you need to be able to make mortgage payments out of your own income, which could be quite a burden. Three important cash flow considerations you should always keep in mind:

1. *It might be possible to find a tenant.* It is rarely practical to work on a fixer-upper in a big way if tenants are in the house at the time. No matter how cooperative someone might seem, a tenant will resent construction noise and dust, and rightly so. If the repairs are restricted to landscaping and outside painting only, they will not be a problem. You could generate rental income while performing outside cosmetic work.

Some landlords believe that they can get a tenant to cooperate by offering a place for reduced rent in exchange for the inconvenience. It usually does not work. The tenant will find major construction inconvenient and invasive and will quickly forget about having given up something for reduced rent. As long as your work will take you inside the property, you and a tenant will only be in each other's way.

2. *You have to continue paying on your mortgage loan no matter how long the work takes.* The risk in working on a fixer-upper is that those loan payments have to continue. The work probably will take longer than you plan, and the more time that elapses the more severe your cash flow problem becomes. Try to plan for the worst case, allowing an extra month, at least, to complete the work you are planning to do. As you get into a project, you will most likely discover additional problems in need of repair. Part of your projection of cash needs must include the monthly mortgage payment.

3. *Market demand can change suddenly.* You may buy your fixer-upper in one kind of market and end up selling it only a few months later in a completely different market. This can be an advantage or a problem. You might buy in a very quiet market, only to find a lot of demand when you finish your renovations—the best of all possible outcomes. Equally possible, though, is that you will buy a fixer-upper in a very hot market, only to discover that the market has gone cold just as you're getting ready to market your property. That means softness in demand and in the price you can expect, so that your profits would be reduced and possibly wiped out.

When you buy a fixer-upper, be aware of the market risk. Keep an eye on the market and try to estimate the length of possible market cycles, to coordinate your holding period to allow yourself time to do the work. While real estate markets generally change gradually and not in sudden, rapid motions like the stock market, sudden adjustments do occur and this is a very real risk or opportunity.

A realistic plan for investing in fixer-uppers is to allow for more time than you expect to have to spend; more cost than you estimate; and more mortgage payments than you would like to have to make. If you are ready to sell but the market is not ready to buy, you can convert the fixed-up property to a rental and wait out the market. But even before you get to that point, you have to ensure that you have enough capital reserve to pay for all the costs of fixing the property *and* the mortgage payment—and you have to allow for more costs than you originally estimate.

If your independent contractor tells you the work will all be completed in two months, don't estimate for just two months of negative cash flow. Keep in mind the following:

✔ The estimate might be too optimistic.
✔ Additional problems might be discovered.
✔ It could take some time to sell, perhaps an additional two months or more.
✔ The market could change between now and then.

If you can quickly convert the fixer-upper into a habitable rental property, you can offset virtually all of these risks. You have 100 percent vacancy while you are performing major work, and cash flow is critical. So if outside work also has to be done, put it off until the major construction has been completed.

LIVING IN THE FIXER-UPPER

One solution to the cash flow problem is to live in the property while it's being renovated. That is not a good idea for everyone. If you have a family and you enjoy your peace and quiet, and if you don't want to live with the three d's of renovation (dust, dirt, and disruption), then living in the property is not for you. If you depend solely on outside labor, it is also not a good idea to live in the property. This idea is best suited to people who will do much of the work themselves and who do not mind temporary inconvenience and complete disruption of schedule.

Living in a house that is in constant disrepair requires a hardy soul, tolerance, and determination. If you are single, you only have to worry about *your* inconvenience. If you are married, make sure your spouse wants to live in the fixer-upper just as much as you do. Tools, building materials, and refuse will be lying around at all times, hidden only by a thin layer of dust on everything—furniture, food, and even you. While this way of life is intolerable to many people, others thrive on it. And it certainly solves the cash flow problem.

Here's how it works: You sell your current home to finance the down payment on a fixer-upper and to create some working capital for repairs. As long as you have lived there for at least two years, current federal tax law exempts you from all income taxes on the first $500,000 of profit—so chances are good you can move without having to give some of your profits to the federal government. (State tax law might be different.) You also locate and put an offer on the fixer-upper. As soon as the deal closes, you move into the property and make it your new primary residence. You complete repairs while also living there the entire time. The mortgage payment is the only payment you need to make, and the interest is deductible from your income tax as an itemized deduction. In comparison, if you stay where you are and buy a fixer-upper, you may have two mortgage payments to make.

When you complete the work, you put the property on the market, with plans to move as soon as the deal closes—perhaps to the next fixer-upper. If you are satisfied with the experience, you might want to repeat this procedure many times. If you use the fixer-upper as your primary residence, it is also possible to repeat the procedure as often as you want without paying any federal taxes. A couple of rules to keep in mind: The property must be your primary residence, and you can avoid taxes no more often than once every two years. So you would have to plan to stay in each property at least two years to be completely free of any federal income tax liabilities.

Example: You sell your primary residence at a profit of $10,000 after living there more than two years. You are not liable for any federal income tax on this profit. You buy a fixer-upper and move into it, making it your primary residence. You fix it up, selling it for a profit of $35,000. If you have lived there less than two years by the time you sell the property, you will be taxed on the profit. If you wait until two years pass to sell, you are not liable for federal income taxes.

If you plan to live in the fixer-upper as you work on it, remember the two-year limitation for deferring taxes on your primary residence. The tax benefits and consequences of investing in real estate should never be the primary consideration, but it is always wise to be aware of the timing of decisions. It would make no sense to close a sale when you have held a property and lived in it for 23 months; by waiting one more month, you could save thousands of dollars in taxes.

You are not allowed to deduct investment expenses when you treat property as your primary residence. However, most of the money you spend in fixer-upper improvements is capitalized, so this limitation is not severe. You can deduct interest and property taxes as itemized deductions, so you still receive the majority of the benefit from investing; it's just reported on a different form. The goal for spending money to improve a property is that every dollar spent should be both necessary and also spent in such a way that it improves market value beyond the amount spent.

LIMITATIONS FOR
REAL ESTATE DEALERS

You could lose many important tax benefits if you operate not under the rules of home ownership or investing, but as a *dealer*. A dealer is not allowed to claim depreciation deductions, or to defer profits from one property to another through an exchange. And because such properties are not primary residences, the dealer is not qualified for the exclusion of federal taxes. So in trying to decide whether a property is to be treated as an investment or a primary residence, there is also a third possibility: that the property will be classified as an asset that you use in your "primary trade or business."

 dealer
an individual who is in the business of buying and selling.

A *dealer property* is not a capital asset. It is bought primarily for sale to a dealer's customers, so it is defined more like business inventory than as a capital asset. Properties are also treated as inventory for tax purposes, meaning no depreciation and no provision for tax-free sale or tax-free exchanges.

 dealer property
a property bought, held, and sold to a customer, as part of the owner's primary trade or business.

What makes you a dealer? If you have a large volume of transactions in real estate, and if you execute transactions frequently, there is a chance you will be classified as a dealer. You have an even greater chance if real estate profits become your primary (or only) source of income. The distinction is made between investing in real estate and being in the business of buying and selling properties.

However, if you are involved actively in the fixer-upper market by moving into properties while you're working on them, you probably will not be classified as a dealer. If you own only one investment property at a time, or if you hold a series of properties over many years and have tenants living in those properties, you will probably not be at risk of being classified as a dealer. By using a fixer-upper as your primary residence, you cannot be classified as a dealer for that particular property.

The distinction is an important one. Dealers are businesspeople rather than investors, so they lose the tax advantages that come with depreciation and favorable tax treatment of some sales. Even though you may think of yourself as strictly an investor, if you buy and sell many properties on a frequent basis, and if real estate becomes your primary source of income, then you probably are a dealer.

CONVERTING TO RENTAL

Most people think about the fixer-upper market in terms of a series of transactions: buy, improve, sell. This is the normal course of events, but that does not mean you have to follow the usual course.

It might make more sense to buy a property, live in it while you are fixing it up, and then refinance it while it is still your primary residence. As long as you live in the property, it is much easier to refinance and get cash out; most lenders will not allow investors to take out cash from refinancing investment properties. With the repair work completed, your property's value should be higher than when it was bought, so you will be eligible for the best available conventional homeowner rates. That means you can reimburse yourself for the cost of materials and labor, as well as getting some compensation for your sweat equity.

As long as the property is your primary residence at the time you apply for a loan, most conventional lenders will allow refinancing. For investment properties, lenders are likely to approve only 70 to 75 percent of appraised value at the most, and will forbid getting out any cash. On your primary residence, however, you can get a loan up to 90 percent of appraised value in most cases *and* possibly take out some cash.

At the time of refinancing the property, you must be using it as a primary residence, and you must intend to remain living there. However, after refinancing, you could later think about converting that property to a rental, depending on changing conditions in the market and your own circumstances. Buying fixer-uppers and doing the improvements leads to several advantages and potential choices, including:

✔ You bought the property as a fixer-upper, getting a good price and owner financing or favorable commercial rates.

✔ Because the property is used as your primary residence, you have the option of selling after living there for two years, without having any federal income tax liability.

✔ As your primary residence, the property is easily refinanced at good rates, for a higher percentage of market value, and in improved condition (thus, higher market value).

✔ If you later decide to convert the property to an investment, you can depreciate the building's purchase value and the cost of all capital improvements.

✔ As long as you don't become a dealer, you can later sell the investment property and defer profits through a like-kind exchange.

If you plan ahead carefully and remain aware of restrictions, you can benefit from buying in the fixer-upper market. The key is cash flow. The range of possibilities is broad: combining fixer-upper with landlording, fast turn-around, or living in the property. Depending on your circumstances, all of these are possibilities worth your consideration. All of these possibilities also ensure that you remain an active investor. The next chapter describes the alternative: passive investing in real estate.

Chapter 12

Passive Investments

abusive tax shelter
any investment program designed primarily to reduce tax liabilities rather than offering economic return to investors.

active income
under tax regulations, income from salaries, wages, and self-employment.

In the 1970s and early 1980s, the federal tax rules were set up so that many people were able to completely avoid paying any federal taxes. Abuse of the system was widespread and the *abusive tax shelter* was a favored vehicle for annual tax planning. Loopholes enabled the sophisticated person to escape liability.

However, in the mid-1980s this situation changed. Congress passed a series of reform bills between 1981 and 1986 to do away with the loopholes enabling people to avoid their legal tax liabilities. By classifying some forms of income as "passive" and restricting the amount of passive losses an individual is allowed to claim each year, the abusive tax shelter industry was shut down.

The new tax regulations defined all forms of income in three broad classifications. First, *active income* is all income earned from salaries and wages or from self-employment. The second group, called *portfolio income*, includes what is generally thought of as investment income: interest, dividends, and capital gains. Third is *passive income*, the new category, which is all income from activities you do not control yourself. This included all income from the kinds of programs previously used as abusive tax shelters. The tax code classifies real estate as a passive activity.

PASSIVE LOSS LIMITATIONS

The federal tax code limits the deductibility of any passive losses. In general, passive losses cannot be deducted except to the extent that they are offset by passive gains in the same year. Any excess passive losses have to be carried forward and applied against passive gains in the following year.

Example: An investor has passive losses of $4000 every year in an oil and gas exploration investment. Those losses cannot be deducted, unless the investor can offset up to $4000 in passive income during the same year. Any unused losses have to be carried over to future tax years.

Formerly, passive losses were completely deductible. It was possible to save more in taxes than the amount invested, so investors had every incentive to invest in such programs. The passive loss limitation changed all of that. The new rules did away with abusive shelters. Fortunately, one exception to the passive loss limitation rules was made, and that was for real estate investments. Congress recognized that well-planned real estate investments were economically viable and not abusive as were other types of passive activities. If you have passive losses from real estate investments, you can deduct those losses if you meet the following five requirements:

1. *Your net passive losses cannot exceed $25,000 in any one year*. You can offset real estate losses against other income, as long as your loss does not exceed $25,000. This allowance extends *only* to real estate passive losses. Any excess losses are carried forward, subject to the same restrictions in the following year.

2. *You have to actively be involved in managing your real estate investments*. You must be an *active participant* to qualify for passive loss deductions. That means you have to make decisions about which tenants to approve, hire others to make repairs and maintain the property, and manage the financial transactions. If you hire a property

portfolio income
under tax regulations, income from investments including interest, dividends, and capital gains.

passive income
under tax regulations, any income from activities not under the individual's direct control.

active participant
an individual who directly makes management decisions (e.g., arranges for repairs and other services, collects and deposits rents, pays bills, and performs other necessary routines to maintain the investment).

management company, you will still be an active participant as long as you continue to confer and review regularly with the manager.

3. *You own at least 10 percent of the property.* It is possible to own property jointly with other people as a joint venture, small business corporation, or general partnership. This is not a problem as far as passive loss deductions are concerned, as long as you meet the other requirements *and* own 10 percent or more of the property.

4. *You are not a passive participant by definition.* You must own property directly, meaning you lose the right to a deduction of passive losses if you are a *limited partner*. A limited partner has no voice in management, by contract; a general partner has all the rights and responsibilities for management of properties.

5. *Your gross income (adjusted), not including property losses, is less than $100,000.* Another limitation on deductibility of passive losses is based on your level of *adjusted gross income* based on the federal income tax return. If the adjusted gross income (not including passive losses from real estate) is less than $100,000, then the deduction is allowed in full. However, for every dollar of adjusted gross income above $100,000, the deduction is reduced by 50 cents. So once adjusted gross income reaches $150,000, no deductibility is allowed for passive losses.

PARTNERSHIP INVESTMENTS

At first glance, a *limited partnership* looks like a practical way to invest in real estate while limiting risk. People with a small amount to invest (often only $1000 to $2000) can buy units (similar to shares in a corporation) in a limited partnership. The partnership then buys properties, often large properties like shopping centers or industrial parks. The profits are shared among general partners (who manage the property and assume unlimited risk) and limited partners (who do not manage properties and have limited risk).

The organization formed in this way is called a

limited partner

an investor who does not manage property directly, but owns units in a limited partnership. Such agreements provide that general partners perform all management duties, and that limited partners have no voice in property decisions. Effectively, limited partners own a portion of the partnership, which, in turn, buys and manages property. Limited partners' liability is limited to only the dollar amount of their actual investment.

program and invests as a single entity. Otherwise, it would be too complicated for hundreds and perhaps thousands of individuals to transact business together. Partnerships are convenient, especially if many people are involved.

The sponsors of limited partnerships emphasize the convenience of pooled investing, often projecting large profits in the future and offering current and future tax benefits to participants. Sponsors also like to point out that while general partners live with unlimited exposure to risk, limited partners are exposed to risk only to the extent of the dollar amount they have invested.

The convenience and limited liability are big selling points. But historically, most limited partnerships have not been profitable, at least not to the limited partners. Under today's rules, passive losses cannot be deducted, so there are no tax incentives whatsoever to owning shares in such deals. Most investors today know better than to put their money into limited partnerships.

Economically sound partnerships will work well, but only if they are profitable. Losses have no value. They should be formed by general partners with a lot of real estate experience *and* a track record of forming profitable programs in the past. Because you would not invest in a limited partnership to benefit from tax losses, be sure the motivation is sound economically.

 adjusted gross income under federal tax rules, the total of wages and salaries, interest and dividends, net self-employment income, and capital gains, adjusted for contributions to retirement plans, moving expenses, alimony, self-employed health insurance premiums, and part of self-employment taxes paid. For most people, the amount on the bottom line of the first page of their federal form 1040.

THE STRUCTURE OF THE PROGRAM

Some people invest in limited partnerships in the belief that a well-managed program will produce profits. In such cases, it is advisable to invest in a *specified program*. This type of partnership has a particular property or project in mind. It simply makes sense to know how and where your money will be invested before you decide which program to buy. This is more desirable than the alternative, buying units of a *blind pool*. In the latter type of program, the general partners indicate the types of property they will build or develop, but they do not have any properties identified specifically at the time

limited partnership
an investment program in which general partners manage property and accept unlimited liability, and in which limited partners do not participate in management decisions, and have limited liability.

 program
a limited partnership or other organization formed to invest capital as a single entity from the pooled investment funds of many individuals.

 **specified program**
a limited partnership formed to buy or develop a specifically identified property.

units are being sold. One potential problem with the blind pool is that of investment policies. Without having identified exactly how the investment capital will be spent, the whole idea lacks a plan. You might want to invest in a program that uses no leverage, so that cash flow risks are minimized. In a blind pool, the general partners might identify an opportunity requiring leverage and decide to go that route. Limited partners have virtually no control.

The structure of the limited partnership involves much more than the division between management and liability to general or limited partners. The program also spells out exactly how each type of partner will be paid from profits. Remember, the terms and policies were probably written by the general partners. This could mean that the limited partners have little chance of profiting at all. For example, many programs will state that the general partners are to be paid a specified amount at a specified time, even if the program does not make a profit. The conditions will also spell out how profits will be divided down the road upon sale of properties —and there again, general partners might be entitled to the lion's share of profits.

All of the information you need to know before you invest in any program, including sharing of profits, types of properties, degree of leverage if any, and the experience of the general partners, is supposed to be fully disclosed in a program *prospectus*. Read the prospectus thoroughly before investing any money. While it is not very interesting or exciting to read, the prospectus contains information that is crucial for you to have, for your own protection.

Here's how limited partnership investing works: The program is formed to pool together the capital of a number of limited partners—hundreds, perhaps thousands of people. The limited partners are silent partners in just about every respect. They cannot participate in management decisions, nor in managing the properties themselves. They are not consulted about purchases or sales or other management decisions. This is all handled by the general partners, who provide their services to the part-

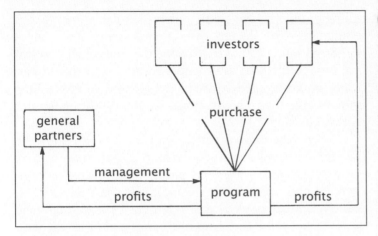

FIGURE 12.1 Limited partnership.

blind pool
a limited partnership formed with a general plan for the types of properties to purchase or develop, but without having any specific properties identified at the time the partnership is formed.

nership in exchange for a "management fee," often paid up front. Other profits, if any, are shared among general and limited partners based on a formula. In studying a prospectus of a program, be sure to look into the details of compensation arrangements. You might discover that the limited partner is far down the chain of compensation, so that the chances of ever getting any profits are remote at best. The structure of the limited partnership is summarized at Figure 12.1.

SELLING PARTNERSHIP UNITS

Units in the limited partnership are marketed in much the same way as a new stock offering. In that respect, the limited partnership offering looks very much like the shares being sold in a new offer of corporate shares.

The *issuer*, usually the general partners themselves (or sometimes another company that is backing the general partners financially), markets units by forming a *syndicate*. This is a management company designed specifically for the purpose of selling units in the limited partnership. Within the syndicate are member organizations and sales associates collectively called the *selling group*. These companies are usually securities broker-dealers. The

prospectus
(also called **offering document**)
a disclosure report published by the sponsors of a limited partnership, for potential investors. All important economic, tax, financial, and management policies and conditions are to be explained fully in the prospectus, and investors should read the prospectus before buying.

issuer
(also called **sponsor**)
the individuals (usually the same people who are the partnership's general partners) or company that makes shares available to investors.

syndicate
an organization formed to manage the group of sales representatives (the selling group) responsible for selling units in the partnership.

selling group
the broker-dealer members of a syndicate whose sales associates and representatives sell units to investors in limited partnership programs.

selling group may have only one broker-dealer member or it might involve dozens of companies and hundreds of registered representatives. Finally, the individual investor is approached by the salespeople employed by the broker-dealer, and those people are paid a commission for selling units to investors. The organization of a syndicate is summarized in Figure 12.2.

While the limited partnership might seem a lot like the organizational structure of a corporation, there are important differences. General partners may act like management and investors might look like shareholders, but publicly traded stock is easily bought or sold, and each day's market value is easy to find. This is not the case with limited partnerships.

The units in the limited partnership have no ready market. Even so, in the decade of the 1980s, investors

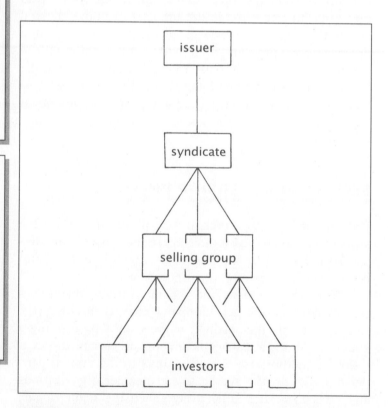

FIGURE 12.2 Syndicate.

bought $135 billion in limited partnership shares.* In the stock market, buyers can invariably find sellers if they are willing to pay the current per-share value. And sellers can find buyers as long as they are willing to sell at the going price at that moment. But with limited partnership units, there is no auction marketplace. When a limited partner wants to sell units, buyers are scarce. Some companies have been formed specifically to buy up limited partnership shares, but they usually are only willing to deal with sellers for deeply discounted prices.

Limited partnerships have no liquidity, in the sense that there is no market for used shares. This is, perhaps, the most serious flaw in such programs, without even considering the complete lack of tax benefits. It is not unusual for sellers to have to accept discounts up to 50 percent just to dump these unwanted units.

THE REIT

Investors want economically sound, liquid alternatives to limited partnerships, with a good historical record for producing returns, *and* with good liquidity. Limited partnerships lack these desirable attributes.

While limited partnerships were big in the 1970s and 1980s, the tax benefits are gone and those days are not likely to return. Today, limited partnerships generating tax losses have absolutely no value. So investors, having abandoned such programs, have begun looking elsewhere. Many have found an acceptable alternative in the *real estate investment trust*, also called a REIT. This is an investment company that pools investment money from many individuals to buy and manage real estate, while providing an open market for shares. REIT shares can be bought or sold through stockbrokers, just like shares of stock.

By law, REITs are not allowed to pass on any tax ben-

 **real estate investment trust (REIT)** a trust formed as a pool of investment capital from many investors, for the purpose of investing in real estate. Profits or losses are passed on to investors each year, and shares can be traded on the open market through stockbrokers.

*William Fulton and Morris Newman, "Fool Me Twice," *California Business*, July/August 1991, pp. 22–23.

efits to investors. Even if losses are generated, they would not be tax deductible. The REIT's management has every motive to form an organization that will report net profits and positive cash flow. For investors who do not want to manage their holdings directly and who are not investing primarily for tax benefits, the REIT is the best choice. The ability to buy and sell on the auction market adds to the attractiveness of the REIT. For investors with passive losses seeking passive income to offset those losses, the REIT provides a sensible investment of choice. The REIT is probably the best investment for generating passive income.

The REIT is formed as a pool of investors' capital. You can buy REIT shares from the REIT management, a financial planner, or a brokerage firm at the time the program is first formed. Shares can be bought or sold later through the brokerage firm. Current values are listed in the financial press just like stocks, and are traded publicly. Another distinction about the REIT compared to limited partnerships: As a general rule the REIT does not employ leverage. Considering that tax benefits cannot be passed on to investors, there is no incentive to borrow money and leverage the program. So the majority of REITs buy property with cash. This dramatically reduces cash flow risks. Profits tend to be higher than in any leveraged program, because interest is usually the largest real estate expense, regardless of how or where you invest.

With many investors participating, there is no need to borrow funds. With a lot of investment capital in hand, the REIT's management is able to define the size and scope of the organization and the number and type of properties it will acquire. Breakeven of occupancy rates is dramatically lower than in any leveraged program, further reducing investment and market risk.

The REIT is designed to generate cash profits to its investors, while providing management services to them as well. The REIT's purpose—positive cash flow with passive income—is far better for everyone in the current tax climate than negative cash flow and worthless passive losses. Profits are paid to investors in the form of divi-

TABLE 12.1 REIT Annual Return (for all categories of REITs)			
Year	Return	Year	Return
1972	11.19%	1985	5.92%
1973	−27.22	1986	19.18
1974	−42.23	1987	−10.67
1975	36.34	1988	11.36
1976	48.97	1989	−1.81
1977	19.08	1990	−17.35
1978	−1.64	1991	35.68
1979	30.53	1992	12.18
1980	28.02	1993	18.55
1981	8.58	1994	0.81
1982	31.64	1995	18.31
1983	25.47	1996	35.75
1984	14.82		

Source: National Association of Real Estate Investment Trusts.

dends. The REIT is required by law to pass through no less than 95 percent of its profits.

Market performance of REITs has been impressive. In 16 of the past 25 years—64 percent of the time—REIT investors gained double-digit returns on their investments.* The record, which includes all categories of REITs, is summarized in Table 12.1 and in Figure 12.3.

You might think of a REIT as a mutual fund that specializes in real estate rather than in stocks and bonds. Many of the same rules apply to the form of the organization, tax treatment, liability, reporting, and the level of regulatory oversight and disclosure required. In looking for a REIT investment, make a clear distinction among the three major classifications:

*National Association of Real Estate Investment Trusts (NAREIT). Annual total return is for all forms of REITs. Additional information can be found at the NAREIT Web site (http://www.nareit.com).

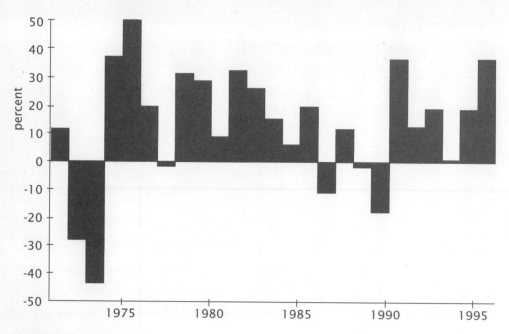

FIGURE 12.3   REIT annual return. *Source:* National Association of Real Estate Investment Trusts.

equity REIT

a real estate investment trust that buys property directly, seeking current income and future appreciation.

1. *REITs that own real estate.* The first category is the *equity REIT*, which is a program designed to buy property and hold it for current income and future appreciation in market value. If the program involves no borrowed money, the potential return on investment is higher than average. The trust itself is the legal owner of property, and each shareholder owns shares in the trust. (The status of a REIT investor is the same as that of a corporate shareholder.) Equity REITs have experienced consistently high returns for investors since REITs were first conceived in 1972, even during periods when other types of REITs were losing money.

2. *REITs that lend money to others.* A second classification is the REIT designed to act as a lender. The *mortgage REIT* takes no equity position but funds development of projects or the purchase of existing projects. For many years, REITs generally had a very bad reputation, due primarily to trouble experienced by mortgage REITs. In 1973 and 1974, several mortgage REITs loaned excessively to developers to build projects, and those projects were not finished. As a consequence, those REITs had large losses, and all REIT markets gained a negative reputation as a result. The losses in the early 1970s have led to a more conservative approach by many REIT companies. Some continue to lend money for development, while the more cautious programs are designed to make loans on only already-built projects that the borrower wants to buy and that are generating cash flow adequate to repay those loans.

3. *REITs that combine goals.* It often makes sense to take an equity position with some capital, and a debt position with the rest, as a form of diversification. The *hybrid REIT* is designed to take advantage of the current market conditions, and to modify its policies as those conditions emerge and change. Some of the REIT capital is used to buy properties, and the balance is used to lend to others and generate interest income.

Another way to divide up the REIT market is by determining whether the program is finite. Some REITs identify a date by which they intend to close out their holdings and liquidate the trust; others continue on indefinitely. Arguments can be made favoring either of these approaches. While a closing date might be desirable, it is impossible to know whether the market conditions on that date in the future will make closing positions wise at that time. Secondly, since shares can be traded freely on the auction market, it might not be necessary to provide investors with an assurance of a liquidation date.

If you are interested in investing in the REIT market, you should first determine the risk level. For any type of REIT, you should know whether the REI intends to borrow money, what types of properties it will buy, and whether it will deal with existing properties or development (either for equity or for debt investing). More conservative programs will avoid getting into the development side. If a REIT ends up foreclosing on unfinished projects, investors should expect to lose money on those deals. While such activity can be potentially extremely profitable, it comes with correspondingly higher risks.

Even with a REIT that is considered conservative

mortgage REIT
a real estate investment trust that acts as lender in real estate transactions, loaning capital to organizations to purchase real estate, with loans secured by the real estate itself. This REIT is designed to generate current income in the form of interest.

hybrid REIT
a real estate investment trust that combines equity and debt, and modifies its position in the market according to changing market conditions. The hybrid REIT's investment goal is to combine market appreciation from equity investments with current income from debt positions.

and relatively safe, you should evaluate risks. Make sure the trust's management has considerable experience in designing programs and in managing real estate. Read the prospectus and make sure you know who will be running the programs. Many are operated by organizations that have been in the business for many years; others may have little or no real estate experience.

INVESTING IN MORTGAGES

You don't need to buy a mortgage REIT to become a debt investor in real estate. You can also lend money through an organized company that works like a mutual fund, but offers mortgage investments instead of stocks and bonds. Whenever an individual seller is asked to carry a loan, that is a request to convert an equity position to a debt position, at least for part of the equity. While such a one-to-one contract might be troubling to many, the alternative—investing with many others in a diversified program—is more comforting, because risks are spread around and the program is managed professionally.

 **mortgage pool**
an organized program consisting of the pooled capital of many investors, managed by a small group of real estate debt experts, that invests the pooled funds in mortgages, all secured by real estate.

You can buy shares in a *mortgage pool*, which works much like a mutual fund. A professional management team organizes the investment capital of many investors, and invests that money in blocks of mortgages transferred from others (usually conventional lenders). The largest volume in mortgage pools occurs in a few government-sponsored organizations, including FNMA (Federal National Mortgage Association, also called "Fannie Mae") and GNMA (Government National Mortgage Association, also called "Ginnie Mae"). Other, more specialized organizations also participate in the formation of pools. This activity is collectively referred to in the mortgage business as the secondary market.

The mortgage pool provides a needed service, both to the real estate buyer and to the real estate investor. In today's conventional lending business, the majority of loans granted by banks have to meet strict standards imposed by the secondary market. The agencies in the secondary market buy the loans from the original lender to form mortgage pools, which frees up the reserve of those lenders to make new loans. This process is illustrated in Figure 12.4.

Four advantages of investing through a mortgage pool are:

1. *You don't have to deal with collections or any other matters concerning the borrower.* In a mortgage pool, you never have to worry about a borrower being late with the payment; chasing after delinquent borrowers and bounced checks; or ultimately, having to foreclose on a property in

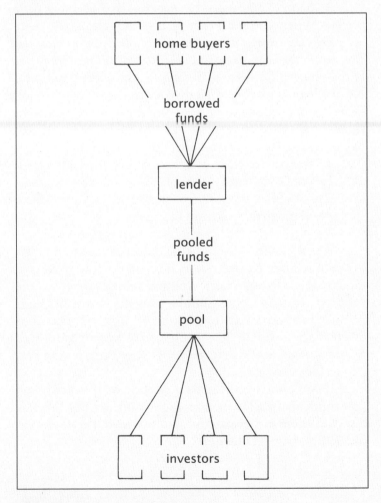

FIGURE 12.4 Mortgage pool.

default. All of these matters are handled by the pool's professional management, dealing with hundreds or even thousands of loans within the pool. The original lender often continues to service the loan, meaning many of the routine tasks of collecting and reporting are delegated back to the bank or savings institution. In either case, you as investor do not have to worry about the details.

2. *You enjoy the benefit of diversification.* Because a large number of mortgages are placed in each pool, your relatively small investment amount benefits from the broad diversification of investing with many others.

3. *Shares in the mortgage pool can be traded with little trouble.* When you lend money to a buyer directly, there are only three ways to get out of the deal. First, you can wait until the loan is repaid. Second, if the borrower defaults you would have to foreclose. Or third, you could sell the loan at a substantial discount. In a mortgage pool, shares can be bought or sold on the market. Value of shares is dictated by overall yield to investors, principal balances, and time until maturity of the portfolio.

4. *You receive current income on a dependable schedule.* The pool's management mails checks to each investor in the pool either monthly or quarterly. This provides a steady and predictable stream of income.

If you like the idea of being a debt investor and buying debt secured by real estate, but you don't want to deal directly with a single borrower, the mortgage pool is the solution. However, you should consult with a financial planner before purchasing shares. All financial decisions of this nature should be coordinated as part of an overall financial plan, and mortgage pools might not be the best choice for everyone.

If you do not want to deal directly with tenants, and you think that REITs or mortgage pools are not the way for you, there are even more alternatives. These are explained in the next chapter.

Other Ways to Invest

Most real estate investors start out in the single-family housing market. For example, you might convert your home to a rental when it's time to move up rather than selling. Or you might refinance your home and use the proceeds for a down payment on a second home, which you will use as a rental. Single-family housing is familiar, is relatively easy to finance, and historically has outpaced inflation. There are good reasons to be comfortable in this market; there are also other investment alternatives you might consider.

MULTIFAMILY RESIDENTIAL PROPERTY

The single-family house is, without a doubt, the most popular form of real estate investing. It is well understood, historically profitable, and has a ready market—either of new home buyers or of tenants. Even in markets with an excessive number of apartment rentals, a large portion of the market prefers a house over an apartment. From the investor's point of view, the rate of return on single-family housing is the standard against which non–real estate investments are measured.

That does not mean that single-family housing represents the only viable market. The time may come when you, as an investor, may want to move beyond single-family housing and explore multiple-unit investments as well—including duplexes, triplexes, fourplexes, and apartment buildings. Housing with four or fewer units tends to hold and increase value closely with single-family housing when compared to inflation, and cash flow often is far better than with the one-tenant house. Only 2 percent of American households are two- to four-unit sizes. For example, in markets in which the typical house can be rented for $800, you might be able to rent duplex units for $500 to $600 each.

A study of all American households reveals the important role that multiunit housing plays in the total picture:*

Ownership of single-family home	56%
Renting in multiunit setting of more than four units	15%
Renting in single-family homes	12%
All other arrangements	17%
Total	100%

Duplexes as investment properties will probably be appraised using the income approach. So even when a single-family house generates less rental income than a comparably-sized duplex of the same market value, the duplex might be valued higher or lower, all depending on the total amount of rent generated. This is perplexing and it points out one of the quirks in appraisal standards and procedures. The market advantage to you, as a potential buyer, should not be overlooked. You may be able to find lower-priced duplexes that yield better cash flow than you can get from a single-unit property, with a lower down payment and lower mortgage payment as well.

The trends look good for apartment investing. An-

*Source: U.S. Bureau of the Census and 1993 American Housing Survey, cited in Apartment Living in America, 1996, p. 36.

nual rates of return for investors in apartment properties have averaged about 12 percent since 1994, the best result of all types of real estate investing. With expectations of U.S. population increases of 60 million people in the next 25 years, demand should continue strongly, coming both from young adults entering the housing market for the first time and retirees seeking smaller living spaces.*

COMMERCIAL AND INDUSTRIAL PROPERTY

Even in areas where residential demand is high and housing prices are rising, there might be an entirely different market for commercial and industrial properties. You cannot apply residential market knowledge to judge this separate market.

Tenants in commercial and industrial properties are likely to hold long-term leases. Certain types of buildings are subject to zoning controls, environmental restrictions or mitigation, and regulatory oversight that never applies to residential properties. The markets for commercial and industrial properties are determined by retail sales levels; manufacturing companies need space in properly zoned areas; and there are many other related factors. None of those are directly related to residential market factors, even though industrial and commercial trends certainly affect residential supply and demand. As far as market value and the supply and demand for these nonresidential properties go, the market is entirely different and separate.

As medium-size cities and suburban areas adjust to new living trends, demand for commercial space will be especially different in the future. When you begin to understand which trends are at work in commercial districts,

---

*Source: Emerging Trends in Real Estate: 1997, Equitable Real Estate Investment Management, Inc., and Real Estate Research Corporation (citing survey data from 150 real estate investors, property executives, developers, analysts, economists, and planners; and the U.S. Bureau of the Census), pp. 42–43.

you realize that seemingly small decisions by planners can cause a boom or a ghost town. One study claims that the aging baby boom population is not a positive trend for retail commercial demand in the future. With the largest segment of the population estimated to be in the 45 to 64 age group by the year 2010,* retail demand will be flat. Contract spending per year from 1986 to 1996 averaged $15 to $16 billion per year, but that will fall to below $15 billion on average between now and 2010.†

building lot

a parcel of land zoned and approved for improvements such as a house, commercial property, or other uses allowed by that zoning.

INVESTING IN RAW LAND

The thought of buying land as a speculator has caught the fancy of many investors. Although fortunes have been made in land speculation, returns generally reflect the higher risk levels involved in buying into the unknown and, all too often, reflect the naïveté of those whose plans did not work out.

Make a clear distinction among different types of land. A platted lot sold as homestead is not the same as raw land; in fact, it is vastly different. A *building lot* is prepared and zoned for building, and will cost more than comparable *raw land*. Raw land lacks some or all of what are known as the six *basic services*: water and sewer systems, paved roads, storm drainage system, garbage collection, and electricity.

raw land

a parcel of land or acreage not zoned for any specific purpose, or zoned but lacking in basic services and, thus, not yet buildable.

In some areas, building lots are approved without all six basic services. For example, in a rural area, local zoning might not require paved roads or garbage collection, or might allow septic systems in place of a sewer system and a small water association or wells in place of a public water provider.

Raw land as a speculative investment is further defined by the fact that, at least for now, no developers have

*Source: Joint Center for Housing Studies of Harvard University, cited in *Changes in Construction Markets the Next 15 Years*, American Institute of Architects, 1996, p. 7.

†Source: F. W. Dodge and AIA, *Changes in Construction Markets the Next 15 Years*, American Institute of Architects, 1996, p. 14.

plans for the area and the city or county is not anticipating promoting growth there or bringing roads and utilities through. Because of this, such raw land is usually also cheap. Because your goal will be to buy land at a very low price and then sell it at a profit, you will hope to recognize the *path of progress* before anyone else does. By the time everyone knows where growth is going, land values will be higher and the opportunity to buy cheaply will be gone.

Some novice speculators are unrealistic about the potential for earning profits from land speculation. You have to be willing and able to invest your capital for many years, without generating income. While speculation, by its nature, is designed to generate the largest possible profit in the shortest amount of time possible, it doesn't always work out that way. The reality is that, once you begin speculating, you learn that the market has its own schedule, and the path of progress may be forged with painful slowness. The advice of one expert is worth remembering: "Investors must not be deceived by the apparent high profit of land speculation. Because the land produces no income, a long holding period and selling terms that draw the speculator into a virtual partnership with the developer always results in reduced yields."*

The path of progress might be very obvious, but with uncertain timing. You might know, for example, that a stretch of undeveloped land along a major transportation corridor will be developed with growth; but you cannot be certain about *when* that will happen—in 20 months or in 20 years. If you are willing to buy raw land to speculate on future profits, you have to be willing to wait out the market.

Four guidelines for buying raw land:

1. *Be aware of the shape of the land.* Squares and rectangles hold their value better than oddly-shaped parcels, and tend to increase in value at a greater rate. Odd shapes translate to wasted space and, in the future, resistance from buyers. If you are competing with other sellers at

basic services
services required in order for land to be ready for improvements, normally required under zoning rules before improvements can be completed or, if partially lacking, subject to use restrictions until the services are provided. The six common basic services are water, sewer, paved roads, drainage system, garbage collection, and electricity.

---

*Jerry T. Ferguson and Robert H. Plattner, "Profits from Land Speculation May Be Disappointing," *Real Estate Review*, 1992, p. 73.

that time, the traditional square and rectangular parcels will move on the market more rapidly. For planning purposes, it is easier to work with standard-shaped lots.

2. *Buy in the right topography.* Avoid buying land containing sharp inclines and drops. The price of land reflects the topography, so be sure you know *why* some land is available at bargain prices. An ideal building lot is located on flat, dry land, close to sheltering tree lines or rises. Avoid flood zones and rough terrain, which make unsuitable building lots, and are not likely to realize a good rise in future market value.

3. *Think in terms of buffers.* What is located near the land? If you are planning to buy industrial land and residential areas are nearby, you certainly will be required to provide noise and sight buffers. If you think the land is residential, but it is close to tracks or highways, you will also need to consider the need for buffering. If you are speculating only and do not plan to develop the land yourself, you should still consider these potential problems; it is certain that a future buyer will ask the same questions.

4. *Always see the land yourself beforehand.* This is essential. Even if you are familiar with an area, you need to see and walk the land before you consider putting in an offer. Avoid buying land in another part of the country where you won't have an opportunity to see it in advance. What sounds like a great deal could end up being useless desert land, craggy rock impossible to develop, or a wetland in the middle of a swamp. Land swindles are not unusual, even today with improved regulation and communication. If you don't protect yourself, you could be taken.

Whenever you buy land directly from a developer, always insist on seeing the property report. This is a disclosure report explaining all of the plans and promises made by the developer. For example, if the developer is committed to providing the six basic services, you should know ahead of time whether the cost of those services is included in your price—and that answer should be in writing. If it is not included, you will be required to pay assessments later on.

Also be aware of the important difference between a planned improvement and a proposed improvement. Never buy under pressure, and never agree to any contract terms that are not put in writing. Hire an attorney who specializes in real estate law, or a land use consultant familiar with land transactions, to help you investigate and evaluate land before you buy.

Consult with your state's consumer affairs office regarding any inquiries or complaints involving land developers or land offers in your state. For transactions across state lines, write or call:

Office of Interstate Land Sales Registration
Department of Housing and Urban Development
451 Seventh Street, SW
Washington, DC 20410
Telephone: (202)708-0502

With diligent investigation and a good, clear vision of the future, you might want to invest some of your capital in raw land. As long as you know the risks and accept them and if you research carefully, raw land does offer diversification. And if you are convinced that you know where the next big shopping center or industrial part will be going, you could take steps to buy that acreage.

Chapter 14

Setting Your Investment Goals

As a real estate investor, you may want to develop a long-term financial plan. This will help you gain perspective on real estate and its place in your overall plan, long-term goals for yourself and your family, what kind of future you envision, and what steps you need to take now to ensure the level of financial freedom you want when you retire.

Real estate is not the kind of investment that you can enter and leave casually, at least not without a lot of costs involved. Getting into and out of real estate costs money. It is a large commitment and involves risks on several levels, some of which might not be immediately apparent. We have covered in detail the important cash flow risk, for example. Another risk is that, if a real estate investment fails because you cannot afford to keep up mortgage payments, your personal credit is affected. These are important financial considerations. Very few people will ever purchase a single-ticket item more expensive than real estate; it is an awesome responsibility. But like all big decisions, experience overcomes fear, doubt, and uncertainty. The process of buying, managing, and selling gains you knowledge. What you learn along the way—expected or not—is what is generally called experience. It has been said that "Experience is the name everyone gives to their mistakes."*

REAL ESTATE AND THE LONG TERM

Any financial adviser knows that planning is the key to security and financial success. In the financial services industry, a favorite adage is, "No one plans to fail; they simply fail to plan."

So, part of the planning process is to define success. What do you consider the signs of a successful life? Many people think that accumulating wealth and belongings is the central sign of success; others are happy to have their health and retirement security. You need to come up with your own definition, but here is one idea about success that deserves consideration: Success may be defined as achieving complete financial and personal freedom. That allows you to do as you please, while maintaining complete control over how you spend your time.

It is that simple. This outline really defines many of the things we really crave, but perhaps have not put into words. It is not wealth, but the freedom from the burden of worrying about money that really satisfies your financial goals. Some people have extraordinary wealth but remain enslaved by money; that is not success. Others are obsessed with earning money, but they tie their entire lives to that goal—and that is not success. It really is the ability to escape from the need that most people probably want, and would like to aim for in their financial plan.

While failing to plan is a fatal flaw, it is easy to develop a plan as long as it fits with your current income. Real estate has a place in many people's long-term plan because it addresses long-term needs. Many people invest with only the immediate future in mind, believing that a particular stock will rise in value, for example. Real estate takes longer to season in the market; but over many years,

*Oscar Wilde, *Lady Windermere's Fan*, Act III.

mortgages are paid down and cash flow improves, so that investors accumulate equity. It is unusual for people to think about the ramifications of committing themselves to 30 years of mortgage payments, and yet these commitments happen every day. Investors, as well as homeowners, may be so committed on several properties at the same time, and even figure out how to absorb negative cash flow for now, with longer-term goals in mind. Usually, those goals do not include the idea of "getting rich," but are more likely to be aimed at comfort and freedom in retirement.

The best course on which to plan is to recognize the overall principles of planning, and set goals for yourself: achievement of financial freedom, retirement security, and so forth. In addition, identify the steps you can take today to meet known needs in the future, such as saving for a child's college education or insuring your life and health. Apply this procedure to all types of investing, not just real estate. Learn to look at the total picture. A good example is the way many people shop for a mortgage. They tend to concentrate on the interest rate, ignoring comparisons between fixed and variable-rate loans, the origination fees, reputation of the lender, length of time the lender has been in the community, call features in the loan, and other such details. While selecting properties, develop the habit of asking important questions, such as:

✔ How will this community change in the next 10 years? 20 years? 30 years?

✔ What kind of growth is most likely, and how will it affect property values?

✔ Is the bargain price of a property a true bargain, or does it reflect poor equity potential in the future due to the property, the neighborhood, or other factors?

To develop real vision as an investor, ask these tough questions. More than anything else, a good investor is a realist, a person able to look beyond the obvious, confront the truth, and analyze information before making an important decision.

Historically, real estate has been a profitable investment for those who plan well. It works not only for long-term planning, but also provides immediate tax benefits. So if you invest in real estate and decide later to sell, you still have intermediate benefits as well as the potential for capital gains. Financial advisers suggest that the plan should be dictated by your personal goals. If that is true, how do you evaluate real estate, and how do you determine whether it fits with your plan? Do you want future appreciation, immediate income, tax benefits, or all of the above? Planning is not so much a question of whether a particular strategy is beneficial, but rather a process of defining priorities. Real estate may or may not be suitable, depending on how you prioritize and on your income and career status today.

Financial advisers seldom recommend that their clients select real estate. There is a good reason for this: If you decide to invest all of your money in real estate, that hurts the financial adviser in two distinct ways. First, real estate yields no commission to the planner who is also a registered representative authorized by the National Association of Securities Dealers (NASD) to sell securities, so the planner loses income today and in the future, since all of your equity will be tied up in real estate. Second, the planner probably will lose you as a client, because real estate is a long-term investment. Even those planners who charge a consultation fee rather than a commission depend on repeat business from their clients. But once you decide to put your money in real estate, you will be more likely to need advice from a real estate agent, an appraiser, an attorney, and most of all, a loan officer—but not from a financial planner. The professional planner emphasizes stocks or mutual funds as well as other products set up to yield commissions, at the very least, and to require ongoing consultation.

In reality, identifying your personal financial goals is not quite as simple as many commission-based salespeople would have you believe. The question of whether real estate belongs in your plans is a matter of individual choice. Unfortunately, many people never get to the point of determining that, because their planner is pushing for a choice between one of three or four mutual funds. To evaluate real estate and other investments as part of your plan, identify the right financial planning questions you should be asking youself. These include:

1. Are you willing and able to go into debt for a long period of time, to build equity through real estate?

2. Are you willing and able to deal with tenants?

3. Are you confident that real estate prices will rise so that you will be able to sell or refinance in the future?

4. At what age do you plan to retire? How many years remain until your target date? And how does real estate investing fit with this goal?

5. Do you need tax shelter?

6. Do you have capital to invest?

7. Can you afford some periods of negative cash flow?

8. Are you bankable?

9. Do you have a strong desire to directly control your investments?

10. Are you willing to mix your capital and your labor?

The course that financial planning has to take, based on setting goals and then determining priorities to meet them, might point to real estate as part of what you need to include as an investment. It is necessary for you to first become aware of the attributes of real estate—such as the various risks as well as the nature of dealing directly with tenants and having the commitment to a long-term mortgage—before you can determine whether real estate is a good fit. For example, you might like everything about real estate except having to deal with tenants. Among your possible solutions, you might:

✔ Hire a property manager.

✔ Invest in REITs or mortgage pools.

✔ Invest in the fixer-upper market, using each investment as your primary residence.

✔ Accept higher risks through other investments not requiring direct involvement, as a trade-off.

REAL ESTATE AND RETIREMENT PLANNING

Real estate investors are often the very same people who think ahead and plan for the long term, and who recognize the importance of planning for their retirement. Such people also know they cannot simply depend on Social Security for their retirement income. It simply isn't enough and by retirement age, who knows how that program will have changed?

Unless you have an exceptionally generous retirement program where you work, you will need to plan for the long term. You will be responsible for your financial freedom (most people call it financial security) in your retirement years. It might turn out that real estate is one of the best ways to plan, for five reasons:

1. *Tax benefits encourage equity growth.* The tax code encourages investors to use real estate to encourage equity growth. The like-kind exchange rule helps investors to keep their capital invested and to prefer cash flow over capital gains. None of your equity has to be relinquished in the form of taxes. Your rents are further sheltered by depreciation. In comparison with other retirement plans, such as individual retirement accounts (IRAs) and pensions, where income is taxed as it is withdrawn, real estate is much more flexible, allowing you to borrow based on invested equity and enabling you to manage your capital without the rules of other plans restricting access.

2. *You can time your debts.* In real estate, you have a lot of control over the timing of mortgage debt. You can pay off a mortgage in coordination with a planned retirement date, and the longer you have to plan, the easier it is. With mortgage acceleration, you can calculate so far ahead that you can have your debts repaid in the exact year you want to retire. And you don't have to refinance. Simply calculate the payment you have to make each month to prepay your mortgage by the planned date.

3. *Real estate values have outpaced inflation.* With the exception of a few economic downturns, real estate outpaces inflation most of the time. On average, real estate is certainly ahead of the cost of living. The consistency of the long-term record is reassuring. The historical rise in prices, when compared to other popular ways to invest such as the stock market, has been predictable and stable. Inflation is a force that erodes an investment portfolio's value, often producing losses in real spending power above and beyond after-tax profits. Real estate, with its combined solid market performance and annual tax benefits, overcomes this chronic problem faced by many investors.

4. *Real estate is a safe investment.* Buying real estate is one of the safest ways to use and protect your capital. Market and investment risks are slight compared to other long-term investments. Cash flow risks can be mitigated with larger down payments, or through seeking properties that produce positive cash flow. And the higher your tax rate, the better your tax benefit, meaning that after-tax cash flow is affected directly. Real estate is also safe because it can be insured. Homeowner's insurance is not only required; it is one of the ways that your investment is protected from risk.

5. *Real estate can be used for retirement housing.* Your real estate investment can be maintained over the years with tenants paying your mortgage while you benefit from the annual tax advantages; and then, on retirement, with your mortgage paid off, the same property can be converted to a primary residence. Thus, you can live mortgage-free in your retirement.

You will probably not find investments offering high safety and low risk that compare with all of the advantages of real estate. This point—valid comparisons of safety and risk—often is overlooked by investors, and almost always ignored by financial planners. Whenever you hear the advice to forget about accelerating your mortgage and instead put the money in to some higher-yielding investment, always make sure the comparison is a fair one that includes relative risk levels. Make valid comparisons before taking any advice.

DEVELOPING INVESTOR VISION

Whether you decide to invest in real estate or place your money elsewhere, you need to develop a vision of your own future, set a sensible course, and take action according to what that course requires. Be aware, in the selection of investment products, of the double problem everyone faces: inflation and taxes.

A conservative investment may be worse than no investment at all, if you are losing on a net basis. That is to say, you are not doing well if the combined effect of taxes and inflation leaves you will less than you started with. To find out if you are suffering from this problem, first reduce your profits by the amount paid in the form of taxes. Next, reduce the entire account's value by the percentage of inflation reported for the past year. If the outcome is negative, you are losing money. Even in periods of so-called low to moderate inflation, many people investing their savings in bank certificates of deposit are barely keeping pace with inflation. And since their profits are taxed, they may be losing money as well as spending power. This is not the right way to save for retirement.

In comparison, investments like real estate provide a unique form of protection against both inflation and taxes. The historical growth in real estate values has outpaced inflation consistently, a benefit you don't get by leaving money in taxable accounts. And with the ability to defer taxes, you can avoid the annual effects of tax consequences. On the contrary, investment real estate provides you with tax breaks instead of liabilities.

To develop long-term vision, you will have to accept some level of risk, such as illiquidity and perhaps some negative cash flow. You might have to put up with tenants, at least for a few years until you can afford to hire a property management company. You might even discover that tenant relationships are not that bad, and that you won't have to spend as much time or energy as you thought.

The risks involved with real estate might become more acceptable when compared with alternatives and when thought of in the long term. Remember, the relationship between risk and reward is direct, even predictable. You need to make these decisions: How much reward (profit) do you want and need from your investments? And how much risk (inconvenience, illiquidity, negative cash flow, debt) can you afford to achieve your personal goals? Your acceptable zone is found by comparing these two sides.

These are the important issues for real estate investors. The energy and effort, of course, go into visiting with real estate agents, negotiating prices, and watching the market; talking to prospective tenants and to lenders; collect rent from reluctant tenants; putting up with the many roles you are forced to assume as landlord; and deciding when or if to refinance or sell. These are management problems. Ultimately, your most important decision is determining your own long-term policies. Is real estate suitable for you? If not now, when will it be? What form of investing will work best?

You will discover as a real estate investor that the day-to-day management decisions are worth tolerating as long as your long-term plan still makes sense, and as long as real estate provides you with success in meeting your goals. And as financial advisers like to tell their clients, planning is critical if you want to reach your investment goals. The greatest mistake you can make is failing to develop any plan whatsoever; the process and effort of making your plan is your first step toward personal financial freedom.

Appendix

This Appendix contains two texts. First is Section 1031 of the Internal Revenue Code; second is Section 312 from the Taxpayer Relief Act of 1997. Remember, all tax laws are subject to further updates by Congress.

INTERNAL REVENUE CODE, SECTION 1031: EXCHANGE OF PROPERTY HELD FOR PRODUCTIVE USE OF INVESTMENT

[Sec. 1031(a)]

(a) Nonrecognition of gain or loss from exchanges solely in kind.

(1) In general.—No gain or loss shall be recognized on the exchange of property held for productive use in a trade or business or for investment if such property is exchanged solely for property of like kind which is to be held for productive use in a trade or business, or for investment.

(2) Exception.—This subsection shall not apply to any exchange of:

(A) stocks in trade or other property held primarily for sale,

(B) stocks, bonds, or notes,

(C) other securities or evidences of indebtedness or interest,

(D) interests in a partnership,

(E) certificates of trust or beneficial interests, or

(F) choses in action.

For purposes of this section, an interest in a partnership which had in effect a valid election under section 761(k) to be excluded from the application of all subchapter K shall be treated as an interest in each of the assets of such partnership and not as an interest in a partnership.

(3) Requirement that property be identified and that exchange be completed not more than 180 days after transfer of exchanged property.—For purposes of this subsection, any property received by the taxpayer shall be treated as property which is not like-kind property if:

(A) such property is not identified as property to be received in the exchange on or before the day which is 45 days after the date on which the taxpayer transfers the property relinquished in the exchange, or

(B) such property is received after the earlier of:

(i) the day which is 180 days after the date on which the taxpayer transfers the property relinquished in the exchange, or

(ii) the due date (determined with regard to extension) for the transferor's return of the tax imposed by this chapter for the taxable year in which the transfer of the relinquished property occurs.

[Sec. 1031(b)]
(b) Gain from exchanges not solely in kind.—If an exchange would be within the provisions of subsection (a), of section 1035(a), of section 1036(a), or of section 1037(a), if it were not for the fact that the property received in exchange consists not only of property permitted by such provisions to be received without the recognition of gain, but also of other property or money, then the gain, if any, to the recipient shall be recognized, but in an amount not in excess of the sum of such money and the fair market value of such other property.

[Sec. 1031(c)]
(c) Losses from exchanges not solely in kind.—If an exchange would be within the provisions of subsection (a), of section 1035(a), of section 1036(a), or of section 1037(a), if it were not for the fact that the property received in exchange consists not only of property permitted by such provisions to be received without the recognition

of gain or loss, but also of other property or money, then no loss from the exchange shall be recognized.

[Sec. 1031(d)]
(d) Basis.—If property was acquired on an exchange described in this section, section 1035(a), section 1036(a), or section 1037(a), then the basis shall be the same as that of the property exchanged, decreased in the amount of any money received by the taxpayer and increased in the amount of gain or decreased in the amount of loss to the taxpayer that was recognized on such exchange. If the property so acquired consisted in part of the type of property permitted by this section, section 1035(a), section 1036(a), or section 1037(a), to be received without the recognition of gain or loss, and in part of other property, the basis provided in this subsection shall be allocated between the properties (other than money) received, and for the purpose of the allocation there shall be assigned to such other property an amount equivalent to its fair market value at the date of the exchange. For purposes of this section, section 1035(a), and section 1036(a), where as part of the consideration to the taxpayer another party to the exchange assumed a liability of the taxpayer or acquired from the taxpayer property subject to a liability, such assumption or acquisition (in the amount of the liability) shall be considered as money received by the taxpayer on the exchange.

[Sec. 1031(e)]
(e) Exchanges of livestock of different sexes.—For purposes of this section, livestock of different sexes are not property of a like kind.

[Sec. 1031(f)]
(f) Special rules for exchanges between related persons.—
    (1) In general.—If—
        (A) a taxpayer exchanges property with a related person,
        (B) there is nonrecognition of gain or loss by the taxpayer under this section with respect to the exchange of such property (determined without regard to this subsection), and

(C) before the date 2 years after the date of the last transfer which was part of such exchange—

    (i) the related person disposes of such property, or

    (ii) the taxpayer disposes of property received in the exchange rom the related person which was of like kind of the property transferred by the taxpayer,

there shall be no nonrecognition of gain or loss under this section to the taxpayer with respect to such exchange; except that any gain or loss recognized by the taxpayer by reason of this subsection shall be taken into account as of the date on which the disposition referred to in subparagraph (C) occurs.

(2) Certain dispositions not taken into account.—For purposes of paragraph (1)(C), there shall not be taken into account any disposition:

(A) after the earlier of the death of the taxpayer or the death of the related person,

(B) in a compulsory or involuntary conversion (within the meaning of section 1033) if the exchange occurred before the threat or imminence of such conversion, or

(C) with respect to which it is established to the satisfaction of the Secretary that neither the exchange nor such disposition had as one of its principal purposes the avoidance of Federal income tax.

(3) Related person.—For purposes of this subsection, the term "related person" means any person bearing a relationship to the taxpayer as described in section 267(b) or 707(b)(1).

(4) Treatment of certain transactions.—This section shall not apply to any exchange which is part of a transaction (or series of transactions) structured to avoid the purposes of this subsection.

[Sec. 1031(g)]

(g) Special rules where substantial diminution of risk:

(1) In general.—If paragraph (2) applies to any property for any period, the running of the period set

forth in subsection (f)(1)(C) with respect to such property shall be suspended during such period.

(2) Property to which subsection applies.—This paragraph shall apply to any property for the period during which the holder's risk of loss with respect to the property is substantially diminished by:

(A) the holding of a put with respect to such property,

(B) the holding by another person of a right to acquire such property, or

(C) a short sale or any other transaction.

[Sec. 1031(h)]
(h) Special rules for foreign real property.—For purposes of this section:

(1) Real property.—Real property located in the United States and real property located outside the United States are not property of a like kind.

(2) Personal property.*

TAXPAYER RELIEF ACT OF 1997, SECTION 312: EXEMPTION FROM TAX FOR GAIN ON SALE OF PRINCIPAL RESIDENCE

(a) In General.—Section 121 (relating to one-time exclusion of gain from sale of principal residence by individual who has attained age 55) is amended to read as follows:

"SEC. 121. EXCLUSION OF GAIN FROM SALE OF PRINCIPAL RESIDENCE.
"(a) Exclusion.—Gross income shall not include gain from the sale or exchange of property if, during the 5-year period ending on the date of the sale or exchange, such property has been owned and used by the taxpayer as the taxpayer's principal residence for periods aggregating 2 years or more.

*Details of this subsection are excluded as they refer to like-kind exchanges other than real estate.

"(b) Limitations.—

"(1) In general.—The amount of gain excluded from gross income under subsection (a) with respect to any sale or exchange shall not exceed $250,000.

"(2) $500,000 limitation for certain joint returns.— Paragraph (1) shall be applied by substituting '$500,000' for '$250,000' if—

"(A) a husband and wife make a joint return for the taxable year of the sale or exchange of the property,

"(B) either spouse meets the ownership requirements of subsection (a) with respect to such property,

"(C) both spouses meet the use requirements of subsection (a) with respect to such property, and

"(D) neither spouse is ineligible for the benefits of subsection (a) with respect to such property by reason of paragraph (3).

"(3) Application to only 1 sale or exchange every 2 years.—

"(A) In general—Subsection (a) shall not apply to any sale or exchange by the taxpayer if, during the 2-year period ending on the date of such sale or exchange, there was any other sale or exchange by the taxpayer to which subsection (a) applied.

"(B) Pre-May 7, 1997, sales not taken into account.—Subparagraph (A) shall be applied without regard to any sale or exchange before May 7, 1997.

"(c) Exclusion for Taxpayers Failing to Meet Certain Requirements.—

"(1) In general.—In the case of a sale or exchange to which this subsection applies, the ownership and use requirements of subsection (a) shall not apply and subsection (b)(3) shall not apply; but the amount of gain excluded from gross income under subsection (a) with respect to such sale or exchange shall not exceed—

"(A) the amount which bears the same ratio to the amount which would be so excluded under this section if such requirements had been met, as

"(B) the shorter of—

"(i) the aggregate periods, during the 5-year period ending on the date of such sale or exchange, such property has been owned and used by the taxpayer as the taxpayer's principal residence, or

"(ii) the period after the date of the most recent prior sale or exchange by the taxpayer to which subsection (a) applied and before the date of such sale or exchange, bears to 2 years.

"(2) Sales and exchanges to which subsection applies.—This subsection shall apply to any sale or exchange if—

(A) subsection (a) would not (but for this subsection) apply to such sale or exchange by reason of—

"(i) a failure to meet the ownership and use requirements of subsection (a), or

"(ii) subsection (b)(3), and

"(B) such sale or exchange is by reason of a change in place of employment, health, or, to the extent provided in regulations, unforeseen circumstances.

"(d) Special Rules.—

"(1) Joint returns.—If a husband and wife make a joint return for the taxable year of the sale or exchange of the property, subsections (a) and (c) shall apply if either spouse meets the ownership and use requirements of subsection (a) with respect to such property.

"(2) Property of deceased spouse.—For purposes of this section, in the case of an unmarried individual whose spouse is deceased on the date of the sale or exchange of property, the period such unmarried individual owned and used such property shall include the period such deceased spouse owned and used such property before death.

"(3) Property owned by spouse or former spouse— For purposes of this section—

"(A) Property transferred to individual from spouse or former spouse.—In the case of an individual holding property transferred to such individual in a transaction described in section 1041(a), the period such individual owns such property shall include the period the transferor owned the property.

"(B) Property used by former spouse pursuant to divorce decree, etc.—Solely for purposes of this section, an individual shall be treated as using property as such individual's principal residence during any period of ownership while such individual's spouse or former spouse is granted use of the property under a divorce or separation instrument (as defined in section 71(b)(2)).

"(4) Tenant-stockholder in cooperative housing corporation.—For purposes of this section, if the taxpayer holds stock as a tenant-stockholder (as defined in section 216) in a cooperative housing corporation (as defined in such section), then—

"(A) the holding requirements of subsection (a) shall be applied to the holding of such stock, and

"(B) the use requirements of subsection (a) shall be applied to the house or apartment which the taxpayer was entitled to occupy as such stockholder.

"(5) Involuntary conversions.—

"(A) In general.—For purposes of this section, the destruction, theft, seizure, requisition, or condemnation of property shall be treated as the sale of such property.

"(B) Application of section 1033.—In applying section 1033 (relating to involuntary conversions), the amount realized from the sale or exchange of property shall be treated as being the amount determined without regard to this section, reduced by the amount of gain not included in gross income pursuant to this section.

"(C) Property acquired after involuntary conversion.—If the basis of the property sold or exchanged is determined (in whole or in part) under section 1033(b) (relating to basis of property acquired through involuntary conversion), then the holding and use by the taxpayer of the converted property shall be treated as holding and use by the taxpayer of the property sold or exchanged.

"(6) Recognition of gain attributable to depreciation.—Subsection (a) shall not apply to so much of the gain from the sale of any property as does not exceed the portion of the depreciation adjustments (as defined in section 1250(b)(3)) attributable to periods after May 6, 1997, in respect of such property.

"(7) Determination of use during periods of out-of-residence care.—In the case of a taxpayer who—

"(A) becomes physically or mentally incapable of self-care, and

"(B) owns property and uses such property as the taxpayer's principal residence during the 5-year period described in subsection (a) for periods aggregating at least 1 year,

then the taxpayer shall be treated as using such property as the taxpayer's principal residence during any time during such 5-year period in which the taxpayer owns the property and resides in any facility (including a nursing home) licensed by a State or political subdivision to care for an individual in the taxpayer's condition.

"(8) Sales of remainder interests.—For purposes of this section—

"(A) In general.—At the election of the taxpayer, this section shall not fail to apply to the sale or exchange of an interest in a principal residence by reason of such interest being a remainder interest in such residence, but this section shall not apply to any other interest in such residence which is sold or exchanged separately.

"(B) Exception for sales to related parties.—Subparagraph (A) shall not apply to any sale to, or exchange with, any person who bears a relationship to the taxpayer which is described in section 267(b) or 707(b).

"(e) Denial of Exclusion for Expatriates.—This section shall not apply to any sale or exchange by an individual if the treatment provided by section 877(a)(1) applies to such individual.

"(f) Election to Have Section Not Apply.—This section shall not apply to any sale or exchange with respect to which the taxpayer elects not to have this section apply.

"(g) Residences Acquired in Rollovers Under Section 1034.—For purposes of this section, in the case of property the acquisition of which by the taxpayer resulted under section 1034 (as in effect on the day before the date of the enactment of this section) in the non-recognition of any part of the gain realized on the sale or exchange of another residence, in determining the period for which the taxpayer has owned and used such property as the taxpayer's principal residence, there shall be included the aggregate periods for which such other residence (and each prior residence taken into account under section 1223(7) in determining the holding period of such property) had been so owned and used.".

(b) Repeal of Non-recognition of Gain on Rollover of Principal Residence.—Section 1034 (relating to rollover of gain on sale of principal residence) is hereby repealed.

(c) Exception from Reporting.—Subsection (e) of section 6045 (relating to return required in the case of real estate transactions) is amended by adding at the end the following new paragraph:

"(5) Exception for sales or exchanges of certain principal residences.—

"(A) In general—Paragraph (1) shall not apply to any sale or exchange of a residence for $250,000 or less if the person referred to in paragraph (2) receives written assurance in a form acceptable to the Secretary from the seller that—

"(i) such residence is the principal residence (within the meaning of section 121) of the seller,

"(ii) if the Secretary requires the inclusion on the return under subsection (a) of information as to whether there is federally subsidized mortgage financing assistance with respect to the mortgage on residences, that there is no such assistance with respect to the mortgage on such residence, and

"(iii) the full amount of the gain on such sale or exchange is excludable from gross income under section 121.

If such assurance includes an assurance that the seller is married, the preceding sentence shall be applied by substituting '$500,000' for '$250,000'.

The Secretary may by regulation increase the dollar amounts under this subparagraph if the Secretary determines that such an increase will not materially reduce revenues to the Treasury.

"(B) Seller.—For purposes of this paragraph, the term 'seller' includes the person relinquishing the residence in an exchange."

(d) Conforming Amendments.—

(1) The following provisions of the Internal Revenue Code of 1986 are each amended by striking "section 1034" and inserting "section 121": sections 25(e)(7), 56(e)(1)(A), 56(e)(3)(B)(i), 143(i)(1)(C)(i)(I), 163(h)(4)(A)(i)(I), 280A(d)(4)(A), 464(f)(3)(B)(i), 1033(h)(4), 1274(c)(3)(B), 6334(a)(13), and 7872(f)(11)(A).

(2) Paragraph (4) of section 32(c) is amended by striking "(as defined in section 1034(h)(3))" and by adding at the end the following new sentence: "For purposes of the preceding sentence, the term 'extended active duty' means any period of active duty pursuant to a call or order to such duty for a period in excess of 90 days or for an indefinite period.".

(3) Subparagraph (A) of 143(m)(6) is amended by inserting "(as in effect on the day before the date of the enactment of the Taxpayer Relief Act of 1997)" after "1034(e)".

(4) Subsection (e) of section 216 is amended by striking "such exchange qualifies for non-recognition of gain under section 1034(f)" and inserting "such dwelling unit is used as his principal residence (within the meaning of section 121)".

(5) Section 512(a)(3)(D) is amended by inserting "(as in effect on the day before the date of the enactment of the Taxpayer Relief Act of 1997)" after "1034".

(6) Paragraph (7) of section 1016(a) is amended by inserting "(as in effect on the day before the date of the enactment of the Taxpayer Relief Act of 1997)" after "1034" and by inserting "(as so in effect)" after "1034(e)".

(7) Paragraph (3) of section 1033(k) is amended to read as follows:

"(3) For exclusion from gross income of gain from

involuntary conversion of principal residence, see section 121.".

(8) Subsection (e) of section 1038 is amended to read as follows:

"(e) Principal Residences.—If—

"(1) subsection (a) applies to a reacquisition of real property with respect to the sale of which gain was not recognized under section 121 (relating to gain on sale of principal residence); and

"(2) within 1 year after the date of the reacquisition of such property by the seller, such property is resold by him, then, under regulations prescribed by the Secretary, subsections (b), (c), and (d) of this section shall not apply to the reacquisition of such property and, for purposes of applying section 121, the resale of such property shall be treated as a part of the transaction constituting the original sale of such property.".

(9) Paragraph (7) of section 1223 is amended by inserting "(as in effect on the day before the date of the enactment of the Taxpayer Relief Act of 1997)" after "1034".

(10)(A) Subsection (d) of section 1250 is amended by striking paragraph (7) and by re-designating paragraphs (9) and (10) as paragraphs (7) and (8), respectively.

(B) Subsection (e) of section 1250 is amended by striking paragraph (3).

(11) Subsection (c) of section 6012 is amended by striking "(relating to one-time exclusion of gain from sale of principal residence by individual who has attained age 55)" and inserting "(relating to gain from sale of principal residence)".

(12) Paragraph (2) of section 6212(c) is amended by striking subparagraph (C) and by re-designating the succeeding subparagraphs accordingly.

(13) Section 6504 is amended by striking paragraph (4) and by re-designating the succeeding paragraphs accordingly.

(14) The item relating to section 121 in the table of sections for part III of subchapter B of chapter 1 is amended to read as follows:

"Sec. 121. Exclusion of gain from sale of principal residence.".

(15) The table of sections for part III of subchapter O of chapter 1 is amended by striking the item relating to section 1034.

(d) Effective Date.—

(1) In general.—The amendments made by this section shall apply to sales and exchanges after May 6, 1997.

(2) Sales before date of enactment.—At the election of the taxpayer, the amendments made by this section shall not apply to any sale or exchange before the date of the enactment of this Act.

(3) Certain sales within 2 years after date of enactment.—Section 121 of the Internal Revenue Code of 1986 (as amended by this section) shall be applied without regard to subsection (c)(2)(B) thereof in the case of any sale or exchange of property during the 2-year period beginning on the date of the enactment of this Act if the taxpayer held such property on the date of the enactment of this Act and fails to meet the ownership and use requirements of subsection (a) thereof with respect to such property.

(4) Binding contracts.—At the election of the taxpayer, the amendments made by this section shall not apply to a sale or exchange after the date of the enactment of this Act, if—

(A) such sale or exchange is pursuant to a contract which was binding on such date, or

(B) without regard to such amendments, gain would not be recognized under section 1034 of the Internal Revenue Code of 1986 (as in effect on the day before the date of the enactment of this Act) on such sale or exchange by reason of a new residence acquired on or before such date or with respect to the acquisition of which by the taxpayer a binding contract was in effect on such date.

This paragraph shall not apply to any sale or exchange by an individual if the treatment provided by section 877(a)(1) of the Internal Revenue Code of 1986 applies to such individual.

abusive tax shelter any investment program designed primarily to reduce tax liabilities rather than offering economic return to investors.

accelerated depreciation a form of depreciation allowing more deduction in the earlier years of the recovery period, with less depreciation claimed in the later years.

acceptance agreement to the terms presented in an offer. Offer and acceptance must exist before a contract can come into being.

accrual method a method for reporting income and expenses as earned or incurred. Income is reported in the year it is earned, regardless of whether you receive payment then. Expenses are deducted in the year incurred, even if paid in the following year.

active income under tax regulations, income from salaries, wages, and self-employment.

active participant an individual who directly makes management decisions (e.g., arranges for repairs and other services, collects and deposits rents, pays bills, and performs other necessary routines to maintain the investment).

adjustable-rate mortgage (ARM) a loan in which the future interest rate may change, with that change determined by an index of rates. The frequency and amount of change are limited by the mortgage contract.

adjusted basis for the purpose of computing capital gains or losses, the original purchase price plus closing costs paid at the time of purchase, plus the cost value of improvements done while the property was held, less all depreciation claimed.

adjusted gross income under federal tax rules, the total of wages and salaries, interest and dividends, net self-employment income, and capital gains, adjusted for contributions to retirement plans, moving expenses, alimony, self-employed health insurance premiums, and part of self-employment taxes paid. For most people, the amount on the bottom line of the first page of their federal form 1040.

adjusted sales price for the purpose of computing capital gains or losses, the sales price plus closing costs paid at the time of sale.

after-tax cash flow cash flow with the tax benefits and savings taken into account. This number might be substantially different from pretax cash flow, especially when depreciation reduces tax liabilities.

agency an area of law concerning one person's actions undertaken on behalf of another. Agents assume duties and responsibilities according to a contract, and perform under specific guidelines.

agent an individual representing the interests of another person (the principal) in contract law. In real estate, the agent is a sales associate acting in the role of either listing or selling agent. The principal is the seller of that property.

all-risk insurance (also called **HO-3**) a form of hazard insurance offering protection against all losses to the dwelling except any named exclusions; and for 18 named perils on personal property.

alternative income approach a variation on the income approach of appraisal, under which gross rent multipliers are calculated for comparable properties, and the average is used to calculate value on the subject property.

amortization the repayment terms of a loan, including the required principal and interest, based on the interest rate and the period of time allowed to pay down, or amortize, the loan to zero.

annualized return a rate of return expressed for the average 12-month period. When a return occurs over a period other than one full year, it does not reflect an accurate annual rate; the annualized return enables consistent comparisons between investments by expressing all returns as though earned in a single, average year.

appraisal the process of estimating current market value of a property, based on the value of comparable properties that sold recently, income generated by a property, the estimated cost required to replace a property of similar size and quality, or a combination of these methods.

assessed value the value of property for the purpose of calculating and collecting property taxes. That value is broken down between land and buildings, and can be used to calculate depreciation basis.

asset a property owned by the individual or business; something of value. Real estate, for example, is an asset. Its gross value is recorded on a balance sheet as an asset, and the balance of the mortgage owed is listed as a liability.

assumption a feature in a loan providing that the borrower can allow a future buyer to take over payments on the loan, as well as responsibility for repayment, without permission from the lender.

balance sheet a statement listing all assets, liabilities, and net worth of a business or individual. Assets (things you own) minus liabilities (amounts you owe to others) equals net worth, or equity. The balance sheet lists the dollar value in these three classifications as of a specified date.

balloon mortgage a mortgage containing a series of payments over a period of time (often three to five years), followed by a single "balloon" payment representing the entire outstanding balance of the loan.

bankable a term describing a person's ability to qualify for loans with conventional lenders. To be bankable, the ratio of debt to income has to be low enough to meet the lender's standards.

basic insurance (also called **HO-1**) a form of hazard insurance offering only minimal coverage. Only 11 named perils are covered.

basic services services required in order for land to be ready for improvements, normally required under zoning rules before improvements can be completed or, if partially lacking, subject to use restrictions until the services are provided. The six common basic services are water, sewer, paved roads, drainage system, garbage collection, and electricity.

basis the cost of the building on your property, plus improvements and fixtures, which can be depreciated but not claimed as deductions. In computing the profit upon sale of investment property, land is included in basis; but land cannot be depreciated.

blind pool a limited partnership formed with a general plan for the types of properties to purchase or develop, but without having any specific properties identified at the time the partnership is formed.

breakeven the rent required to cover all monthly payments and operating expenses, expressed as a percentage of maximum rent.

bridge loan a loan granted temporarily, pending the borrower's finding permanent financing. Bridge loans are used by investors who have a property for sale but want to close a new deal immediately, without having to wait for one transaction before closing the other. Also called "gap financing," the bridge loan may require a higher interest rate than the market rate, but provides flexibility to the borrower.

broad insurance (also called **HO-2**) a form of hazard insurance offering protection for 18 named perils.

broker the individual responsible for matching a buyer's offer to a seller's listing, usually working through agents employed as salespersons by the brokerage firm. The broker is responsible for all of the actions and statements of these agents.

building lot a parcel of land zoned and approved for improvements such as a house, commercial property, or other uses allowed by that zoning.

buy-down mortgage a mortgage in which an initial interest rate is reduced by prepayment. The rate is reduced according to the prepayment, which is also called "discount points."

buyer's market a condition in which there is a plentiful supply of properties on the market, and not enough available buyers to purchase the entire inventory; from the seller's perspective, a slow market.

call feature a clause in the mortgage contract giving the lender the right to demand full payment of the unpaid loan balance at some point in the future. Lenders may "call" a loan if market interest rates have risen far above a loan's fixed rate, or if the borrower is chronically late with monthly payments.

cap a limit on the amount of increase a lender may impose under the terms of an adjustable-rate mortgage. The annual cap specifies the maximum annual increase, and the lifetime cap specifies the overall increase the lender is allowed to pass along to the borrower.

capital expenditure money spent on improvements to rental property, including buildings and all permanent fixtures. These cannot be deducted as expenses, but are depreciated.

capital gain or loss a gain or loss resulting from holding investment property, which is subject to capital gains tax rather than tax on ordinary income. Capital gains and losses are reported on a special schedule as part of the federal income tax return.

capitalization setting up of capital expenditures as assets subject to depreciation. Capitalized assets are not deducted as expenses but are instead written off through depreciation over a period of years mandated by tax regulations.

cap rate a percentage rate of return, short for "capitalization rate." This is used both to estimate value and to determine whether rents are in line with market rents, based on the purchase price. Properties may be compared by applying a standard cap rate for the region to several different properties, as a test of acceptability of the profit level from a particular property.

carry a term describing a seller's holding a note for part of the debt owed by the buyer. The seller helps a buyer close the deal by providing part of the purchase price as a loan.

cash flow the amount of money received from rental income each month, minus the amount paid out in mortgage payments, the purchase of capital assets, and payment of operating expenses. Cash flow is not the same as profit, since it includes nondeductible payments.

cash method a method for reporting income and expenses at the time cash is exchanged. All income is reported in the year it is received, and all expenses are deducted in the year paid.

clear title a title held without disputes concerning ownership or liens against the property; all liens are agreed to, identified, and not in dispute.

commercial property nonresidential property, operated for business use. It requires adequate traffic and parking, delivery areas, and room for storage of inventory.

compound interest interest calculated on the remaining balance of debt; or the accumulation of interest based on both the principal and accrued interest.

comprehensive insurance (also called **HO-5**) a form of hazard insurance offering protection against all losses except named exclusions, on both dwellings and personal property.

condominium insurance (also called **HO-6**) a form of hazard insurance offering protection against losses to personal property and structural losses within the unit, but excluding losses to the outside of buildings and to common areas.

conformity the tendency for property in one area and with common zoning to be similar to other properties in the area and with the same zoning. Conforming homes, for example, tend to be similar in lot size, number of rooms, and other features. Nonconforming properties tend to be limited in their potential market value.

consideration the reward, benefit, or payment given by one person to another as part of the contract, with equal consideration being provided by the other side. A payment is consideration for property; turning over title to that property is consideration exchanged for the payment.

contingencies terms in a contract qualifying the agreement by stating that for the deal to go forward, one side or the other agrees to meet certain conditions. Typical contingencies include qualifying for financing and completion of inspections.

conventional financing lending obtained from traditional sources, such as banks, savings and loan associations, and mutual savings banks.

cost approach an appraisal method that establishes value based on what it would cost to acquire a similar or identical property, given values of land as well as replacement or reproduction value of improvements.

creative financing any variation on the standard fixed-rate or adjustable-rate loan, or alteration in the terms of the mortgage contract, designed to make a financing deal work.

dealer an individual who is in the business of buying and selling.

dealer property a property bought, held, and sold to a customer, as part of the owner's primary trade or business.

deferred gain a capital gain on investment property, put off until a future date. The property must be replaced within a time limit by another property costing as much as or more than the property that was sold.

deferred maintenance work required to properly maintain or upgrade a property, which has accumulated over time and has not been done. Examples include old, chipped paint; broken windows; leaking gutters; unrepaired pest damage; sagging foundations; outdated plumbing, electrical, or heating systems; and leaking roofs.

depreciation an annual expense representing part of a capital asset's basis. Depreciation is deducted as a noncash expense each year, and reduces the basis in the investment property as it is claimed as an expense.

discount rate the interest rate charged to banks when they borrow from other Federal Reserve banks.

diversification a strategy of spreading risk among different markets, regions, or types of property, with a potential for future price increase. This lowers the risk that a single change in the market will adversely affect all properties in the same manner.

due on sale clause a clause in a mortgage agreement stating that the entire outstanding balance of the mortgage loan is due and payable immediately upon sale of the property.

earned income income earned in a specific month or year, even though the actual payment might not be made until later.

earnest money deposit a deposit, made by check or promissory note, presented by the proposed buyer at the time an offer is made. If the buyer's offer is accepted and the contract is later breached, the earnest money deposit may be forfeited.

equity the portion of real estate you own. In the case of a property bought for $100,000 with a $58,000 mortgage owing, the equity is the difference, or $42,000.

equity buildup the process of reducing debt by accumulating equity in the property over a period of time. Without accelerating the payments, the rate of equity buildup with a long-term loan is very slow. The more extended the term, the more slowly equity builds up.

equity dividend rate a calculation comparing cash flow with the investment amount. The rate includes all investment in the property—original purchase level plus all capital expenditures.

equity line of credit a form of loan in which the lender provides the borrower a maximum line of credit secured by equity in real estate. The borrower can draw as much as necessary up to the maximum.

equity REIT a real estate investment trust that buys property directly, seeking current income and future appreciation.

equity return a percentage of return calculated by adding cash income to principal reduction and then dividing the result by the investment base (purchase price).

escrow the process of completing contractually required steps, such as obtaining financing, completing inspection work, paying and transferring funds, and recording changes in title, and of checking and clearing title to the property to ensure that all liens have been identified and are satisfied by closing.

first mortgage a mortgage that has first priority for payment in the event of default and foreclosure. When a borrower fails to make required payments on a mortgage, the lender forecloses. The first mortgage holder is paid first; other mortgage holders are paid from the remaining equity, if any.

fixed-rate mortgage (FRM) a loan in which the interest rate will not change during the contract period, as a matter of contract.

fixer-upper a property requiring repairs, either cosmetic or structural, in order for it to gain its full potential market value.

free and clear a term describing real estate owned without any outstanding debts. The owner is free of mortgages and other liens, and has clear title.

functional obsolescence a form of obsolescence arising from changes in systems and uses of the building, rendering that building impractical or out of date.

general ledger the document for recording monthly transactions and summarizing the breakdown between total expense and subsidiary records.

gross rent multiplier (GRM) a calculation used by appraisers to set value for income property. Sales prices of recently sold properties are divided by monthly rents. The result is the gross rent multiplier. An appraiser performs this calculation for several comparable properties, and then applies the average GRM to the rents received on the property being appraised. This produces an estimate of market value.

growth stocks stocks expected to increase in value over time.

half-year convention a rule often used in calculating depreciation of personal property, which assumes that on average, assets are purchased and placed into service halfway through the year. The first year's depreciation is allowed for only half the year, and a half-year's worth is left to take up at the end of the recovery period.

highest and best use the use of property for the most profitable, efficient, and appropriate purpose, given the zoning and other restrictions placed on the land. Property not being utilized at its highest and best use will have less value than other, comparable properties, based on this standard.

hybrid REIT a real estate investment trust that combines equity and debt, and modifies its position in the market according to changing market conditions. The hybrid REIT's investment goal is to combine market appreciation from equity investments with current income from debt positions.

illiquid asset any asset that cannot be converted to cash within a short period of time, such as real estate.

impounds charges added to interest and principal to cover property taxes and insurance, and possibly other costs. The lender collects an estimated amount necessary to make periodic payments, and then submits those payments on the borrower's behalf.

income approach an appraisal method establishing market value on the basis of current and potential income that can be generated from the property.

income statement a statement that summarizes the income, expenses, and profits for a period of time, often one full year, for a corporation or for an investment portfolio.

incurred expense expense that applies to a specific month or year, regardless of when payment is actually made.

industrial property property used for manufacturing, trucking, storage, warehousing, transportation, and other specialized uses. Industrially zoned areas tend to have noise and traffic levels and other hazards not compatible with residential land use nor with most types of commercial land use.

issuer (also called **sponsor**) the individuals (usually the same people who are the partnership's general partners) or company that makes shares available to investors.

lease option an arrangement in which someone leases a property and buys an option to purchase that property for a specified price on or before a specified date in the future.

legal description a description of property identifying location and boundaries as well as lot size, as recorded on plot maps.

level debt service periodic payments that remain the same every month. While the payment is level, it consists of principal and interest, divided according to the current outstanding loan balance. As the loan balance becomes lower, the portion of the level payment going to the principal gradually increases.

leverage the use of a limited amount of capital to purchase more than a single property, increasing potential gain as well as risk level.

liability the amount of debt owed by a company or individual as of a specified date. Liabilities are listed on the balance sheet to offset assets. For example, current mortgage balances are liabilities against real estate assets.

like-kind exchange (also called a 1031 exchange, referencing the Internal Revenue Code section) an exchange of one investment property for another of the same type, with taxes deferred. In order to qualify, investment real estate has to be replaced with other investment real estate. As long as the new property is bought within 180 days of the sale and costs as much as or more than the old property, all of the gain is deferred. If the new property does not cost as much, the shortfall is taxed in the year of the sale.

limited partner an investor who does not manage property directly, but owns units in a limited partnership. Such agreements provide that general partners perform all management duties, and that limited partners have no voice in property decisions. Effectively, limited partners own a portion of the partnership, which, in turn, buys and manages property. Limited partners' liability is limited to only the dollar amount of their actual investment.

limited partnership an investment program in which general partners manage property and accept unlimited liability, and in which limited partners do not participate in management decisions, and have limited liability.

liquidity the condition of an investment asset in terms of how quickly it can be converted into cash.

listing agent the agent who enters into a listing contract with a seller, agreeing to find a buyer and to represent that seller's interests in negotiating a contract. The listing agent is always entitled to a commission, even when a different agent finds a buyer.

loan-to-value ratio a ratio used by lenders to limit the amount they will loan on a property. The appraised value is multiplied by the maximum percentage the lender will allow, resulting in the maximum possible loan amount the lender will approve. The ratio is expressed by dividing the proposed loan amount by the appraised value, with the answer representing a percentage.

locational obsolescence a form of obsolescence caused by changes in zoning and uses of buildings, including property designed for purposes for which a market no longer exists.

market comparison approach an appraisal method based on values of similar homes in the same neighborhood or in similar neighborhoods that have sold in the recent past.

market economy a market in which prices are not set, but vary with purely economic factors, specifically supply and demand.

market value the current value of property according to the price it would command on the market, which reflects current supply and demand levels and whether the property is being utilized at its highest and best use.

meeting of minds an agreement to terms, when both sides in the contract know what the agreement states. Without a meeting of minds there is no contract. In a real estate contract, one side agrees to sell a property and the other agrees to purchase that property. However, if they have not agreed on the price, there is not a meeting of minds.

mid-month convention a rule for calculating depreciation for buildings and improvements, which assumes that on average, assets are purchased and put into service halfway through the month in which they are purchased. The first year's depreciation is calculated from the mid-month forward, with the excess assigned to the final year of the depreciation term.

mixed use zoning that allows residential as well as other uses (commercial, industrial, recreational) in the same area; or an area that lacks zoning altogether.

money supply the amount of currency in circulation at any given time, plus demand deposits (savings accounts immediately available to depositors) in banks and other financial institutions.

mortgage acceleration a technique for reducing interest costs. By paying additional amounts to principal, the outstanding balance is reduced, so interest is reduced as well, having the effect of lowering the interest cost and speeding up the repayment term.

mortgage pool an organized program consisting of the pooled capital of many investors, managed by a small group of real estate debt experts, that invests the pooled funds in mortgages, all secured by real estate.

mortgage REIT a real estate investment trust that acts as lender in real estate transactions, loaning capital to organizations to purchase real estate, with loans secured by the real estate itself. This REIT is designed to generate current income in the form of interest.

motivated seller a seller who is very anxious to sell, meaning that seller is more willing than a firm seller to negotiate on the price and other terms.

negative cash flow the condition in which payments are greater than receipts.

net worth equity; capital; the net value of a business or investment portfolio. Net worth is the difference between assets (the value of things you own) minus liabilities (amounts you owe to others).

occupancy rate (1) the opposite of vacancy rate: the number of units occupied, divided by total units; (2) in multiple-unit buildings, the total rentable area divided by the total area of the building.

offer the proposed terms of a contract in real estate. The offer is put forward and must be accepted by the other side before a contract can exist.

older home insurance (also called **HO-8**) a form of hazard insurance designed to replace losses to serviceable condition, but not to duplicate quality of workmanship or materials.

ordinary income income earned from salaries and wages, interest or dividends, self-employment, partnerships or trusts, rentals, and other sources not subject to capital gains tax.

overimprovement condition of property that has been improved beyond the scope of other properties in the same area, so that the property is nonconforming.

passive income under tax regulations, any income from activities not under the individual's direct control.

path of progress the direction of growth and development in the near future, in which currently raw land will increase in value; the place to buy raw land.

performance an action required as part of the contract. If one side fails to perform, the contract is breached. Examples of performance include paying a down payment, obtaining financing by a deadline, performing repair work, or transferring title.

physical obsolescence a form of obsolescence resulting from physical condition or features, such as investment property that cannot be fully utilized at a profit due to expensive internal systems resulting in high utility costs or recurring high maintenance, and a decline in potential rental value that results from those conditions.

point one percent of the loan amount; an additional charge in the form of advance interest payment, added on as a fee assessed for getting the loan. Points are also called "loan fees."

portfolio an investment term describing all of the holdings owned by one investor. In real estate, the portfolio refers to all of the properties owned or controlled, plus other investments. It may include equity assets (ownership of property) as well as debt investments (loans made to others, which earn interest).

portfolio income under tax regulations, income from investments including interest, dividends, and capital gains.

portfolio loan a loan kept on the lender's books and not sold on the secondary market, or kept for a specified period of time before being sold; lenders tend to charge higher fees and interest rates for portfolio loans.

positive cash flow a situation in which cash receipts are greater than cash payments.

prequalification the process of review by a lender of the income, assets, and credit of a prospective borrower. The purpose is to determine, first, whether the borrower is qualified to borrow and, second, the maximum amount the lender will be able to approve.

primary residence the property in which you live, defined under tax rules for the purpose of excluding profits upon sale, as the house you lived in for at least two of the past five years.

program a limited partnership or other organization formed to invest capital as a single entity from the pooled investment funds of many individuals.

proration a division of liabilities at the time of closing between buyer and seller, usually based on the number of days before and after closing date over which the liability applies. Proration is used for interest, taxes, assessments, and utilities, as well as rental income if the property is rented out. The seller is responsible for prorations up to and including the date of closing; the buyer is responsible for the portion of the expense applied to the period after closing.

prospectus (also called **offering document**) a disclosure report published by the sponsors of a limited partnership, for potential investors. All important economic, tax, financial, and management policies and conditions are to be explained fully in the prospectus, and investors should read the prospectus before buying.

raw land a parcel of land or acreage not zoned for any specific purpose, or zoned but lacking in basic services and, thus, not yet buildable.

real estate land and all permanent improvements on it, including buildings.

real estate cycle the trends in real estate values, affected by ever-changing levels of supply and demand. The cycle describes changes in construction activity, available supply of real estate for sale, credit available for financing, interest rates, population and job demographics, and attitudes among buyers and sellers at any given point.

real estate investment trust (REIT) a trust formed as a pool of investment capital from many investors, for the purpose of investing in real estate. Profits or losses are passed on to investors each year, and shares can be traded on the open market through stockbrokers.

real property real estate plus the rights attached to it, such as leases, easements, and estates.

Realtor a trademark name of the National Association of Realtors (NAR). Members using this title agree to conduct themselves according to a Realtors' Code of Ethics, and are subject to the rules of the association.

reconveyances documents filed at closing on the payment of a lien or mortgage, acknowledging that the debt has been satisfied.

recovery period under depreciation rules, the number of years over which depreciation is claimed; within each recovery period, certain kinds of depreciation can be used.

renter's insurance (also called **HO-4**) a form of hazard insurance offering protection against losses to personal property only, with no coverage for losses to buildings.

replacement cost the cost required to replace a building to the same functional condition and purpose that it serves today, based on the current cost of material and labor; but not necessarily to duplicate the same quality of workmanship using materials of identical quality as the original.

reproduction cost the estimated cost to replace an existing building using the same quality of workmanship and materials as in the original.

reserve requirements the rule stating that lenders have to establish reserves for loans granted and keep a minimum required amount of cash on hand to cover future losses.

residential property property designed for living, including single-family homes, duplexes and flats, triplexes, apartments, and other multifamily buildings.

return on equity a percentage of return calculated by dividing annual net income by equity.

rights intangible assets added onto real estate, which have value not because of the land itself, but because of the advantages those rights provide.

rollover mortgage a mortgage containing fixed-rate terms for a specified period of time, after which the contract continues but the interest rate is renegotiated, or "rolled over" for a new term.

seasoned real estate real estate that has been owned long enough for market value and equity to accumulate.

secondary market the market for the purchase of loans written by conventional institutions. Agencies in this market buy loans to form pools; shares in pools are sold to investors who want to earn interest. The pool works like a mutual fund for mortgages rather than stocks.

second mortgage also called a "junior lien," a mortgage not in first position in the event of default. The second mortgage holder is paid only after the first mortgage holder is paid, and only if enough equity remains in the property.

seller financing a financing arrangement in which the property owner agrees for the buyer to purchase the property partly with cash and partly by the seller providing a mortgage. The seller assumes the role of lender, and the buyer agrees to make monthly payments to the seller, with interest.

seller's market a condition in which many buyers are competing for a relatively small inventory of available properties; a fast market, in which prices tend to be driven upward by high demand.

selling agent the agent who locates the buyer and brings an offer to the seller. The selling agent is an agent of the seller and is entitled to a commission if the deal goes through.

selling group the broker-dealer members of a syndicate whose sales associates and representatives sell units to investors in limited partnership programs.

specified program a limited partnership formed to buy or develop a specifically identified property.

speculator an investor who buys property with the goal of earning the greatest possible profit in the shortest possible time.

spread the percentage difference between an asked price of a property and the price at which it sold. As a tool for judging conditions of the market, the recent average spread and the trend in spreads indicate the relative strength or weakness in prices.

straight-line depreciation a form of depreciation in which an identical amount is deducted each year in the recovery period, until the entire basis has been fully depreciated.

subject property a property that is being appraised.

subsidiary record a record for breaking down an expense by property. The expense account within the general ledger is broken into several subsidiary accounts, one for each property, so that expenses can be tracked not only by expense classification, but also by property.

supply and demand the economic conditions in the market that affect prices. When demand is greater than supply, prices tend to rise; when supply is greater than demand, prices tend to fall.

sweat equity equity that comes from the owner's labor rather than from growing market demand or reduction of a loan's balance; equity you develop from working on a fixer-upper yourself.

syndicate an organization formed to manage the group of sales representatives (the selling group) responsible for selling units in the partnership.

tax avoidance the reduction of taxes through planning and timing of income and expenses, within the law.

tax deferral delaying tax liabilities until future years, often as a part of a long-term plan. This practice is especially beneficial when taxable income is expected to be lower in the future than it is today, so that delayed profits will be taxed at a lower rate.

tax evasion falsifying a tax return, failing to provide complete information, or reporting untrue information on the return, for the purpose of illegally reducing tax liabilities.

tax planning a review of income and expenses throughout the year, undertaken for the purposes of estimating tax liabilities ahead of time, seeking ways to legally reduce taxes, planning transactions according to the present situation, and ensuring compliance with the tax rules.

teaser an initial interest rate charged on an adjustable-rate mortgage, well below the current market rate, offered by a lender in order to attract new business. After a few months, the teaser is replaced with a higher interest rate.

time value of money the basic series of rules concerning accumulation of interest over a period of time; compounding and its effect; and return to lenders (or, on the other side, the cost to borrowers). The longer the period of time that money accumulates with interest, the higher the time value of the money. The time involved determines the real benefit or consequence of interest.

title company a company specializing in establishing title to real property, including identification of all existing liens on property. The title company issues a title insurance policy insuring that all liens have been disclosed at the time of closing.

title insurance policy a special form of insurance issued by a title company to insure the buyer against any undiscovered liens on the property. The coverage is paid by a single premium during escrow, and remains in force as long as the buyer owns the property.

total return a rate of return including a calculation of capital gain, net rental income, and tax benefits received during the holding period; expressed in terms of average annual rate of return.

vacancy rate the percentage of rental units in apartments and other multiunit buildings that are not occupied by tenants. Average vacancy rates are used as an indicator by lenders and appraisers to estimate average annual rental income.

weighted average the average interest rate of two loans, when both the outstanding loan amounts and the interest rates are different. The larger-balance loan is given proportionately more weight to reflect a true average interest rate.

yield a rate of return comparing annual rent income with the cost of the property.

Index